AF604024

ON MANAGEMENT, LEADERSHIP AND LIFE

Snigdha Mohanty

INDIA • SINGAPORE • MALAYSIA

Copyright © Snigdha Mohanty 2023
All Rights Reserved.

ISBN 979-8-89133-752-7

This book has been published with all efforts taken to make the material error-free after the consent of the author. However, the author and the publisher do not assume and hereby disclaim any liability to any party for any loss, damage, or disruption caused by errors or omissions, whether such errors or omissions result from negligence, accident, or any other cause.

While every effort has been made to avoid any mistake or omission, this publication is being sold on the condition and understanding that neither the author nor the publishers or printers would be liable in any manner to any person by reason of any mistake or omission in this publication or for any action taken or omitted to be taken or advice rendered or accepted on the basis of this work. For any defect in printing or binding the publishers will be liable only to replace the defective copy by another copy of this work then available.

Dedication

I dedicate this to my mother, and all the *mothers* on this planet – mothers, fathers, grandparents, wives, sisters, daughters, brothers, husbands and whosoever has ever 'mothered' anyone!

Contents

PART III

Acknowledgement and Disclaimers

First and foremost, I owe it to my mother and sister-in-law that I developed an interest in cooking in the first place, and then, post-marriage/post-motherhood, needed to keep on fine-tuning and perfecting my own culinary skills, thanks especially to my children and other family members, turning it into one of my passions somewhere along the journey! In the process, as I was also in a job that needed me to understand and handle people of diverse kinds and status, I developed the skill of being keenly and reflectively observant. There are umpteen others – persons in my life as well as materials in various media, from whom I have learnt, and am still learning many new recipes and experimenting/improvising. That process of learning, improvising, and exploring *newness,* in itself, has been very rewarding and enriching for me, facilitating my insights. It is not possible to take all names individually; so, I just want to express my gratitude to one and all in my life, as I have learnt and gained from each of them directly and indirectly. My own managerial experiences on the job, mindful observation, and reflection on my own experiences in kitchen and research on Internet have helped me a lot in formalising my ideas and inferences. I am especially grateful to God and my organisation that during my professional career in service sector, I had got opportunities to have formal training inputs in management and leadership, too, many of which helped me pick up invaluable insights and fine-tuned my own leadership style on ground for effectiveness. No wonder, while working in kitchen, I see so many parallels to management and leadership anywhere else.

Although whatever insights and deductions and inferences shared in this book are entirely my personal understandings, I am alive to the fact that there may be many who share my thoughts. And there may also be many who may dub it as undue eulogising of a basic level daily chore like cooking. I respect all views.

I shall be very grateful to every reader for having spared their valuable time to read through this book. Hope they find some value or at least a connect to my insights, and recall from their own experiences how most of the lessons learnt in our humble kitchen indeed apply to bigger canvases of workplace and life as such.

Last but not the least, I acknowledge with great appreciation the support extended by the Team at Notion Press in publishing this book.

DISCLAIMERS:

No.1 By highlighting the fact that our humble kitchen teaches us many critical lessons in management, leadership, and life philosophy, I do not maintain that these lessons are not available to be picked up and imbibed from elsewhere – in fields other than kitchen management and through formal management courses! The prime reason I seek to shine on this immensely educative platform that our kitchen provides, and the invaluable lessons it throws at us is two-fold:

i. It is usually NOT acknowledged what a great and honourable place kitchen is to work in, like any other professional field.
ii. Often cooking and kitchen management is looked down upon, especially when run by women in the family as a wholetime engagement. They are neither financially evaluated/rewarded, nor acknowledged in terms of their great contributions to the well-being, productivity, and success of others.

Just as we say *in general* that the Men in Uniform guard our borders through sleepless nights, so that we civilians can sleep at night peacefully, why cannot we gracefully admit, our Women in Aprons hold the fort at home and ensure our nourishment so that we, the so-called working lot, can go out and excel in our chosen professions? (Men include Women in those roles, and the vice versa. There is no intention to stereotype any gender's role in any way.)

No.2 Some of my insights and inferences are drawn in the *specific context* of Indian homes and work culture, e.g., observations in the context of maids, doing utensils, cleaning etc. These may not be so in advanced countries where these basic kitchen management chores have become mostly machine driven, and cooked/half-cooked food is majorly outsourced.

Notwithstanding the above, I am sure, everywhere, kitchen must be throwing up numerous similar/other situations that hold important life and management lessons for keenly observing eyes.

No. 3 I also do not maintain that *every* mother, *every* cook, or *everyone* who manages kitchen responsibilities for a long time learns all the lessons that our humble kitchen throws up. That depends on the personal qualities of the individual concerned; whether they have the 'eyes' to notice subtle points, develop insights, and the ability to learn. But yes, kitchen does impact the majority, as it often 'pushes' them to act!

Introduction

An Ode to Cooking, Kitchen, and Mother

Goal and purpose orientation, Self-discipline, decision making, planning and review, flexibility, focus, multi-tasking, time management, budgeting, resource management, optimum utilisation, whole spectrum view/the big picture, value of dispensability and indispensability, diversity in basket, waste consciousness, redemption and salvaging, delegation, outsourcing, leading from front, mentoring, motivation and inner drive, problem solving, crisis management, innovation, creativity, stress management, attitude towards life ...... Well, well, well... sounds like a barrage of exotic management jargons suddenly leaping out of nowhere. Not really! I am, indeed, talking about *cooking* and the *homely kitchen,* and how a *mother** manages it with love, care, understanding and inexhaustible innovativeness day in and day out for years together, almost without a break and perhaps no one even noticing what it takes to keep doing it. Kitchen to me is one of the least recognised but greatest citadels of learning some of the fundamental lessons in not only management and leadership, but also in life philosophy.

At times, I have heard Management Gurus and great leaders saying: if you truly wish to learn the lessons of management, just keenly observe your mother. The term 'mother' immediately creates an image of a loving person toiling the best part of her time and life to fix meals on your table – day in and day out, for years on – that are tasty, healthy, diverse, within budget and on time when you really need it! Sorry, I keep harping on 'day in and day out for years together', because there lies the real catch. Hold a small glass of water in your hand; it does not weigh a wee bit. But keep holding it for a long period, you will realise how uncomfortable it is! Same with daily cooking and all other mundane routines relating to maintenance.

Go under the surface and analyse her style of functioning, the goals she sets for herself by role-consciousness and maternal instinct aligned to the bigger *purpose in her life,* as well as the principles she lives by, albeit never documented. And you would be overwhelmed by the profound insights that it would give you on management, leadership, and the philosophy on how to live.

I love cooking! And honestly, I find it one of the most creative things on earth. Ever tried to count how many recipes are prepared around the world out of a limited number of ingredients? And how many variations are still waiting to be experimented? Simply amazing!

And of course, the saying goes – the way to one's heart lies through one's stomach. How true! It feels like heaven when my children shout out, "Hey, Mama! It was yu..m.m....y!" And of course, the kick you get when others, too, admire and lick their fingers.

I would add one more feather to this cap. *Cooking is a real stress buster.* It's when I cook that I sing to my heart's glory.

I was not a fulltime homemaker always. I was in a public sector job for close to 26 years, before I left my job some years back to pursue my other passions. While in service, normally I used to have very little time for myself or my hobbies. But as a matter of principle, I prepared the breakfast, tiffin for school/office, and lunch for the family in the morning. I had carved out a few hours' time in the morning before I left for office. Advantages of cooking the lunch myself in the morning before leaving for office at 9/9.30 a.m. were manifold:

– Ended up managing my morning time better than it would have been possible, had I relied on a hired hand with the associated uncertainties about her regularity and punctuality. In fact, this ensured that I was never late for office. (Not that I had not tried delegation; it did not work for me in the morning, as it was a trade-off between punctuality plus quality of food on one hand, and less burden on me for things I was able to take care of, at that time. Yes, I had delegated dinner to a hired hand, as there, the trade-off was between 'lesser quality food' and 'No food on time'!)

- Got to nurture that most vital emotional bond with family through my gesture of cooking for them, despite lack of time for being with the family as much as I would have liked to.
- Got to retain and sharpen my own cooking skills, one of the life skills most useful till the last breath.
- Enjoyed my creations. Cooking can be very innovative and creative, if you enjoy it. And the bonus of engaging in anything creative is: it acts like a very effective mood booster and stress buster, by shifting your energy and attention in positive direction. It indeed helped me start my office work with a recharged mind.
- Enjoyed singing while cooking and thus, got to maintain my singing talent even without real practice. After all these years, I am reaping the benefit of still having a good voice quality now, on which I can work with pleasure and a sense of legitimate pride.

I think, those are quite enough to motivate anyone, at least me, to continue with my rendezvous with recipes. I am still an avid experimenter of new recipes for tasty, simple, and healthy food from all accessible sources. I also firmly believe that a healthy body facilitates a healthy mind and overall wellness of a person. After all, health is wealth, and the entrance key to this wealth lies in right food.

Something profound that I learnt from cooking regularly even during my most hectic phase, as I realise now in retrospect, is: the importance of inculcating two immensely necessary qualities for true success in any field: i. the discipline of planning and *being prepared* on one hand, and ii. the art of *being flexible* to handle uncertainties on the other hand, *without being tied to those plans*. When one is purpose-oriented and learns the fine art of maintaining a balance between these two seemingly opposite qualities of rigidity and flexibility, not only your effectiveness as a leader/ manager increases, but your entire life experience becomes balanced and soothing, not unduly weighed down towards any one extreme.

Cooking is also not about combining *ingredients* only, it is more significantly about *proportions, balance, process, complementarity, and final delivery* as well. Balance in taste, texture, and nutrition is an absolute necessity for delivery of all those dimensions to our palate and body.

Similarly, in our day-to-day life, it is about proportions and balance between various roles that we play, various feelings and emotions, various competing goals, and interests! Without this *sense of balance,* we fail to deliver in all spheres- be it cooking, or relationships, or professional commitments, or personal fulfilment. *How fulfilling and worthwhile our life is will depend on our ability to balance! And kitchen does help us immensely to learn and cultivate this valuable trait.*

Further, it offers great learning opportunities to develop our *ability to observe beneath the obvious.* To notice those fine lines of differences that we must reckon in many fields of our life to stay on the right track. The fine line between fixing responsibility and blaming; between taking responsibility and inability to fix responsibility where it belongs, between being considerate and being weak/pliable, between arrogance and confidence, arrogance and assertiveness, firmness, and stubbornness, etc. Because kitchen with all its insights and lessons makes us a well-rounded personality.

In kitchen, you pick up the knack of knowing how much is just right cooking, neither overdone nor underdone. And you also get to know that this 'knack' does not come to you in one trial. *You learn this by doing that same thing again and again, failing a few times, till you perfect* your observation. Is it not said that *practice makes one perfect*? For example, while preparing ghee (clarified butter) out of malai (cream), only repeated trials would make you an adept in knowing when to stop cooking by looking at the colour of the remains... dark brown but not burnt, and the aroma. You overcook for a second, and your clarified butter gives a burnt smell. You undercook it; your ghee finally does not smell as aromatic as it should, nor does it look great. I am sanguine, just like me, others must have spoilt the ghee a few times before getting it right. Thus, you learn here a huge lesson in management, leadership, and life philosophy - *do not be afraid of failures; indeed, failure is a part of success.*

There are many such lessons that our humble kitchen can teach us, which I have tried to bring out in this book. Needless to mention, those are only illustrative; and do not comprise a fully exhaustive list. As one develops a sharp sense of observation, one would find many more lessons *for oneself* from even apparently very insignificant incidents.

Another hugely significant dimension about managing and analysing kitchen affairs is that it makes us truly appreciate and value 'food.' Food is necessary for our very existence. We all know that. Yet do we value it the way we should? Do we feel sensitive to the plight of those who are starving, and feel compassionate enough to share? Do we see beyond, to appreciate what one must pour-in to bring food to our table day in and day out? Are we able to draw the gems of wisdom and great lessons of management that get practised in managing food? Time to pause, and ponder.

Let us get going, and explore what lessons the humble homely kitchen holds for us!

It may sound blasphemous, but I dare say: If you are the one managing your kitchen, and you happen to be a manager in your profession, then how you manage your kitchen gives a fair preview of what kind of a manager and leader you are in the workspace.

Because it is here that you learn the difference between 'being' and 'appearing', and more significantly, you actually start 'becoming' what you learn. What a bigger life lesson you need to learn when deep down you understand that mere learning at an intellectual level is not enough; it is more about "being" everything that you learn in course of life.

That is, you learn not just to *go* through life, but *grow* through life.

I might mention here that I was asked a very straight question by my daughter: "Who are you writing this for?" My target readers.

Well, to be honest, I had not thought about this so pin-pointedly. After early retirement, I had started journaling my thoughts and insights gained from my own experiences as I was getting very interested to notice more and more parallels in managing kitchen and managing anywhere else. Despite having no age-related problems nor time-related problems post-retirement, there have been times when I felt like hiring a hand for cooking, thinking this would give me more time to pursue other important stuff. But whenever I started tossing with the idea of employing a full-time cook, and then did the pros-cons analysis given the lack of availability of decent and/or dependable/professional cooks in my part of the country, coupled with the diverse needs and rigid timetables of my family members, every time I ended up with the same decision of continuing it on my own till I can. I started becoming more observant and more reflective. Gradually, it made me very anguished and sad to observe continuously a toxic tendency on the part of many these days to waste food, to show low respect for household chores, to increasingly outsource food choosing more unhealthy versions of fast food etc. Moreover, post-retirement when I mingled more with homemakers of all ages, it really hit me hard to realise what enormous emotional pain these women must be going through for want of an identity of their own despite being very talented and sacrificing so much for the family. In this scenario, I found my habit of journaling very helpful as creative outbursts. That is when, very recently, I thought of sharing all my thoughts in the form of a book.

So, to answer my daughter, I would say:

Firstly, it is a special tribute from me to all the home-makers. I expect mothers* and homemakers to read this book as the title can have an immediate direct connect for them. I wish to tell them how whole-some they are as human beings; how whole-some they are in their role as a nurturer and care-giver; and what a high level of managerial skills they possess and practice in everything they do for feeding their families! They should feel good that the immense contributions they are making toward the *well-being* of others are being acknowledged openly in this book and with all sincerity. I would like them to *feel* their share of legitimate pride and self-respect.

Secondly, I hope the title attracts the management trainees, as also anyone working in the managerial roles, especially at bottom and medium rungs to explore if they find any practical tips relevant to them. Yes, top leadership demands a far more complex set of traits-skills-competence, but unless you perfect the fundamental skills and attitudes to manage and lead, moving up the ladder might break you eventually.

And thirdly, I hope, anyone who is curious enough about terms like 'Management', 'Leadership' and 'Life' lessons would rise above the apparent triviality of the word "kitchen" in the title of the book, and its auto-mode association with women and household chores only. This brings everyone who loves reading into the ambit of my target group!

I believe, one must read voraciously for the sake of reading, and not just read contents carrying titles suggesting a direct link to their fields of work. Reading is like entering a Treasure House, having no idea on what could be your invaluable surprise finds, till you explore.

If after going through my book, even one person develops a new pair of eyes for those who run the kitchens, gets inspired to learn this life skill and carries forward a few lessons as appropriate to their workplace and life, I would be glad and grateful that my efforts have been worthwhile.

And I would add at the end of this Note, *last but not the least:*

If my book inspires anyone, who used to lack cooking skills for reasons whatsoever, to learn this skill and cook when needed with an understanding that not only is cooking a life skill, but also a *must* for promoting gender equality, then I would feel truly fulfilled. We lecture on the need for gender equality every now and then, but do not back it up by enough action. Responsibility to ensure food to the family as per the usual stereotyping of gender-based roles is one of the primary things that almost ties up otherwise talented women. Unless men first share this one domestic responsibility with their women, how would their women go out and pursue their professions free of guilt and worries? So, here is a beckoning for all: Do treat cooking as respectable a job as any other work; learn it, and share this responsibility in your family!

AUTHOR NOTES:

*i. As already indicated in my Dedication, the term 'Mother' is used in this book to include mother/wife/daughter/father/cook/chef/stay-at-home husband/own self, irrespective of gender and relationship, i.e., anyone who 'mothers' - i.e., nurtures by providing food and care for nourishment on a regular basis. This may please be kept in mind all through while reading this book, to prevent further stereotyping of a mother's role on gender basis happening inadvertently in readers' minds!

ii. In order to be gender-neutral in structure of sentences, I have used pronouns in plural form even for subjects cited in singular form, although that goes against correct grammar conventionally. For example, "No leader can ensure this unless *they* know each team member as an individual first."

Part I

A Cry-Out

I am *Food*.

I am all over there in everyone's life - from morning beverage till the night meal, not only for the basic *sustenance* and *nourishment* of the *body*, but also for the rejuvenation of *mind*. Even no *celebration* can ever be thought of without me. Strangely, people binge on me even in depression; or while in a state of heightened creativity.

I am quite amused to see, how some people not only eat to live, but also live to eat, quite often.

I know I am indispensable to the human life *literally*. Why only the humans, I am indispensable to all living kinds- animals, birds, and plants, too. Man is not only responsible to protect, grow and preserve the sources of *me* for themselves, but also has a duty not to plunder the same to the extent of starving the other living species of their natural sustenance. Our forefathers did realise this in great depth, so much so that, in many cultures/religions, it is a normal practice for people to offer prayers to God before every meal, to express gratitude for HIS grace and blessings in ensuring *me* for survival. And that makes me contemplative.

On one hand, it gives me a wonderful sense of fulfilment when I nurture and nourish everyone's health, and also offer an outlet for expression of the inexhaustible *creativity* of people who experiment with *me* with passion. *It is amazing how with only a limited number of ingredients, people create unlimited varieties of dishes across the world!* My day is made when I save a starving person from the pangs of hunger; when I make a sick person spring back to life; when I see people relish and *bond* over me; or when I see people generously *share* me with the needy. To cut it short,

I stand *fulfilled* when I make people *healthy, happy, and ready to take on the other challenges of their lives.* I am a *prerequisite* for human *existence* itself.

But alas! How many people *value* me rightly? Yes, one thing is for sure: everyone notices my absence. Then why the *value* of my *presence* is so pathetically downplayed, I wonder. When millions are starving elsewhere, there is ostentatious consumption of me far beyond requirement or purpose. Mindless wastages are so common-be it at home, in eat-outs, in feasts and celebrations! Aren't humans supposed to have a mind with a conscience and power to discriminate the right from the wrong?

Sorry, I can't help brooding and questioning. How many people *care* to take me in right *kind-combination-manner*? How many spare a thought for the Mother Nature who provides all that goes into me? How many truly appreciate what the mother (or anyone in charge of cooking daily at home) pours into serving 3-4 meals a day, day in and day out, for years together throughout her life? How many recognise her love, compassion, personal sacrifices, sense of service with self-effacing traits, her great managerial skills [whether she has attended a business school or not]?

Forget about appreciating what goes into my *nutrition and taste* aspects; how many even pause to observe what *rich lessons of effective management and life philosophy* actually get practised there in bringing *me* to your table every single time? I need not lecture on this. Just notice the details, do yourself a few times and reflect. All lessons will come to you crystal clear. You would automatically become a great student of management and leadership, well prepared in foundational lessons, ready to learn more and the higher inputs.

The greatest lesson that you can learn as you manage me is how to develop a sense of proportion and balance in every dish as well as in every meal. After all, the goal is*: I must be wholesome, nutritious, tasty, and yet, within budget.* And the purpose is: *health and happiness.* Take these lessons to every sphere of your duties and responsibilities if you wish to lead a balanced, synergised, and wholesome life.

Moreover, playing with me can prove to be one of the biggest *stress-busters* since it diverts your attention completely when it fills you with a drive to create something worthwhile. On top of that, just think about the element of self-dependence it brings in. At times, I really pity those who *all the time depend* on others for as basic a need as me. That is nothing but compromising with your own independence. Yes, if professional, reliable, and affordable help is available, you may (and should) *delegate* or *outsource* me at least partly for diverting your time to more important tasks. But as you do so, take care never to lose your own ability and willingness to take charge, and feed yourself and your loved ones, when necessary.

Think a little bit more about me. Have you ever thought of some of the *core values* that you have taken for granted in the person who has brought me on your platter? Like, trustworthiness, dependability, punctuality, quality-consciousness, care, and concern for your tastes & preferences. In short, you are taking for granted that food has been served with utmost care ensuring what is *right for you*. If you appreciate this, then is it not warranted that you too, as a person as well as a professional, must bring all these values into your relationships and engagements with others? *Well, that is how I teach life philosophy, too.*

Well, I am not just a *job-once done and forgotten;* I am your *attitude*. How you treat *me* mirrors how you treat your own self, your own profession, and your own life. *Do you waste food on your plate habitually?* Do you let ingredients or cooked food rut and just throw into dustbins? Beware, you might be living your life half-ways, not enjoying anything to its fullest, not putting in your best in whatever you do, not feeling content and grateful for what you have now, thereby allowing leakage of vital energy that you could otherwise put in to making efforts for a better life. Are you eating junk food most of the times by choice? Look at yourself deeply. You might just be prone to getting carried away by the outward shine of things and people rather than the content, *their inner worth*; and/or you might be suffering from a lack of self-control and discipline. Or, may be, you have a tendency to choose the easier. If that be so, how far will you go in life in terms of achieving true success and happiness? Please pay attention to *me*. While preparing me, or having me, are you attentive to what you are thinking? What mood you are in? What quality of vibrations are you putting into me? Watch out: it's all a play of energy and vibration. If impure, it will simply neutralise my beneficial effects, or may even contaminate *me* as I go inside your system, just to align with *your* state of *being at that moment*. You must have heard the saying: some people just don't keep healthy whatever they eat.

Remember, to a great extent, *you are what you eat*. What you eat impacts your body and mind equally. So, learn to respect *me*, appreciate the person who relentlessly serves you to bring me on your table, and always eat right with right thoughts, intentions, and vibrations. Take a fresh look at the valuable role that the 'mothers' play in your lives, and how often you tend to speak derogatory and dismissively about them. Stop, and start appreciating.

And yes, *share* me with as many as possible - especially the starving and the needy. Abundance flows, not from hoarding, but from sharing. And see the magic unfold in your life.

After all, I am *Food*. With *me* you may or may not exist*; but without me, you surely cannot exist beyond a short while!*

Mindscape and Skills

How Kitchen shapes our *Mindscape* in a fundamental way and helps us build multi-skills is simply mind-blowing!

What one can learn from keenly observing the processes involved in cooking and running a kitchen on a regular basis and how a regular cook handles them can simply be transformational. No wonder, as I have already mentioned in my introduction, Management Gurus suggest management students to observe their mothers keenly and reflect, if they are truly interested in learning lessons in Management!

Our humble kitchen is an amazing experience when we look at how it can teach us not only culinary skills, but many *core values* that we must imbibe and/or reinforce to lead a fulfilling life:

- Self-discipline and Sense of responsibility
- Integrity
- Honesty
- punctuality
- Empathy
- Sense of Appreciation (in every sense... motivate, understand)
- Acceptance, Co-existence, and redemption/reclaiming people
- Equity and equality
- Trustworthiness
- Dependability
- credibility
- Persistence
- Creativity
- Simplicity
- Respect for Nature
- 'Learning' as a value
- Purpose orientation

- Courage
- Love
- Compassion
- Patience
- Diligence
- Decisiveness
- Self-dependence
- Inter dependence
- Humility
- Sense of service
- Sense of Sacrifice
- Sense of Observation (beyond the obvious and beyond the surface and beyond the ordinary)

And many more. Goes without saying, the above list is just indicative, not exhaustive, and in no particular order.

At a core level, all human beings are endowed with these fundamental universal values. We call it our *Inner Compass*. But not all have their Inner Compass securely in place in their *conscious* mode of living. Kitchen helps us, by putting us into various types of existential situations, to bring up these values from within and bring them into practice in our day-to-day lives. As a result, our entire *MINDSCAPE* undergoes a phenomenally beautiful change. When these values start working together - one building on others - what emerges is a beautiful CHARACTER! So, the much talked about *Character Building* that we essentially aim at in Education, happens continuously in our humble kitchen, unobserved and unacknowledged most of the time. Imagine how beautiful our life would be if all this learning happens under observant eyes, picked up, reinforced, refined, and applied effectively 'out there.'

As we take charge of kitchen, these values usually get embedded in us over time, some even very early, and get reflected in the ways we handle our work and life. It, so to say, greatly shapes our mindset- the attitude with which we look at things/people/situations, as well as the techniques and strategies we bring into our action/responses in various situations. Especially some of the early and quick lessons on values refine our mindset positively and constructively, which, going forward, get reflected in a better *ability to deal with not only problems but every kind of situation with sensibility and sensitivity to larger issues* involved in any matter. Perhaps, this is one of the reasons why women intuitively display strong leadership and managerial skills at work, in general. Just an observation from own experience. Otherwise, *work* has no gender, and so is the case with maturity and leadership.

Let us look at just three examples in brief. There are many more that we would discuss as we proceed.

Example 1: Self-Discipline and Sense of Responsibility.

These two values get imbibed in the kitchen faster than we can think of. If you observe young girls, before marriage at their parental homes and after marriage in the In-laws' home, or even own home with husband alone, where she is expected routinely to share/take over kitchen operations, you will understand what I wish to get across. Once the young girl *accepts* looking after 'food for the family' as *'her share'* of the household chores, she just first *'shows up'* for the task, no matter what. When you are in charge of food, you cannot afford to be whimsical about whether you feel like cooking or not, or whether you are free that time to cook or not. NO. The simple realization dawns: cooking has to be attended to as per set food timings. Punctuality is not an option here- it is a rule to be adhered to, except in very rare cases of other exigencies. So, first show up! This urge to attend to an assigned job, without excuses, is the first and fundamental requirement of a Sense of Responsibility, and Self-Discipline! Going forward, obviously she picks up different recipes and cooking techniques (value of learning and creativity), preparing on her own (gaining self-reliance), maintaining health and taste quotients (love, care, sense of service etc.) and many other valuable traits. Look at your mothers in charge of kitchen. Even when she is ill and there is no aid/ alternative to ensure meals for the family you would find her managing to prepare at least something modest to feed, but on time. This is Sense of Responsibility of a high order, at times self-effacing!

Can you think of any successful person who has achieved anything without self-discipline or a sense of responsibility?

Example 2: Care and Concern for others

The entire engagement in kitchen on a regular basis in an optimal manner calls for a genuine sense of care and concern for others- for those who you are serving. And as 'others' are your family members whom you love, that sense of care and concern emerges from within automatically and gradually takes a deep root in your overall character. Once something becomes characteristic of someone, it gets demonstrated in all other situations as well. Think about leadership and managerial effectiveness now. Is not genuine care and concern for both people and your Organisation an indispensable quality for that?

Example 3: Integrity. Doing the right thing even when you know that no one is watching.

My daughter is strict about NOT using refined oils in her dishes. She is fine only with Olive oil, Mustard oil, butter, and pure ghee (clarified butter). To ensure this, I use only these 4 fats for dishes that we all would be having, including her. If we feel like having deep-fried snacks at times, I would use Refined Oil for our share; but use olive oil for deep-frying her share. Point is: *no matter what, I would never cheat her, nor would any mother!*

Now think about this: If occasionally, I cheat and prepare a dish using refined oil, do you think she would even come to know? NO. The spices we use in Indian curries are so many and so flavoursome that refined oil, if used in a small quantity for a large batch of curry/pan fry/tempering would hardly make much of a difference to the taste. No. 2: Since childhood, her body is already used to refined oil for almost 3 decades, and it is only a few years back that she stopped taking refined oil. So, I don't think, occasional consumption of refined oil in insignificant quantity would actually affect her system and health very badly. BUT does this mean, I would actually cheat her? NO, I don't and I can't. My love and concern for her would never allow me to do that. Cooking for the family brings up from within the value of 'integrity,' that lies within every human being.

Similarly, your integrity will not let you use barred/unhealthy/expired ingredients in your cooking even if no one would know; will not let you compromise with basic cleanliness in your cooking environment. You won't leave dishes open to let flies sit on them and serve the same food to your family. Etc. Just observe how shabbily things are managed in many small-time food joints. There can be many more examples in kitchen. Just because no one is watching while you are cooking, would you, say, order something from outside and serve that as if you have cooked? Would you put ingredients one of your family members is allergic to, just to avoid more work in cooking separately for them? You are a bit tired, not exactly ill. Would you make that an excuse too often and stop cooking for the family without making alternative arrangements for their food? No, your *clarity on purpose* behind why you are running the kitchen, and your commitment to your responsibility derived from that purpose would not allow you to be unreliable in any sense.

There can be many ways to cheat as no one is watching while you cook. But there is a strong value – *integrity*- that guides you not to cheat as the others involved are your loved ones in the first place, and secondly, no mother, in fact, no self-respecting person can ever face their own self-condemnation if they cheat. So, integrity as a core value, gets reinforced/imbibed in our homely kitchen like in nowhere else. Once acting with integrity becomes habitual, it also gets reflected in your other engagements/interactions/transactions outside the kitchen.

As we proceed, we shall observe how great values, as enumerated earlier and more, develop in kitchen.

Besides a positive mindset, running a kitchen also helps us immensely in becoming multi-skilled. The specific lessons that can be learnt from kitchen are innumerable and varied. Ultimately every lesson has a combination of both attitudinal and technique-related dimensions. After all, how we act and behave is influenced by our *attitude*, our existing *knowledge* (what we already know about handling that issue), and the extent of our *ability to learn* further (for newer solutions and perspectives). Hence, for ease of listing and comprehending, we shall try to find out and discuss the important lessons (in no particular order, as it is impossible to segregate the over-lapping) and values, in forthcoming portions of this book. Needless to mention, the variety of lessons learnt implies similar variety in the skills being imparted and picked up through these lessons. The first obvious core skill that one picks up in the kitchen is the culinary skills. The ability to cook food is no less than a major life skill. The sooner we, irrespective of gender/role/social status, understand this fact, the better! Moreover, cooking (its processes and techniques) also teaches you many other skills useful in management, leadership, and life, as we would discuss in Part II.

Apart from the important values and managerial skills, running a kitchen teaches you to learn multiple skills by becoming a 'jack of all trades'- say a plumber at times when the drain chokes in the kitchen sink, an electrician when the tube needs be changed immediately, a gas technician when you need to replace a cylinder, a healer when minor injuries are to be tended to, an organizer when you fit everything in some kind of order within the small space available in the kitchen for retrieving quickly when needed, a salesperson when you have to convince your children to eat healthy stuff like say, vegetables that they hate, a bit of a mentor/teacher when you make your children learn a few recipes, and the like.

Let us now discuss the perspectives, insights, lessons, values, skills, and attitude that we learn from cooking and kitchen in greater details in coming pages. We shall deliberate on these lessons and skills, not in isolation or individually, but in an intertwined manner so that their significant contextual import is not lost. Moreover, no value or trait or skill works independently of others. One always acts on and reacts to many more, thus building upon one another, or weakening the chain!

And let me proclaim: all these soft skills we imbibe from kitchen are like 'pivoting skills', a concept that has emerged lately in the corporate-world in the context of career-switches, especially in the technology world. A pivot skill is a competency gained in a previous career that is transferable to a current profession. Companies are also said to *pivot* when they change their line of business, but use their learnings, strengths, and competencies from the past business in the new business. Similarly, in human lives, too, pivoting is essential as we must learn our fundamental lessons from our past experiences and carry their essence as we move on or change direction. These are pivotal, foundational and do not get obsolete or irrelevant, no matter where you go. As we proceed with our thoughts in this book, we can draw an unquestionable parallel between the skills and attitude we learn from kitchen and the same needed in any sphere of life, be it professional, personal, or social, for life to be fulfilling and meaningful.

Part II

Perspectives/Insights/Lessons

As mentioned earlier, it is amazing how kitchen with its big and small challenges, apparently small and insignificant situations, can hold very important and useful lessons for us – to imbibe core values, develop right attitude, learn various skills and tactics for effective management and leading a fulfilling overall life. We just need be mindful, open-minded, keenly observant, and graceful in receiving these messages as they unfold.

Let us deliberate a bit in detail.

1. Just Begin!

Beginning a task is having it half-done! So goes the saying. This is also one of the earliest lessons we learn in the kitchen.

Cooking, as it may turn out, is a drudgery, at least for the simple reason that there is no break from it. No one can live without food. No one can outsource it for ever. More so, when we have a family to feed, with different tastes and preferences, timings, and other health requirements. So, it becomes almost a burdensome responsibility, although the cooking job *per se* is rather simple. Besides, it has to be done. No respite! This indispensability of cooking tasks very soon teaches the 'mothers' learn the valuable lesson: *Just Start!*

Once we are actually inside the kitchen and start, it really gets over in no time. 'A thousand-mile journey begins with a single step'. We all have heard it, or even might have said it to others to motivate them to overcome the reasons for their procrastination. But we truly get what it means and *internalise it* to become a part of our own character when we run a kitchen on a regular basis for a long period. We also gradually learn how to keep *reinventing* this routine job of cooking to add that extra rub of freshness in course of time through our *innovativeness and creativity*. We start picking up many lessons and philosophical insights as we do this job on a continuous basis, and that *sustains our interest*.

The importance of this lesson can be fully appreciated when we look at it against the backdrop of our usual tendency *to procrastinate*.

All of us must have, at some time or other, somehow procrastinated doing some tasks. Reasons could be many:

- Simple inertia or laziness, especially when it is a boring job, or a new task or a new way of doing. We simply *don't feel like* doing, despite knowing that with laziness we fail to achieve much, whereas true growth calls for diligence.
- Reluctance to do something, especially if we *perceive* that as difficult, or a drudgery, or below our dignity.
- Fear of failure and associated ridicule if something is new and challenging
- Expectation of 'Perfect' conditions. Some people have a habit of waiting for things and circumstances to be perfect *as per their perception* before they start a job. This also is a manifestation of fear of failure and perfectionism. These people want to do everything perfectly without a margin for any failure. And hence, keep procrastinating.
- Indecisiveness. At times, we defer things just because we can't make up our mind whether to do it or not. Yes, it is good to think through a matter before jumping into action. But beyond a reasonable limit, too much time taken to decide may be symptomatic of paralysis of analysis, can be counterproductive, or amount to missing an opportunity.
- Anger. Yes, at times we resist out of anger when *asked to* do something. Lack of volition leads to irritation if pressurised and thus, to procrastination.

While managing a kitchen on a regular basis, that involves many more things other than pure cooking – especially the cleanliness related chores, many or all of the above reasons might surface to fuel a procrastinating tendency. Whatever the reason, procrastination has never helped anyone.

And the antidote to procrastination is 'Just Begin'! This is one of the earliest and most important lessons that we learn in the kitchen, alongside the first lesson on self -discipline: *Show up*!

Especially, when you are new to the kitchen. Your lack of skill might trigger a fear of failure. Your perception about the drudgeries in kitchen might trigger a strong reluctance. But very soon, you get to learn, if you just show up in the kitchen, rest of the things start rolling.

Similarly, when the maid absents, we have to do many jobs we ordinarily don't do ourselves like doing the soiled utensils, cleaning the kitchen platform etc. Not used to cleaning the soiled utensils we may go near the sink, but so long as we just do not BEGIN, there will be terrible resistance and hesitancy to actually do that dirty job! Believe me, once we start cleaning, in no time we would also be done with that job, however tedious and shabby it might look in the beginning. Not only you finish that job, you also start learning how to fine tune the entire process for a faster and better result, as you do it yourself a few more times!

So, when my maid remains absent, I actually end up feeling glad that by doing these mundane, dirty chores, once in a while, I get a chance to learn and re-learn some of the fundamental life lessons:

i. If a job is to be done, we must simply begin. Mere beginning is the job half done. The rest in any case gets done.

ii. Although we all wish to always stay clean, cleanliness does not descend from the blue. Yes, there are tools for many tasks to avoid the rigour (dishwasher), or to avoid getting dirty (gloves). Use them by all means whenever you can. But there are times, when you really have to get dirty to get clean. Dishwasher does not clean all types of utensils; you have to manually do at least some of these soiled dishes. Platform must be wiped clean, for which you may have to use your hands. Clogged kitchen sink cannot be cleaned 100% in gloves; you may have to dirty your fingers at times to pull out some slimy thing choking it. Etc. Once you understand and accept this fact, you would get over the resistance to that cleaning job, which in any case, is indispensable.

iii. There is a world of difference in *looking clean* and *being clean*. Doing the utensils can drive this home like nothing else. Just rinse and most of your soiled utensils will *look* clean. But they *are not*, actually! Bacteria and fine dirt may still be residing there. To be clean, it must be free of toxic elements. Extend this learning to every sphere in life. Be clean, don't just look clean. Kitchen teaches us the lesson of integrity and honesty in a most effective manner, when we look at all the so-called mundane tasks required to be done, from a philosophical stand point.

iv. An ability to appreciate also comes naturally to you when you do temporarily a tedious task that is being otherwise done by your maid almost regularly, that too a number of times on the same day in different houses that she works in. You not only learn to appreciate her contribution to make your life easier, but also develop empathy and compassion for her realising how much hardships these maids have to go through daily just to make both ends meet!

This is just one type of situation that drives you to begin first. There are many more tasks which might make you feel resistance even to start; but once started, they do get finished with ease. Ever peeled whole pomegranates to de-seed? Or say, peeling a load of green peas or corns? Or say, storing freshly procured green vegetables and fruits in the fridge with space constraints? These are small tasks, but personally make me procrastinate at least once or twice! So boring and time-taking. You need patience, too. But once I remind myself the lesson of *Just Begin*, miracle happens and there I am, starting and finished with the job!

Another associated lesson that we get to learn along with 'Just Start' is *'Eat the frog first'*. The idea behind this saying is to identify one challenging task (the frog) and complete the task as the first thing in your schedule (eating it). Thus, it is the process of identifying your most difficult, but unavoidable, task of the day and finishing it before doing other things. In the context of kitchen, there could be many 'frogs' depending on what is unavoidable, but appeals to you the least personally. Yes, some of the kitchen tasks, especially the cleaning chores are the most unappealing ones when we ordinarily have many other odd jobs every day. But cleaning is absolutely unavoidable. So, the sooner we are done with these, the better. Finishing those irritating/difficult 'Must-Do's releases us from negative energies like resistance and tension to give our undivided attention to other important tasks.

Is not this lesson of 'eating frogs first' to tackle the least-appealing, but important and unavoidable, tasks on your to-do list first, rather than avoiding or deferring them, a great practical tip for effectiveness in professional workspace too?

Our humble kitchen, thus, makes us learn how to overcome procrastination and simply begin the task, i.e., *start action,* which is fundamental to success in all the spheres in our lives.

2. Purpose and Goal Orientation

No! Great ideas/concepts like 'Purpose Orientation' do not get into our mind in a jiffy when we initially enter the kitchen. What happens on ground is that as we move on discharging our responsibilities as a nurturer, feeding the family being one of those critical asks, purpose orientation as a core value (and goal setting as a significant action point for that) gathers clarity in one's conscious mind and gets deeply embedded in one's character over a fairly long period of working in kitchen. Every such nurturer gets to sense it at least sub-consciously very soon. Some take a reasonable time to recognise it consciously, some may take longer; but sooner or later, kitchen instils the sense of purpose in every mother.

Although not one of the *initial* lessons taught by kitchen, I would like to talk about this in the beginning itself, as ultimately this is the underlying bedrock on which every significant other value/lesson/attitude rests. This, in fact, gives *context* to every experience and every insight that we are going to talk about.

"Perfection of Means and a confusion of Ends seem to characterise our age."

– Albert Einstein

Gaining clarity on this one lesson would rescue us from the *'confusion of ends"!*

"When you are inspired by some great purpose, some extraordinary project, all your thoughts break their bonds: Your mind transcends limitations, your consciousness expands in every direction, and you find yourself in a new, great, and wonderful world. Dormant forces, faculties and talents become alive, and you discover yourself to be a greater person by far than you ever dreamed yourself to be."

– Pantanjali (c. 1st to 3rd Century B.C.) Indian master and founder of Yoga

I am reminded of this quote whenever I reflect on how a deep sense of purpose in everything we do, even in as limited a context as cooking for the family, truly transforms our whole character, and our ways of doing things, bringing out the best in us, that too, in alignment with the universal human values!

It is amazing how observing my mother in kitchen, and many others, and later, a lot of self-observation as I was living a life of a *working-mother,* helped me pick up from my homely kitchen deep insights into *Purpose Orientation and Goal Setting* – the most basic lessons in Effective Management and Leadership. The *ultimate* in life lessons, too. Until we realise what our *purpose of living* is, life does not get meaningful; nor can we give meaning to life, just by going through it. And no growth is ever possible if we do not ponder over anything, do not reflect, and introspect on why and how we want to do something, and what are we looking forward to achieving out of doing that.

Means, Ends and Purpose! Kitchen is a place where you automatically get launched into this inquiry, consciously or subconsciously.

So, let us ponder: Why does a mother, or the woman of the family, or for that matter anyone, cook?

Let's talk about mothers and women of the family first. Ask this question and you get a prompt reply: "Well, it's her job!"

Sure?

Since time immemorial, perhaps ever since the idea of 'family' came into being, it has been the role of the woman/women of the family to bring food to the table so that everyone eats to live and grow. That practice might have started during those early days of human civilisation, evolved out of a sheer convenience factor in division of labour between males and females. This might be because men are physically and emotionally/ sentimentally better endowed by Nature to do the outside tough jobs like hunting, growing food (i.e., procuring raw material for food) as they go about ensuring the security side. *While women are better endowed by Nature to nurture by bearing and raising children*, that requires them to stay indoor for most part, and so they are better placed to take care of all chores inside the house. Women *holding the fort as the men are out*!

Over time, for very many reasons that we all know about more or less, *this convenient mode of division of labour of the olden times became the unwritten law, leading to stereo-typing of roles for men and women, and eventual misjudging of capabilities on that basis.* (It is heartening that despite age-old constraints for women, we are now in a world that witnesses women managing all fronts with equal competence and valour.)

Well yes; even now, a woman, once married, ordinarily cooks for the husband and family. I am using the term 'ordinarily' as things have changed quite a bit in today's scenario with options available to employ cooks/order food from outside/dine outside etc., and sharing of household chores by both partners in some cases. Notwithstanding such social progress, even now, it is seen as *The Duty* of the woman of the house to ensure food for the family day in and day out- irrespective of whether she is also earning, going out or not.

But whatever may be the compulsion, *when she accepts this as her responsibility*, especially when a *mother* cooks for the family, does she look at this as merely her 'job'? No! It is not just a job; she sees it as a shining part of her 'role' as a Nurturer. She sees what a great opportunity she has got through this responsibility to make *her* invaluable *contribution* to the *well-being of her loved ones.*

Notice the difference...the moment she realises who she would be doing it for, i.e. the people she loves and cares for, who also love and care for her (that's what she likes to believe at least), *cooking is no longer a mere job*, that she can do rough-shod. It is her *contribution to their well- being.* She does it as perfectly as possible, pouring in all her talent, love, and care; yet may feel at times that she has fallen short- that is the kind of *sense of responsibility and ownership* that she starts bringing in to her so-called job. Enjoying it, rather than feeling weighed down by that feeling of responsibility and the drudgery of its routine. She, not so strangely, feels greatly enthused and empowered to just put her best foot forward every time she cooks, to do better and better.

She is now clear that the purpose of her task of cooking is to ensure the well-being of family and bonding, and she knows what goals she must keep for herself to achieve so that her purpose gets fulfilled. Let us list out some of the important goals she sets for herself:

a. providing food on time,
b. food cooked must be healthy, balanced in nutrition-i.e., nourishing,
c. food must be tasty and appealing to the preferences of the family members,
d. special needs of each individual family member must be met,
e. variety in food must be maintained from meal to meal over time to combat boredom,
f. simplicity of recipes for the most part, easy sourcing of ingredients, timely inventory management, avoidance of wastage etc. must be ensured.

Etc.

Love is always an important and indispensable ingredient in all cooking! It is said, without this ingredient, no dish turns out great ever. For professional cooks, it may be love for their own creations, while for a mother it is love for the family as well as for her own creations.

Truly, every act that we perform must be autographed by excellence! As much in the homely kitchen, as in the corporate world, or anywhere else.

Imagine how fast a person who manages kitchen, or has been observing this intently and understands the way we should look at the purpose of what we are doing whether for our family or for a living, can develop this *purpose orientation* in their work sphere as well and pick up the skill of setting appropriate goals aligned to that purpose! For example, such a person would be quick to understand that the purpose of any organisation they work for is not *profit* alone, but a *shared development of all stake–holders* (owners, shareholders, employees, customers, and all down the supply chain, and the community at large).Similarly, their goal will not be merely giving and achieving sale targets set for products and services, but to create and sustain valued *relationships* with customers by offering *solutions* to their problems as well as anticipated needs.

With clarity on purpose, it becomes easy for anyone to learn not only the skill of setting goals to achieve success, but also the skill of always aligning those goals with the ultimate purpose. Because *goalposts many a time tend to shift from the original position with changes in time and circumstances,* much of which cannot be predicted with precision and correctness in advance while setting goals. The *purpose, however, is something that must remain uncompromised/unchanged.* So, a true leader has to demonstrate this skill of continuously keeping the *goals aligned to purpose* even if it means to course-correct, amend or drop some goals and set new ones.

These insights carried forward from the humble kitchen can also help us inculcate a habit of asking 'whys' at significant points– ultimately developing a quest for the purpose of our life itself.

3. Show Up: Self-Discipline

Let me now get back to 'Just Begin'. Easier said than done, until and unless one finds and inculcates the *self-discipline* to *show up* every single time for the task, no matter what.

Kitchen teaches us in no ambiguous terms the need for Self-Discipline and the values of Structure and Routine in this context, as also in the context of many important things in life. In fact, I would say, the kitchen responsibilities almost *push* us to pick up the lessons on Self-Discipline quite early on.

Reasons are very simple. Already mentioned earlier. Food is indispensable for everyone to live. Not only indispensable, its intake also must follow almost a regular timetable. Timings of meals have to be *aligned to* our body requirements (biological clock) as well as daily work schedule to discharge personal and professional duties and responsibilities. So, a casual approach to planning, preparing/sourcing, and having meals is simply not sustainable. On one hand, such elements of indispensability and strict regularity of cooking tasks make it quite burdensome. On the other hand, the 'mundaneness' and general perception about many aspects of cooking and kitchen maintenance as 'intellectually not stimulating' (at times even *looked down upon* as an ordinary lowly job), could be a big dampener on many occasions, and you simply *'don't feel like'* going to the kitchen only. It takes a high degree of self-discipline to combat this avoidance tendency in the first place; show up for the task every time, and just begin it!

Self-discipline is primarily driven by Purpose, Passion, and Love, as well as the recognition of the fact that TIME is our most precious, yet non-manufacturable, non-renewable resource.

When we know the *purpose* behind anything and realise why we are doing or must do something, we shall be more inclined, or even excited, to *show up* for that job in the first place, overcoming inertia or resistance, if any. It is said, each of us exists for a purpose, and it is our duty to find and carry out that purpose. IKIGAI in Japanese culture – must have heard about it. It says the same thing: Everyone has a purpose, or reason to be here; and it lies within. Meaning of life is found in finding and living one's IKIGAI. When you have a clear understanding of that purpose, you also gather an idea on what constitute your big goals aligned to that purpose, and *how your daily tasks fit within these big goals.* This ensures that you are much more likely to complete these tasks, than if you look at those tasks in isolation, without keeping in view the bigger picture.

Look at the mother – how she finds her purpose (i.e., *contributing to the wellness of her family*) in the mundane kitchen routines! She simply shows up even while having health issues, and fixes the meals 3-4 times a day. This is nothing but purpose-driven sense of responsibility. Or in other words, *self-discipline* to attend to the needed chores. Look at the millions of working wives/mothers across the spectrum of professions! You would be simply flabbergasted if you observe the degree of self-discipline they bring into discharging their hugely diverse responsibilities in multitude of roles spanning personal and professional areas, taking all the constraints in their stride.

Kitchen teaches you soon that the biggest driver of self-discipline is to have a reason to do the task. Even if at the beginning you don't know what all exactly is to be done, just start and do something of that every day. In course of time, the other necessary steps will be revealed before you. For example, if you want to be a professional singer, do your voice exercises like alankara/sargam every day, and practice singing every day. Write something every day if you want to be a writer. Becoming a great writer does not happen overnight. Your purpose itself will be sufficient motivation to do the necessary tasks. Cooking is a beautiful example of this. Almost everyone enters the kitchen as a novice, an amateur, and mostly reluctant. But the compelling reasons for which one enters the kitchen brings on self-discipline to start and complete the meals, perfecting/improvising the dishes in course of time. Unless you find these compelling reasons (the purpose, or passion, or at least love for those you would be catering to) very soon, you are likely to get daunted by the regularity, rigour, and boredom of cooking and kitchen management.

No wonder, from time immemorial numerous famous philosophers have emphasised that self-discipline starts with finding your purpose and it is all about finding compelling reasons to do something, then committing yourself to that task or activity till the very end.

Similarly, if we are truly *passionate* about something, then we stay ever-ready and enthusiastic to take up that despite the hardships along the way or even the sacrifices of other comforts it might require. We enjoy doing that and bring in self-discipline to focus on that activity without wasting precious time, or constantly whining about the irritants/discomforts/sacrifices. We can then easily stay out of excuses or blame games for not being able to do our job. For example, creative pursuits. I have a passion for singing, and hence doing regular vocal exercise is a must for me, even if it is not always convenient. I also love tangy and hot food, as also ice creams. But I know, those are harmful for the vocal cords. Vocalists refrain from consuming such stuff. So, although I love them, I control myself, allowing myself to relish them once in a blue moon, may be. Thus, *self-discipline also lies in resisting immediate gratification for longer term good, driven by passion!* Look at the professional chefs, most of whom must have landed in these jobs due to their passion for cooking. Observe how they carry themselves with self-discipline to create new recipes through experiments, and once successful with some recipe, how they stick to the recipe to maintain consistence and uniformity in quality, taste, and flavours in their dishes. Thus, doing something driven by passion does not also give one the license to be free-floating all the time without any self-discipline. *Self-discipline also lies in knowing when to be strict about structure and when to give priority to spirit behind a task.*

Self-discipline necessarily requires us to have power over our mind. Once we clearly realise that we have power only over our own mind and not over outside events, we find mental strength and agility to take inconveniences in our stride as we keep focusing on doing our tasks. Being distressed over small things can easily derail us even before we realise. In such situations, self-discipline helps us to stick to what is within our control. If we embrace and accept what is outside our control, our peace of mind will remain undisturbed and hence, our ability to focus on what we can do will remain unaffected. *In kitchen, there could be umpteen instances which can upset your mood,* like a dish going bad at the last moment, hurting yourself while cooking, an experiment going wrong just when you have no time to replace that by something else, your creations getting no due appreciation etc. etc. But kitchen is a place, where we cannot afford to *cry over the spoilt milk*-something that has already happened. *Instead, it drives us to immediately shift our focus towards how to salvage the dish, or the situation.* What a huge learning! Effective people accept what *is*, and take action to ensure what *can be*.

Similar is the case, when we do something out of *love* and care for others. We know we have to cook for our loved ones. In a sense, we are being looked up to for food by our family with tremendous faith that we would not fail them. That helps imbibe a strong sense of self-discipline in us, the mothers, to meet *their needs* in the best and most cared for manner. *Self-discipline driven by love gives rise to a sense of responsibility that is unmatched and supreme.* If one is in charge of feeding others, will it be okay if she brings meals not as per the set timings and requirements, but as per her sweet will? Makes the breakfast, skips the lunch, delays the dinner! No. Here comes the need for self-discipline in ensuring *what is needed*, that too, *on time.*

In the process, kitchen also teaches us the value of time, and why and how to use it optimally, by setting some form of structure and routine to manage the unavoidable chores. You don't have the whole 24 hours to cook as per your sweet will, as other personal and professional tasks must also be attended to, as required and on time. Thus, for effective management of everything you need to do, first you start realising that TIME is a limited resource (you have 24 hours only a day which cannot be stretched, but can unwittingly be *shrunk by wasting*) and so must be valued, and put to correct use. Or else, your whole life would simply slip away moment-by-moment. *With self-discipline, we avoid squandering away time unawares.*

One more integral dimension of self-discipline is *Consistency*. Not only we have to be driven from within by our purpose-passion-love, and show up and do the job, we must show up and work every day or regularly *with consistency*, without allowing anyone or anything to distract us uncontrollably from doing that task. We must build up our life action by action. Even after finding our purpose and planning effectively, most of us fail to achieve our goals. Why? *We fail because we fail to be consistent in action.*

'Self-Discipline' is the other name of a habit of consistency in action, i.e., finding motivation for doing something again and again, and actually doing that until you start seeing the results. Your ability to keep going on, even if you fail a few times, till you succeed!

So, can we say now, our humble kitchen teaches us constantly to discipline ourselves in small things, so that, from there, we can progress to things of greater value and significance in our lives?

This kind of self-discipline is also warranted in achieving anything worthwhile in life. One who cultivates this in a kitchen can easily carry it forward to other walks of life, especially while having to manage challenging workplaces with limited options.

Let me add, our mundane kitchen responsibility in a unique way makes us thoroughly understand the concept of "Inertia" also. When we start avoiding our kitchen duties on some pretext or other out of lack of self-discipline, we observe very soon that we get a thousand inane excuses not to attend to our kitchen duties. We don't feel like doing; so, we don't do once; 2nd time also we would give in easily to that 'don't feel like doing' mood and procrastinate doing our chores. That is, if we procrastinate once, very likely we would continue to procrastinate – that is inertia- *the tendency to stay in the same position.* Similarly, if we are active, enjoying exploring in the kitchen, getting creative, then most likely, we would continue to be active, creative, and happy. This is also inertia – *of staying active*.

This understanding is immensely helpful in life to get over the resistance to do things that need to be done, whether you like it or not.

4. Structure and Routine

Consistency in action calls for some sort of structure and routine.

As a working mother, there was a time when I had to finish a lot of cooking before 8.45 am in the morning, after which I used to have hardly 30-45 mins to get ready and leave for office. Lot of cooking means lots of cooking, indeed – tiffin for school and office, lunch; plus, breakfast! For 4, at times, 6 members. Add to that own daily morning ablutions. Obviously, it takes some minimum time of 3 to3 ½ hours to complete all chores even with my quite high level of expertise by then. Thus, my alarm to wake up was set for 4.45 am, with a 2nd one at 5 am, that still left a margin of say about 20-30 mins to be out of kitchen by 8.45am. *That was my planning with a structure and routine, to which I used to stick to, no matter what. And it worked.* Most of the times, I used to be too tired particularly while in Mumbai (having to work hard physically both at home and in commuting to-and-fro office by local train and buses and autos- having a few hours to sleep at night). Yet, the self-discipline imbibed over years to follow the *routine* regularly with only occasional slips did serve me very effectively. As I have mentioned somewhere earlier, I am a punctuality freak – could never accept being late to office due to reasons *within* my control.

Yes, I had also put in place some other facilitating *'structures'* for my household chores, like employing maids for doing utensils, sweeping, and mopping, and for preparing dinner. Yes, it was not possible for me to do dinner due to time constraints after reaching late at night from office. So, engaging a helping hand, and outsourcing on days she was absent, is a sort of 'structure' to deliver in kitchen management. Similar to the organisational structure for deliverables at different levels of management and operations 😊 We will talk about delegation, outsourcing etc. later on. In kitchens of joint families, you would find very nice division of labour as also collaborations, which are like *invisible but set structures*. So much of work would get done without overlaps or collisions, so that 'too many cooks spoil the broth' kind of situations are averted. These are kind of *structures* in the context of kitchen management.

Let us look at structures and routine from another perspective.

Surprises thrill, but not always.

Can you be comfortable and most efficient in a kitchen in which ingredients are stored without any orderliness whatsoever- today here, tomorrow there? Some degree of *structure and orderly arrangement* must be brought into our kitchen storage for ease of operating. This way, you don't spoil a dish looking for a small ingredient at the nick of the moment, neither do you waste time in first taking out 100% of different things needed to cook a dish.

Can you be okay if you are sitting on dining table ready for breakfast *at your usual time*, but pat comes the surprise: no breakfast or lunch today; only an early supper! NO! There has to be some structure for *meal timings*, with very occasional diversions, may be once in a blue moon, for compelling reasons.

Similarly, even if some *staple dishes* are repetitive, e.g., rice, roti, dal, green vegetables, these are almost indispensable *on our platter*. We must have these for meeting some of our basic nutrient requirements. Then we are free to add other dishes, some even fancy or just tasty to elevate our platter. These staple food dishes give the *anchors* to our food, leaving space for experimentation thereafter. Just think about it: you are a rice-eater, and your main meal is lunch, that keeps you in a properly energised state for the whole day as per your work schedule. Would you like to be surprised with rice one day, upma some other day, or dhokla still some other day? No! Your lunch Thali must have rice, or at least some version of rice like pulao/biriyani/khichudi as a must (set structure), while the spirit behind the meal (complete nutrition, taste, and preference) can be taken care of through some expected and some surprises built into side dishes.

Similarly, in life we have to go through the motion of some basic chores. We must not get bored with something the moment it becomes routinely repetitive and throw all anchors to wild winds in the name of flexibility or experimentation – then it becomes *drifting* and not experimenting.

So, the point is: Self-discipline requires showing up, starting action and consistency in action over a period of time for the desired outcome. Consistency, in turn, requires us to pick up the skills of putting in place some needed structures and routines, which must be adhered to with occasional diversions only for reasons good enough to let the structure go by.

Everyone in charge of cooking and kitchen learns this value of putting in place routines and structures, and gradually acquires the skills to frame these depending upon personal factors, and inculcates self-discipline to adhere to these. Such people, while working in their professional workplaces, are more likely to create, appreciate and follow, the formal/informal structures for ultimate delivery of goods/services. The element of lackadaisical attitude to implementation of policies automatically reduces thereby.

As I figure out, the plus points of structuring certain activities are:

a. Ensures that the activity gets done in the first place.
b. Ensures that some specific periodicity/manner of doing the activity is maintained.
c. Ensures that you *stay on course*; minimising inaction/diversions, on some pretext or the other.

Especially, in the initial phase and if the task is difficult or boring, it is a common human tendency *to procrastinate* and justify that with a whole lot of *other things supposedly needed to be done*. At times, even there are cases wherein we start with a lot of gusto, but let them die off just because we stop doing it altogether, on some pretext or other. If the reason for stopping is worthwhile, then fine. But *if the reason for stopping is flimsy, and actually stems from lack of commitment/discipline, then structures can be of great value to avert such situations and help you do the important things at regular periodicity.*

So, basically, structures help in staying focussed. What a valuable lesson from a homely kitchen!

5. Structure Vs Spirit

Yes, structure lends discipline and continuity/consistency to activities needed to be undertaken.

BUT.... Beware of the trap it sets at times!

Very often, in course of time it is the structure, that becomes the primary target to be ensured, rather than the *purpose* for which this was set up in the first place! *The purpose behind any formal structure has to be 'delivery'/'fructification' of some ultimate pre-determined outcome,* viz. sale of products/services, or inculcation of a mindset/organisational culture, or formation of desirable habits/behavioural patterns. When such purpose behind the structures is not well-communicated, or well-received down the line, the implementing people at different tiers try to uphold structures with religious commitment, but fail to appreciate the *spirit* behind these, and thus fail to achieve the results for which these comprehensive structures were created initially. *Unless you are always alive to the fact that structures are not important for the sake of themselves, but for facilitating implementation of something which will deliver value/result, there is every possibility that, over a period of time, through your unguarded enthusiasm to keep up the sanctity of structures, you would tend to lose sight of the spirit behind.* You unwittingly end up destroying the very purpose behind them, OR, you fail to grab / lose sight of the *newer and better* opportunities coming your way for the same/better results, as your schedule is already so structured that the margin for recognising new opportunities is just not available.

Think of the Review Meetings many of the Organisations usually have in tons. It is a *structure* set up to review performance in key areas, say, monthly, quarterly or in any other periodicity. Plus point: without such a structure which requires that a meeting be held of concerned line functionaries with management to take stock of the affairs, it will not be possible to know whether things are moving on the ground the way they should; how much of the periodic goals have been achieved and what should be the guidelines/roadmap on what to do next etc. etc. Without this structure, it may not even be possible to have all these key people together, given their busy schedules even otherwise, for cross-fertilisation of ideas and further planning. *But it will be self-defeating to have these structured meetings,*

- if the participants do not come after doing their own home work, i.e., assessment of their own status.

- if the periodicity is too frequent to even have some meaningful action in between two meetings.
- if changes in circumstances warrant shift in focus to some other area, but you are fixated about this original plan of action.
- If as higher-ups, you simultaneously drive multiple goals in different directions working at cross-purposes without enough prioritisation and/or allowing reasonable time for execution, and only focus on *monitoring* through umpteen meetings and status reports.

I recollect here, something Mr T.V. Rao, an eminent HRD Guru, said in his book on HRD Mission about *HRD Traps*. He says, HRD (Human Resources Development) is ultimately a philosophy – a way of living and building a work culture. So, it is the *spirit* behind all HRD initiatives like reward, recognition, performance planning etc. which is of paramount importance. But my personal experience in the HRD Department of the Corporate Office of my organisation made me realise how we were actually more particular about the implementation of the HRD initiatives as structures, rather than trying to assess whether the spirit behind these is getting achieved, that is whether actually these actions are having any impact on/changing mindset and work culture, as desired to be brought about through these initiatives.

Sorry, I digressed a bit. But *this is one of the central issues when we deal with structures in any context.* We must gain absolute clarity – *structures are there not for themselves, but for a purpose.* So, if that purpose is getting fulfilled even without strict following of the structure, then so be it, at times. We can also think about this in terms of rigidity vs flexibility of means.

In the context of kitchen, a very good example of structure could be a prescribed RECIPE, setting out all ingredients, their quantity and proportions and exact steps/procedure with exact cooking time periods. There would be some, especially the new cooks, who would rather not try a recipe if following it 100% is not possible, say for want of some ingredients. But a mature cook would see through the recipe for workable combinations and make her own improvisations, instead of outrightly dropping the recipe, and ensure turning up something tasty, healthy with whatever is available at that point of time.

Similarly, timings of meals – an important 'structural process' for kitchen management. Usually, during the whole day, a normal person is supposed to have three wholesome meals with reasonable gaps – breakfast, lunch, and dinner. This is a structure that need be adhered to, in general, for ensuring proper nourishment of our body and physical health, that also has a tremendous impact on our work-abilities as well as mental health. But this does not mean we be so rigid about this time table (structure behind a healthy routine) that we forget how to enjoy life (spirit behind a healthy routine) in small other not-so-harmful ways, once in a while. For example, on Sundays/holidays, we may sleep a bit more, or do some other fun-stuff with very light ready-to-seep liquids, like say, juice/soup/milk/buttermilk etc. and go for a nice and filling *brunch* instead of a breakfast and lunch as per routine timings. We know that home-cooked food is healthy. But at times, we may outsource from good places, if tired, or feel like having a diversion, or having much more important things to do.

This type of skill to know the laid down way to do (structure), but do the best with *available* resources (that includes 'time') without unduly diluting the whole purpose/spirit behind such structures, gets cultivated easily in the kitchen, which is very useful in other spheres as well. This is, in fact, a lesson in structure versus spirit, that can be carried forward from kitchen to all other spheres in life. This can also be seen as another way to understand the need for advance planning *with scope for flexibility.*

6. Planning, Goal setting, Review and Flexibility

Someone once remarked, "Oh! cooking is breeze!"

Yes, may be so when you are *only* cooking, and you are a bit of a pro.

Well, it might be so even for *a hired cook*, who comes and does cooking as per *your menu and instructions,* and leaves. *Simply because when she is cooking, she is only cooking, without owning* the responsibility for the menu, that must be prepared keeping multiple aspects in view; nor they owe the responsibility to ensure requisite provisions and ingredients; nor they usually assume the responsibility for keeping up to a *high* standard of quality in what they are cooking. *It is your, the home makers' call to keep the needed provisions ready, tell them the menu, even teach them the recipes many a times*. Even for *a professional Chef*, who also *only cooks while cooking*, it is *not* a breeze. It comes with a tremendous amount of responsibility, hence stress, to keep up to the set standards of fine dining, excellence, and uniformity of quality parameters! *And for the homemakers, who cook themselves, it is definitely not breeze as when they are cooking, they are not only cooking; they are multi-tasking.* Apart from the *added responsibilities* of all the planning, procuring, and executing in connection with putting meals on the family table, there are scores of other things that a mother-cum-home cook must attend to regularly, including her own professional demands if she is also working. *Now bring in the quantity aspect.* It is one thing to cook only for a few people every day, and absolutely a different burden when cooking has to be done for many people in large quantum when you are used to cooking only a small amount. The sheer physical strain is terrible, forget about the mental pressures of coming through as a perfect host(ess)! No! Cooking is not breeze for mothers in such cases; it can get really tiring! And most importantly, when cooking is done by the home cooks *regularly* without respite, day in and day out for years on, as I keep harping, it is definitely not breeze. Sorry, people who comment so derogatorily about cooking by a mother, do not have their hearts in right place, to say the least!

Food does not appear on your table by MAGIC! It takes a world of sustained planning, procuring, stocking and decision-making, and then cooking each meal. Cooking itself in fact sucks the least of our energy, in normal situations.

Any time you look into my fridge, along with the usual stuff like vegetables, milk, bread, non-Veg etc., you would find a whole lot of ready-to-use spice pastes, home-made spice powders (singly and in combinations), may be some prepared batters, some roti-dough, some boiled potato, some blanched winter vegetables, some frozen peas and corns, some boiled beans and lentils, different categories of dry spice-mix packets from market, etc. I am sanguine, this is pretty much a common practice with regular cooks, especially working wives/mothers. Also, with professional Chefs.

So, here comes the value of '*staying prepared in advance*'- not only to save time, but also to have ready ingredients for plan A/B/C as the situation unfolds, depending upon exigencies. PLANNING! Not only you roughly plan your menu for breakfast, lunch, dinner etc. for the day/following day, you also are in readiness to a significant extent for quite a good number of days. Circumstances still can thwart your plans suddenly. But you have quite an array of basic ingredients to quickly fix something else.

It is mind-blowing how in small and seemingly insignificant ways, kitchen helps one learn the extremely valuable skills of planning and goal setting. Let us see, how.

Once the purpose is clear, the next step is how to achieve that purpose. Obviously, it cannot be a one huge jump. A roadmap is to be made. The journey to the final goal invariably progresses through many smaller goals – the milestones – one at a time.

Preparedness. Is this not an indispensable requirement in every sphere of life? Consciously or sub-consciously, we all imbibe into ourselves and our schedules some degree of preparedness. Goes without saying, when such preparedness is gained *consciously* with some mindful planning, it is definitely going to be more useful and fruitful.

Now let us mindfully observe what goes into managing kitchens on a regular basis.

Planning, of course. Virtually every mother plans, quite in advance, for ingredients/provisions required in the kitchen for a long enough period (*inventory management*); as also *a rough menu* at least for a few days or a week or so (*setting short-term goals*). But so far as the next day meals are concerned, there is definite planning by a mother at least one day in advance. If not put in black and white, which is usually done by some organization-freak/busy mothers, at least something *concrete* takes shape in her mind before she signs off for the day and drops on bed at night. And while deciding menus, she keeps in view stock at home, previous few days' menus, special tastes/requirements of family members etc. – i.e., *not only plan must be feasible for instant execution, but also must work for the family.*

And the beauty lies in the flexibility that is brought into what is already planned, without rigidity, i.e., without killing herself to stick to the plans or routine by any means. Quite often, I end up preparing a completely different menu, keeping all my concerns addressed, if better choices spring up, when I actually get down to cook. At times, despite planning you might lack/run short of some ingredients, or get unannounced guests, or face unpredicted situations like sudden emergencies might come up, when your plan A no longer looks feasible. *When you keep your mind open, surprising things happen.* You remember new dishes, new experiments etc. There you are – quickly ready with a Plan B, C! In fact, at times it even becomes too burdensome to come up with a menu... especially for dinner. You think, think, and think; nothing good strikes; but the moment you are in the kitchen ready to go for the job, superb ideas strike you. Planning for kitchen management thus teaches you to *just stay open to here and now!*

I believe, this is indeed the outcome of always keeping some kind of plans. Planning does the wonder of letting the stress factor go, and frees up your mind. And we know, how much more we tap into with an open mind! And the bonus is: devoid of stress, we start enjoying what we are doing, and often do a great job.

It may sound oxymoronic; *but planning, when understood rightly, gives space to flexibility. Great planning always contains alternatives to achieve the core objectives.* Flexibility does not mean throwing up everything planned to the winds. Nor does it mean compromising with self-discipline to execute. It only means needed open-mindedness and *agility* to abandon plans that do not work on the field and switch to some other plan without losing precious time.

In kitchen, flexibility may mean small little things like changing menu, changing recipe, changing cooking techniques etc. I remember doing this as a working mother in kitchen in morning hours whenever there is shortage of time, as getting late for office was never an option. But my great take-away from these repeated experiences is a *skill to deal with sudden changes in circumstances* when things cannot go as per planning.

Flexibility to deal with sudden changes in circumstances when things do not go as per planning for reasons whatsoever is a major call on leaders and managers for effectiveness – just like need for changing menu, changing recipe on the spot in the context of a changed circumstance in kitchen and cooking.

Reminds me of something Winston Churchill once said,

"The best Generals are those who arrive at the results of planning without being tied to plans."

I say, the same applies to all of us in all spheres of our lives, more so to leaders in challenging roles. The playing fields in work environments are dynamic, and not entirely within your control. So, to successfully deliver the outcomes navigating through a constantly changing playing field, planning must be done with enough scope for necessary agility and flexibility to adapt to, or beat, the changes in the environment.

There is one more significant dimension embedded in these ideas of 'plan, but be flexible'. When we are changing our Plan A, what are we doing effectively? If changing *before* executing, then we are *'reviewing'* our plan in the context of the actual cues/dimensions in the present situation, and modifying/discarding accordingly. If we are modifying/discarding *after* executing, to plan something else for the next time, it only implies we are *'reviewing for evaluation'* of the results of our plan and deciding for the requisite changes in plan and/or implementation for a better result next time. But every time, we are learning to stay alive to the need for a *'review and evaluation'* of any plan, before/after execution, and internalising those skills.

Rings a bell? THE PDCA (Plan-Do-Check-Act) cycle they teach you in any professional management course.

Someone who has learnt these significant lessons on planning and flexibility even from a homely kitchen would find it way easier to do similar exercises in respect of other real-life responsibilities for delivery of an outcome, irrespective of whether they have attended a professional management course or not. *In kitchen, you learn by doing, and that kind of learning gets internalised better in any way.*

These lessons we learn in kitchen are very significant in every situation in life, and especially for effective management and leadership in workplaces. Keep your plans ready; but be open to flexibility. Demonstration of appropriate flexibility as per the demand of the prevailing actual situation is a strength, not weakness, although flexibility in terms of unwarranted changes in plans for lack of faith and conviction in your own action plan, or due to lack of self-discipline, might point to a weakness. And so is rigidity about a set plan a huge weakness as it puts the pre-set plan above its objective, and fails to address the dynamic parameters in your actual environment and hence most likely may prove infructuous and ineffective.

There are some situations in which *backward-planning* is also done in kitchen. At least, I do! When we would be going on a long vacation, and I would have to completely empty out my fridge by consuming the green vegetables, non-veg, and perishables like spice pastes, I resort to backward planning. I make a list of whatever is in there, making a mental note of quantity in each case. Depending upon the stock already in the fridge, I make a detailed menu-plan for some days (at least 3-4 days) *ending with the last meal* before we would be leaving home. Mostly my plan would be to use up all stock and *not to let anything go waste.* Once the menu plan is ready for those days, either I stop further procurement, or if I find a few things wanting, I procure just that much, or give away the excess to the maid before they turn bad. Usually this becomes a week-long execution of multiple small tasks running up to the final day. I am not aware if there is any term in management lexicon equivalent to backward planning. But let me tell you, I have found important parallels in corporate workspace requiring backward planning. *It is evident, backward planning essentially relates to execution of some non-negotiable, non-deferable goal.* While I was in Human Resources Development Department at our Corporate Office, one of our responsibilities was to organise Special Day Celebrations/important Felicitation Programmes of high achievers at the hands of the Top brass. These functions had to be very meticulously planned and organised in perfect coordination with many other departments/outstation offices, as none other than the Chairman used to be the key participant. To ensure that nothing goes off-track at the last moment, we always used to have a *backward planning* on the exact tasks with exact timelines much in advance, with a detailed day-by-day chart for the last week ending with the D-Day. I guess, my kitchen had taught me this lesson well enough by then not to miss it for a carry-forward to a parallel situation in my workplace.

Goal setting

As we all know, 'Goal Setting', particularly within organizational settings, is immensely important, as without setting tangible short-term, medium term and long-term goals, the process for achievement of the final goal neither kick-starts, nor efforts sustained, nor ends successfully. It is a powerful technique that provides a direction to our efforts, focuses our attention, promotes persistence, and increases our confidence by enabling us to pass through milestones – one small goal after another, that, in turn, enables us to *evaluate* our implementational success in right direction and in right measure.

Understanding the importance of goals and the techniques involved in setting achievable goals paves the way for success. Our homely kitchen may be a very insignificant platform to learn the detailed techniques of professional goal setting; but observe keenly and you will be surprised to find how it throws up insights on at least the basic KEY principles of goal-setting in any working area.

No. 1:

Think about the difference between these two scenarios.

a) You just wake up and start thinking, Oh! I have to cook all three meals myself today as the maid is not coming. Maid had informed last evening. A relative is also expected around lunch time. Though not exactly invited for lunch, he might have to be offered lunch as a courtesy. What if he accepts? You have not yet decided on the specific menu for each meal.

b) You get up, knowing that you have to manage everything on your own today as maid had informed last evening that she would not be coming. So before going to bed the previous night, *you have planned the menus,* say, to make dish A and B for breakfast for X number of people; Dish C, D, E, F (G, H already in fridge as left-overs) for X+1 people for lunch (as expecting 1 relative to drop by around that time); and Dish H and J for dinner for X people. In deciding menu, you have taken care not to repeat dishes made in previous 2-3 days as some of your family members just hate it; ensured that ingredients required are at home, as also other miscellaneous factors like specific tastes, preferences, health issues, timing etc.

Picture another simple situation:

You have decided to prepare a *mixed vegetable curry*. Well, one sub-goal is set. Now, compare two situations.

(a) you just stop at that without further planning, till you are actually in the kitchen.

(b) you also decide specifically *which* mixed veg curry to make, i.e., the specific combination of vegetables, spices, and recipe. In my part of the land (Odisha), there are just N number of recipes mixing all sorts/groups of vegetables – local, traditional, winter vegetables, western vegetables, and herbs, etc. and combo of traditional and winter vegetables which are now-a-days available round the year! Most of the times, some beans/legumes like yellow peas/white chickpeas/small black chickpeas etc. are also added to mixed curry and *they need prior soaking*. So, you can get to job without wasting time if you have decided in advance which *specific* recipe to do.

I know, you're getting it; very obvious. The ease, speed, and quality of your 'performance'/achievement of goals will be superior in the second situations when you are in good preparedness with at least some specific plans than in the first (without specific goals).

When you get into a habit of specifying even small sub-goals through your kitchen routine, subconsciously you are likely to carry this habit forward to all other situations. For example, if you have to lose weight, you won't say, "I will regularly exercise and shed my overweight." Rather, you would say: "I will exercise regularly for 30 mins in the morning and reduce weight by about 2kg by the end of the current month."

Which goal is likely to push you to be regular about your exercise, and periodically evaluate how much you have actually lost, i.e., if you achieved your goal or not?

So, the first important insight that leaps out of our humble homely Kitchen is:

Specify your goals clearly.

Setting clearly defined goals leads to better performance. Even empirical research works evince that *clarity of goals* is positively related to overall *motivation* and *satisfaction* in any work space – personal or professional. When goal is clear and precise in mind, it gives us an improved understanding of the tasks at hand, exactly what is required and how it is to be approached, and you start the job without anxiety or wasting time. And the resulting success is a further dose of motivation. Success is, indeed, a pillar of further success in many situations (till of course complacency takes over!). No wonder, when an individual has specific goals to meet, their performance is more pronounced than in the absence of specifics.

No. 2:

Simply watch your own emotions and feelings in kitchen when you are reasonably comfortable with time available to you, and you create a rather good spread with variety of delicious dishes, as against a lazy decision to make do with, say, a khichdi (one pot rice with lentil and vegetables) for lunch! Khichdi is no doubt a complete meal with required nutrition; but sorry, not challenging, if you have the time for a better spread and you are not a novice. *Which option fires your motivation more* – the too-simple one-pot dish or a platter of nicely cooked variety of delicacies which are possible with some extra effort and will be loved by your family?

Picture another situation in kitchen:

You are extra excited and wish to mind-blow your guests with some exquisite, complex, and rare dishes and a huge spread, to impress them with your great culinary skills. *You don't have sufficient time on hand, though*. You don't even have all the unique ingredients; you have not yet perfected your hands on one or two of the rare dishes. Yet, you decide this menu, thinking you may improvise here and there. Very confident move. But in the process, you run short of time and rather mess up a few dishes! The spread also turns up too wide, without complementarity amongst various dishes. In food, lack of balance and complementarity kills even a great 'thali' having dishes that are individually yummy, but do not go together. So, what is the result? How would you feel as the creator/ hostess in this case?

So, while setting goals, keep in mind that goals should neither be too simple, nor too challenging. Too simple goals don't challenge us to push our skills to the limit, as we can achieve them staying within our comfort zone without any demand on us for improvement in performance. If not laced with more demanding goals along the way, it may become very boring soon in the workplace. On the other extreme, too challenging goals *which are not within our ability level in given circumstances,* even after allowing for reasonable stretches, are likely to lead us to frustration, as their *probability of failure* is very high. So, goals set up should be bold enough to challenge our potential ability to a good extent so that we continuously can push the envelope and reach for it. Such challenging goals (which call for more efforts from us vis-à-vis our current level, yet not far beyond our ability level given all the related factors) can improve performance through increased motivation to prove our mettle and increased self-satisfaction at continuous visible improvement in results.

It is not only *achievement/success, but also the anticipation of achievement*/success, that impacts our motivation level for any task. Kitchen throws up this insight time and again. You are happy to cook or try nice dishes because you *anticipate* it would turn out great and yummy and would be liked by all. If you anticipate a disaster, you stop trying only. If we know a goal is challenging yet believe it is within our abilities to accomplish by walking an extra mile, we are more likely to be motivated to complete that task. Hence, while setting goals, be careful about 'what challenges your potential to give your better than current best', along with its feasibility.

So, the second important lesson that gets thrown up by a homely Kitchen is:

Goals must be challenging, yet attainable.

Here we may do well to remember that even so called 'simple' goals also have their own place in goal-setting. *Whether something is simple or challenging or too complex is context-specific!* And the context is the stage-cum- skill level of the doer. Walking for a baby of say 7-8 months is too challenging, while it is not so for a one-year-old! Making tea is too simple a task for a regular cook, while this could be fairly challenging for a novice. When you want your adolescent child to start learning how to roll out a *Roti* (round flat bread made of whole wheat flour), you don't set a goal for a perfectly round shaped roti (that would be too challenging for them); rather you set a goal of getting them to roll out first without any tears/ cracks and with some uniformity of thickness all over (not even 100%), which will be challenging enough, *but attainable* under guidance, for a starter.

No. 3:

Many a times, too challenging tasks also involve high task complexity.

Your young daughter is showing interest in learning cooking. Instead of helping her learn some basic processes and basic recipes like steamed rice, simple lentil, simple fry/curry first, you would teach her a complex recipe (say, Biriyani) by hand-holding, and expect her to replicate it in the very second attempt. What would happen? She would just get *overwhelmed and scared* to try! Will she ever come running again to you to learn cooking? Here, even 'basic' recipes for you would feel like 'challenging' to her as she does not know anything in the first place. In fact, mothers, elderly matriarchs do goal setting very effectively (though subconsciously without naming the processes as per management jargons) while initiating the younger ones to culinary skills.

While deciding on task complexity of any goal, 3 important aspects must be kept in mind. Skill level of the performer, time available for completing the task, and phase of the doer, as well as the overall project.

Goals which are overly complex for the skill level or stage of the doer will very likely kill the motivation for doing it as these would appear impossible to achieve. In all probability, these will become overwhelming with negative impact on morale, motivation, and productivity.

Complexity of any task must also be evaluated in terms of the time allowed for completion. Very simple. Unless the time period allotted for a task is reasonable, the task complexity of even a simple task is *perceived* as high enough to be demotivating, what to speak of challenging tasks. More so for people who reasonably understand the various dimensions of the task and can guess the timeframe reasonably required to complete the overall task. Even 2-minute Maggi takes at least 4-5 mins to get cooked right. If someone already knows that, but asked to do it in 2 mins, she would know the trap. Sufficient (not excessive) time must be allowed to work toward a goal, which should include time and opportunities to review and reassess all factors so asto improve performance.

As emphasised in so many other contexts, stage of the project must also be kept in mind to go for certain levels of task complexity. It is always advisable and effective to keep complexity at lower/comfortable levels in initial stages, so that the process starts, and then can gradually gather momentum with added task complexity, without overwhelming the performers. As an unmarried pampered daughter at home, my mother used to ask me to help her out in kitchen with very simple chores first like boiling the milk, or chopping some vegetables, or making tea. But gradually, I learnt how to roll out *roties*, then how to prepare the dough, then how to roast the roties (going step by step in terms of higher and higher complexity) etc. Now, after all these years of experience in kitchen, I don't get scared to turn out a delicious spread before the family and friends with admirable speed. I have repeated the projects often enough – so the degree of task complexity I am comfortable with is much higher than, say, someone with a short period of kitchen experience.

Always assess the task complexity in terms of skill level, time allotted and stage of the performer in the project to avoid making the goal too overwhelming.

So, the 3rd principle is:

Avoid Task Complexity that overwhelms the performer.

No. 4:

Goals must always flow from *Purpose*. Otherwise, you won't have the requisite *commitment* to these goals. And without high commitment to the goals, you are likely to be shaken off the track the moment obstacles appear. Goal-theorists say that goal performance is strongest when people are committed, and even more so when said goals are difficult (i.e., reasonably challenging goals).

I don't wish to repeat how our homely kitchen helps us pick up this insight on purpose-driven goal setting as we have discussed this in detail in the context of Purpose-orientation and goal-setting earlier in this book. Kindly refer to point. 2. Notwithstanding obstacles, mothers always attend to their kitchen responsibilities with strong commitment to goals and values that they must demonstrate, as they are clear on the 'purpose' behind why they have accepted these responsibilities in the first place. Just want to add that 'purpose' and 'values' are terms that are universally used in a positive sense. You cannot have a 'purpose' to kill someone; you have the *bad motive* to do that.

Point is: goals that we are strongly committed to would elicit our best efforts despite obstacles. And strong commitment can arise when goals are perceived to achieve our ultimate purpose. Further, commitment is higher if these goals are perceived as challenging enough, yet attainable; may be because we love proving our mettle, too.

So, the 4th principle you can learn from kitchen is:

Your goals must be set aligned to your purpose and values (right values) to elicit the needed commitment for attaining them.

No. 5:

It always pays to self-assess our performance on a continuous basis. But that is not enough, as things at times look blurred from too near. So, goal-setting must have in it an in-built window for review by others – both from internal teams as well as from outside.

I am sure, all cooks themselves taste the dish they create, at times during the process, and unfailingly at the end, to find out how the dish has actually turned out. Any committed cook would do this. So, this is the self-evaluation bit. But thereafter, they do request anyone around or children/other family members to taste and ask how it is. A very normal scene in kitchens. "Thoda chakh ke batao, namak mirch sahi hei?" (Pl taste and tell me if it is fine.)

In management jargon, we may term this as *'feedback'* on our performance of the goal. When feedback is immediate, it is easier to determine the degree of success in meeting the goal without loss of precious time, and there is better scope for course-correction accordingly. Moreover, positive feedback has a strong motivational angle. Constructive criticism and negative feedback are also equally helpful as they drive us to re-assess and improve. Or, if on re-assessment, we are satisfied with our own job, it helps to strengthen our spiritual progress in terms of increased ability to take negative opinions in our stride without getting affected. ☺

When feedback is delayed, it weakens the process of goal-achievement in terms of loss of time for corrective action; plus, at times leading to irreversible mistakes. A dish that is too salty for others (say, may not be for you as you eat salt on a higher side) *and already served* cannot be redeemed. Whereas, had this been known earlier even immediately after the dish is made through feedback from others, some salvaging (by adding more hot water to dilute gravy, or adding flour doughs to soak up salt etc.) could have been done.

So, the 5th important insight on goal-setting from kitchen is:

Seek and be open to honest, unambiguous, and immediate feedback on your performance of the goals from significant others even as you are in the process of achieving the goals, without waiting for the completion of the tasks. The more immediate the feedback, the better.

Simply mind-blowing how our homely kitchen is a superb platform to teach us goal-relevant behaviour that focusses our attention on what is needed to be done, motivates us for consistent efforts and energizes our performance.

So, let us put our hands together for our home makers in humble kitchens, for practicing such key techniques of planning, goal setting, review, and flexibility, even without a formal management training!

7. Strategy lies in Quick Thinking and Presence in the Moment

I thought of talking about Strategy, briefly but separately, even though it is already incorporated in the ideas of planning and execution, because ability to strategize is pivotal to successful leadership. Strategy, at the end, is nothing but a plan of action on how to direct as well as where exactly to focus efforts to achieve your overall aim or goals. *But there is a subtle difference between plans and strategies.* Formal management thinking associates Plan with long-term goals and Strategy with short-term goals. As I understand, for ultimate success, we need to play along a combination of overall plan and strategies at all levels. We have already talked about *flexibility* in our planning. Quick strategies usually emerge out of this element of flexibility that we must infuse into our planning and preparedness. So, in brief, strategies focus on short-term goals mostly in a changing operating environment and involve quickness in adjusting/ implementing action plans.

Thus, though *thinking* and *communicating* are the two most important dimensions of any activity relating to planning and execution, they acquire still greater significance in the context of strategy.

It may sound too childish to talk about exotic terms like planning and strategy in the context of kitchen. But we have already done that in earlier segments! Sensibly enough, I believe. Just to add and give another example, let us think this way. *Purpose* behind why mothers take up kitchen responsibility is health and well-being of family. The very basic

Purpose-driven goal is to ensure meals that contain all important nutrients, vitamins, and fiber for nourishment. Planning involves action points on many fronts, but the *basic plan* is about the daily menus for the three main meals and snacks. Now, *strategy* involves making these meal plans in such a way that *each* meal contains at least protein, carb, some fat, some vitamin rich food and some fibrous food, or if that is not possible for each meal on some days for emerging, unpredicted reasons, then at least ensure that for all meals taken together over one day! When on some veg days, I am alone and I have left over rice and left over vegetable curry to finish, and I feel like having pakhala (watered rice) for lunch with which I cannot take any protein like fish (as it is a veg day), my strategy is to keep a good breakfast, have veg fries that go well with pakhala, have roti and left over curry for dinner AND a good helping of homemade cottage cheese (Chhena – a very good protein) simply with some honey and crushed pepper. See, how I built in everything needed over the day at least. This is strategy, not planning. Similarly, *plan* may involve including some bitter vegetables for health reasons; strategy would involve going for some specific recipes that make their bitterness lessen/palatable/even tasty.

The circle for me goes like this: clarity on vision and purpose –> plan to achieve that purpose-> setting goals -> *strategies to communicate* those visions and goals down the line (which is in fact the most important reason behind making strategies, or *Strategic Planning* as it is more correctly known as.) through formulation and communication of *broad* policies and guidelines for achieving the goals. Detailed implementational/operational instructions are the job of those managing the mantle at senior- middle levels. Execution, strategies to adapt to emerging short-term market dimensions on the field, and bottom-up feedback are handled at the lower operational levels. *The process then moves upward for review and re-planning, re-strategizing, i.e., re-thinking at all levels.* So, personally, I always put 'thinking' at the core of everything, including strategy. It is not possible that precise operational instructions for all kinds of situations come from the top. So, middle-level and people delivering on the field must *apply their mind in* a constantly volatile and evolving operational space, and execute strategies, aligned to the broader goals and vision/purpose.

A part of strategic planning, especially for short-term goals, thus must leave space for keeping eyes and ears open for unseen, unplanned, sudden opening of new *windows of opportunities* and the strategy lies in simply grabbing them swiftly without letting them pass. The other day, I had been to the neighborhood Mart and was delighted to see the vegetables and fruits back in the shelves. Initially they were keeping these stocks, but perhaps found these were not moving. The reason was: there were umpteen street vendors in nearby locality selling fresh and varied vegetables and fruits, and generally people used to prefer sourcing from them. So, after a few weeks, the Mart stopped this segment. But recently, because of road widening works by the local government, these street vendors are no longer available. The nearest good vegetable market is far compared to this mart for most of us. But thanks to our luck and *strategic swift action* on part of the Mart in recognizing the sudden window of opportunity opening in this segment, they moved in just 2-3 days and re-started the green grocery segment. Shows, this segment must have been in their strategic thinking all along.

Thus, ultimately, strategy is all about thinking it through and thinking it out, quickly and being 'present' in the moment.

Something similar also keeps on happening in humble kitchens, whether you cook yourself, or you have delegated the core cooking job to hired hands. When cooking is delegated to hired hands, 'thinking' and 'communication' are obvious processes involved. Even when directly cooking, you go through all steps from clarity on purpose till feedback and re-thinking. We have already discussed enough from those angles in earlier segments.

8. Ability to Execute - The Technique of '*One Step At A Time*'

Just knowing the recipes or making menu-plans would not serve your goals of having food for survival and growth. You have to cook, that is, execute. So, goes without saying, kitchen is a platform which shouts out the moment you enter that 'to act', 'to execute' is the core need. This awakens you to similar need for developing execution ability in other fields, too. Not only that, kitchen also teaches you the basics of how to execute.

Have you ever noticed how precisely *'Recipes'* are documented? Or taught by demonstration and verbal explanation? *Step-by-Step!* If a beginner, you follow it exactly and get delighted at how you could complete even a complex dish without messing it up seriously. If a professional Chef, you follow it *precisely* to ensure uniformity in quality-taste-presentation of the dish every time you serve it, as that is what sells, and binds repeat customers. *Thus, the first important tip on effective execution that kitchen gives us is to go step by step.*

To go step by step, a task must always be clearly broken up into smaller tasks that can be done sequentially/simultaneously, so that you don't let the complexity or size of the whole task overwhelm you, or paralyse you. Indeed, this is an effective approach to execute any task anywhere. *Do have a clear idea of the whole, but keep accomplishing part by part* – just as someone climbing a mountain, or even stairs, in darkness would climb focussing on the NEXT step, not looking at the last point to be reached from the starting point itself, though always having it clearly in mind.

Kitchen teaches this lesson very soon as in regular cooking, you don't always have only simple recipes to prepare. Many of the dishes in our cuisine involve a fair amount of complexity. Plus, it is never about just one dish and you are done. As already harped on enough by now, it is about doing multiple dishes multiple times a day, day in and day out. So even for an experienced cook, or an expert Chef, *execution requires an ability to find a method in this madness* (for ensuring successful outcome), *as also a madness in these methods* (for infusing creativity and innovation). *Method manifests in the steps of recipes, while madness in experimentations with twists here and there.* By the way, for a novice especially, any dish may appear challenging in the beginning; thus, needing a step-by-step approach for execution. Thankfully, as you get set in kitchen, very soon you develop the knack of where to go by method and where to give it a go by for excitement and effectiveness in execution.

There is a second important aspect to execution, too. Flexibility! In both planning and execution, 100% rigidity does not pay. Sticking to a recipe for flawless execution does not mean you have to do that 100% of the time without experimenting or improvising. Homely kitchen is a bastion of innovation and creativity as we all know, sometimes even at the risk of real mess-ups. Even professional Chefs go for a little twist here and there to further improvise their proven recipes. *Yes, eventually every cook, while keeping in mind the original recipe, plays around with the ingredients as well as the process at some stage of their own skills and expertise levels, taking a call on their creativity.*

That is to say, the technique for execution not only lies in going step-by-step, it also calls for bringing in some degree of flexibility as needed and as feasible, depending upon the actual field dynamics at various steps at the material time.

If planning and Goal setting is on one side of the coin, on the other side is execution. How well you have planned and set your goals – short term-medium term-long term - will decide how well you execute. And how well you execute will reflect how effective your entire exercise of planning & goal-setting was!

Ultimately, execution is the key. Without execution, even the best of planning is an exercise in futility. Is it not a huge perspective we gain from our humble kitchen?

9. Budgeting

May be in a very basic and rudimentary manner, but surely and gradually, management of own kitchen does make one alive to the need for the skills of budgeting, and helps gaining some key insights thereon. For middle class families like us, especially in not-so-advanced countries like India, food accounts for the major share of our monthly expenses. So, budgeting for food does capture a homemaker's mind in some form or other.

What is budgeting after all? *In simple terms, you estimate your periodic, say, monthly, income/revenues, and anticipated expenses, and bring them to balance somehow including some savings for a rainy day.* If income is expected to fall short, you find out ways to increase income, or curtail expenses. If expenses are expected to leave some surplus of income, you see where you had been doing cost-cutting so far so that you can put in there some more money/resources as required/feasible; or you start considering what *new* avenues you would like to spend on to earn more or have a better standard of living; or simply increase your savings. It is a huge, complex task in the context of Corporate Management, though it is rather uncomplicated in case of home or kitchen management. *But basic understandings and principles are similar.*

So, necessarily the *Step No. 1 in budgeting* is: In advance, calculate or estimate realistically your net income for the period in question (monthly, annual etc.); i.e., income net of unavoidable obligations to pay, like tax, loan instalments, tax saving investments, children's education, mandatory minimum health expenses etc. When we talk of kitchen management, this could be a fixed lump sum that usually households set aside, or directly give into the hands of 'mother' to run the kitchen for the month. In that case, may be, no calculation is involved. You just keep the amount in mind as your anticipated income.

Step no. 2: Track your expenses for a few months in the beginning to have a realistic estimate of likely expenditure in the current time period. In the context of kitchen, mothers usually maintain a daily account notebook, wherein they jot down every single expense made and due in connection with food and kitchen, including maid's salary and bonus. 😊 This happens at least in all middleclass households. Rich people might be engaging Accountants/managers. *But some mechanism to track expenses and make estimates for future is usually put in place.*

Step 3: Factor in special expenses anticipated during that coming budgeted period due to some seasonal expenses, new expenses, emergency fund etc. while designing the budget. For example, in many parts of my country, bonus is paid to maids/caretakers/employees etc. for some special festivals like Dussehra, Diwali, Holi. Moreover, which festival gets celebrated without special food and dining? So, even a homely budget to be realistic, these seasonal expenses must be added to our estimated expenses. And provided for from some source or other even if that means deficit budgeting. Similarly, suppose there is a marriage in the family. Idea is: *these seasonal and special expenses must be built into our budgeting exercise to be fruitful.*

Step 4: Plan how to source the funds – from regular salary, or income on investments or loans etc. etc. Goes without saying, unless we have matching anticipated income from available regular and occasional sources, there is no meaning in keeping any such item on our expenses list.

Step 5: Having done a budgeting exercise, our endeavour must always veer towards continually reviewing our actual figures, and keep making adjustments to stay on budget, if exceeding budget from income side is challenging. Especially, if you have already settled for a deficit budget (excess of expenses over income provided for through borrowings), then you simply cannot go on adding to the deficit recklessly. Instead, you start doing what you have control over – curtail *expenses. For a householder,* increasing income may not be in your hands most of the time.

Carry forward these fundamentals of budgeting to your work unit – big or small, and see how relevant in fact these perspectives are.

Primarily, there are 3 types of budgets: Surplus budget (anticipated income more than anticipated expenditure), Balanced Budget (both AI and AE are equal) and Deficit Budget (AE is greater than AI). In kitchen, ordinarily mothers very assiduously work towards a surplus budget, or at least a balanced budget. However, in larger contexts, like Corporates or Economy, these calculations are at macro level; hence extremely complicated and it is the required growth that drives the budgeting, which mostly results in a controlled deficit budgeting.

Anyways, we can say that prolonged and regular kitchen management does help one pick up the basic insights on budgeting process. It makes clear the utility of budgeting, viz. it helps to prioritise needs, set clear goals, forecast requirements, and find possible sources to fund them. Won't such foundational understandings help one in their workplaces, too, while doing the budgeting exercise for the firm/company?

10. Resource and Inventory Management, and Optimisation of Utilisation

One of the most requisite management skills, especially in operations, is the ability to *manage resources and inventories optimally* – neither falling short, nor stored in excessive quantities thereby locking up scarce funds, not to mention the probability of losing value when these just sit idle (wear and tear, expiration/deterioration of usable intrinsic value, fall in market value in case this need be cleared etc.) Goes without saying, both shortages and excesses of resources and inventories might terribly affect a business.

Watching my mother as I was growing up, and personally managing my kitchen, even as I was working in a corporate job taking care of both domestic and professional fronts, have made me learn so much so deeply and so effectively in this area, that I honestly feel I couldn't have learnt this from any amount of formal management training programmes! I have not only learnt the lessons, but more significantly, these lessons have been so drilled into me as to become my second nature – *a person in perpetual preparedness for eventualities in their operational field at least in terms of the requisite minimum resources.* I am sanguine, this is so with others directly managing kitchen, too. This consciousness automatically gets carried onto our professional areas of operation too, by dint of being an ingrained trait, a second nature.

Look at any homely kitchen. You will always find enough stocks of groceries, especially staples like rice, wheat flour, lentils and legumes, basic spices, and seasonings etc., as also green groceries so that emergencies do not strike for want of these. Every mother develops her methods to keep a tab on the consumption of these, and *replenishes* stocks in time. *Timely replenishment is the key to resource and inventory management in every work area.*

Similarly, there are many other frequently used basic ingredients (goods-*in-process*) like boiled potatoes, boiled lentils, ready-to-use batters, and spice pastes (ginger-garlic paste, mustard paste, onion paste etc.), spice powders (garam masala, some specific curry powders, cinnamon-green cardamom powder, roasted jeera powder etc.), pureed ingredients (like pureed tomato, pureed spinach, coconut milk etc.) which are stored in refrigerator almost on an on-going basis. On holidays, I used to prepare these and store. I also dry-roast certain ingredients like split green grams, semolina, as these can be *stored* for much longer in the open pantry and reduce time required to make many recipes using them later.

So, right storage is another integral part of effective resource management as they prolong the 'best before' date. *And right storage is not just about space for holding and retrieval, but is also about preserving the potency of the stored resources, i.e., the nutrient dimensions.* As in the corporate world of, say, manufacturing or procuring of perishable goods, *cold storage* is an important technique, mothers in kitchen employ some great *techniques* for longer storage like *dry roasting, pickling, deep-frying, fridge-drying of green leaves, fridge, and freezer storage etc.* I store lots of legumes, lentils, and many other dry ingredients in the freezer section in moisture-resistant covers, (like re-cycled cotton bags). Let us note that *longer storage is an important dimension of green act, too,* as by avoiding early wastages, it leads to optimum use of precious ingredients – resources that ultimately come from Mother Earth. Besides, I and many like me also take pleasure in creating a *kitchen garden* at home and growing stuff like mint, curry leaves, holy basil etc. – i.e., herbs that must be used fresh for aroma, but cannot be stored for long in fridge. *Create sources of supply to eat fresh* - this is also a pragmatic way of addressing the issue of storage and resource management.

Point is: On one hand, a kitchen manager *ensures intelligent stocking of essentials* to avert emergencies, and on the other hand, *ensures timely replenishment of all types of required ingredients* (raw materials plus goods-in-process) *for uninterrupted provision of food* (final product) to the family. By the way, staying prepared with certain necessary other ingredients like spice pastes etc. that take time for preparation but very frequently used in recipes, also helps in effective *time management*. This kind of effective management of food is not feasible unless you develop a keen sense of what is required (*right resources*), how much required (*right levels of stock*), when required (*right timings*), how long to store (*right movement of stock before expiry*) and where to store *(right space for storage- open/cold) etc.* Kitchen helps one develop this sense quite soon.

We can say, *optimality* of stock in terms of 'best before' life, periodic requirement of quantity of each, their procurement/replenishment time, and available storage space *drive your inventory management in the kitchen.* It is similar out there, too, in the professional world.

What is Inventory management in management science, after all? It is a systematic approach to sourcing, storing, and selling inventory—both raw materials (components) and finished goods (products), in such ways as to ensure the right stock, at the right levels, in the right place, at the right time, and at the right cost as well as price. Observe how this keeps on getting practised in kitchen all the time.

The habit of always having a "List" gets imbibed in the kitchen for all. For resource/inventory management in kitchen, there is no other way to ensure getting all the required stuff from market in time. In professional life as well as life in general, the need for having a "To-Do" list cannot be over emphasised. Kitchen drills this habit into you very soon, or else you face the music badly!

And the trick is to keep noting down on the list as soon as stock of something comes down to a level that would last you for a specific time period that you almost know from experience (e.g., I note down oil, as I *open* the last bottle at home which is going to last me for about a month; so that well before it gets over, I would have replenished stock.). Thus, *list it before getting over!* That way, you always maintain a minimum necessary stock for your kitchen to keep going, taking care of need for storing, shelf life of different ingredients, as well as space available for storing, both in kitchen and in the refrigerator.

Another important aspect of resource management also lies in optimisation of use of everything that you already have.

A simple illustration of Optimisation of Use: I use cow milk – raw, not pasteurised. From milk, my direct by-products are fresh cream, cottage cheese (by splitting milk), milk solids (*khoya* – by boiling milk till it turns into crystals), curd, butter, whey (butter milk) and clarified butter (pure ghee). But that's not all. While preparing ghee, butter is cooked till ghee gets separated, leaving bits of fried milk solids, called *khuruma.* I do not waste any of the by-products. No need to elaborate on uses of milk, curd, cottage cheese, butter or clarified butter. Let me talk about whey (the watery portion left after churning cream and taking out the fat portion, i.e., butter) and *khuruma.*

I love having whey just as it is as a refreshing drink (*Chhanch*); or flavour it with a bit of crushed ginger-green chilli-fresh coriander plus a dash of seasoning of black salt and salt. It is truly very delicious, refreshing, and nutritious. Not to be wasted! Secondly, I knead wheat flour dough with whey, so that whatever little fat and milk component is left, that goes into the dough making it softer and greasier. So far as *khuruma* is concerned, it can be a great filling, with sugar added to it, in our typical Odia stuffed pithas like *manda, kakara, budha chakuli* etc. THIS is optimisation of use.

(Of course, the way I prepare ghee by storing fresh cream with a bit of curd, not just cream, hardly there are any remains (*khuruma).* But some people do not add curd to cream while storing in fridge and churn only the frozen cream and are left with a lot of remains. They use these as stuffings.)

Similarly, take the example of the banana plant and how kitchen teaches us to optimise its use by using virtually every part of this plant, from inner stem (*manja*) to leaves (for wrap-cooking)!

There are umpteen situations thrown up by kitchen, that drive the mindful, waste-conscious, and creative mothers to optimise use of all resources. No wonder, they carry forward such *orientation towards optimisation* to all other situations in life too. It becomes a deep-rooted part of their attitude towards life.

Is it not similar out there in the professional work place? All the high-sounding terms in management lessons taught to make you learn how to manage resources, viz. procurement, storage, replenishment, finding out alternative/new sources of resources and optimisation of use etc. get better understood, and more importantly, *get practised* easily as a matter of habit, when you have picked up these lessons from kitchen.

Furthermore, you also learn in kitchen that it is very important to recognise the 'right' kind of resources. How can you do your recipes the way you want them to be without having what they need as ingredients? *So, recognising right resources is important*. Similarly in life, if our goal is to live blissfully and purposefully (which indeed all of us wish), then we must recognise what are the 'right' resources for that. What are your resources in life? Wealth? Health? Success, Fame, and Power? Relationships? Well, these *are* necessary, to some extents, for our healthy, comfortable and respectful worldly existence, no doubt. But bliss? Sense of fulfilment? True happiness? Soulful existence? We need these even more, as we move on in life and progressively mature. As life unfolds before us through various situations, we understand these higher needs better and better! And to "cook" that up, right resources/ingredients are qualities like gratitude, honesty, integrity, compassion, empathy, courage, conviction, contentment etc. And we must be mindful always about whether we are having and using these qualities while dealing with life situations. That would be eventually our ultimate resource management in life!

11. Optimising Mess

OMG, kitchen not only teaches you to *optimise use* of everything, it also gives you a hugely pragmatic lesson on optimising mess, some sort of mess that you can treat as comfortable to live with for the time being. It may sound cheesy and oxymoronic, but there is a *'perfect mess,'* and you must learn to always find your own and make peace with it.

Kitchen makes you appreciate the value of *organisation* in various ways- planning, inventory management, storage, structures and schedules, discipline etc. But *simultaneously, it also makes you appreciate that 'Mess,' i.e., lack of complete organisation and planning, is not always messy.*

Bringing onto table four meals a day for the family day in and day out as per an inescapable routine is a huge task that cannot be done efficiently without planning, preparedness, and organisation. True. But that is only half the truth.

Firstly, demands on your time very often are so heavy that something or other does fall on the wayside despite all planning and organisation. Especially the organising part. In the context of kitchen, some dish on an elaborate menu remains unticked for lack of time; some cleaning tasks get deferred; some utensils, ingredients etc. get piled up in an unorganised manner for the time being; etc.

Secondly, too much of pre-planning does not really work well in real-life homely kitchens. For example, if you fix a menu for all 7 days and follow it rigidly, very soon that touch of spontaneity and that excitement of what surprises you can spring up today would be lost, and most likely your family members would hate to have a feel of a hotel-like set menu. Yes, as discussed in resource and inventory management, certain stocks of basic, time-taking ingredients needed for multiple recipes must be kept in a planned way and kept in advance. But it would rather be a headache to plan each dish too much in advance and execute. This way, you yourself would lose drive after sometime for cooking, with opportunities to try out new stuff getting blocked, not to speak of the difficulty that rigidity would entail in respect of stock and menu management. *Ideally, there must be some unplanned windows open to the home cooks always for continued interest and creativity, even if that means a bit of probable mess in execution or organisation at times*. We will talk about how some mess very often leads to creativity in a later segment on innovation and creativity.

Thirdly, 'mess' can also be allowed at times in terms of some compromise in healthiness of food. Sorry, if I shocked you! Take a moment to introspect and you would also start nodding your head in agreement. Eating some fast food, junk food or so-called unhealthy food in terms of fat and spices, at times, or once in a blue moon for a change, or in fun and frolic, rather helps your body develop better immunity system than rigidly ensuring intake of only 'healthy' food all the time. In any case, in this harsh real world, things do not always go as per your needs. Unless you train both your mind and body to positively take in your stride occasional disruptions/discomforts, your sufferings would only get enhanced. Bonus, of course, is the mood-boosting effects of such occasional off-the-routine indulgences, that also have a positive impact on your immune system. Basically, your body stays used to small shocks at irregular, unpredictable intervals. This is like how periodic upsets/adversities in life build up resilience and strength in our character and mental agility.

Fourthly, being comfortable with some kind/level of mess, on which time is saved just by not attending to it then and there, is a part of effective time management. There is a *cost to neatness* – in terms of valuable time and resources. Always arranging things in the kitchen in the name of neatness is likely to eat up your spare time unnecessarily, that could have been otherwise utilised more fruitfully in some other engagements. Do you clean a utensil as soon as it gets dirty? No! You keep them separately and these get attended to only in one-two batches later. Till then, you do carry on with your other chores fully aware of this pending work/mess. Similarly, the kitchen platform. The mess that gets created on it while you are cooking must continue, more or less till all cooking is done, and it becomes the time to clean your work station. *Kitchen reminds us every day that there are certain important things that need stretches of uninterrupted time.* If you start cleaning every little mess immediately, you won't get that time stretch to do the more important stuff.

In fact, in real life, everything needed to be done at any point of time NEVER gets done 100% for all sorts of reasons. So, learning to allow an optimum amount of mess, and stay comfortable with it as you go about doing your other important jobs is indispensable in the real world. What is more, it also helps in creativity. Creative mess is better than idle tidiness.

Mess is supposed to be messy because it is believed to adversely affect your productivity with wastage of time in looking for unarranged, misplaced things, or stressing out at last moments for want of proper planning and organisation. But it may not be true always as we have seen; especially when you choose your own optimum mess often having a *hidden order in the apparent randomness* that is known to you, but may look messy to others. Let me tell you, while in service, I had a tagline for my work station – *Jungle mein Mangal* (meaning, all fine in this forest); and my colleagues totally believed in it😊 All used to amaze, how I could retrieve and use whatever is really needed for any disposal at any time, although apparently, my desk never looked tidy. No wonder, I always love Einstein's great satirical quote, "If a cluttered desk is a sign of a cluttered mind, of what, then, is an empty desk a sign?"

I have personally seen many people, who are moderately disorganised, are actually very efficient and creative. I have also noticed there are small shops with truly a variety of stock, stashed in every bit of space available, but the shopkeeper can within no time access what you need for buying. It is about the hidden order in any mess that counts.

It is a very important lesson in the context of our professional work place, as also life in general. At any point of time in our profession and life, there will be some pending issues, even some long-pending issues, critical issues, current issues-urgent and/or important. In other words, *some kind and quantum of mess*! Unless we learn to be at ease with some amount of mess, that can be attended to later, or must be lived with beyond a period of comfort, we would remain in constant stress, and our quality of current work and mental peace will always be at stake. So always look for that optimum quantum of 'mess' that you can live with and go forward in life, taking those up when their time comes, or just decide to leave them back and go forward. This understanding from kitchen also helps one deal with some critical questions in life whose answers are not easily available, but with time, even these questions become irrelevant! That is, in spirit, living with and living past certain kinds of 'mess'. A hugely important ability for a well-rounded personality. Amazing how our little kitchen has lessons on this, too!

Coming to how creativity at times flows from mess.

History is replete with examples of how innovation sometimes happens *by accident*. Recall the term "Entropy." Generally, *entropy* refers to disorder or uncertainty. But from such disorder, while certain things decay or get destroyed, certain new things emerge and take shape. The discovery of Penicillin by Dr Alexander Fleming by accident is a story worth remembering.

In 1928, Dr Fleming had gone on a holiday without taking full care to organise his laboratory. An uncovered petri dish near an open window got contaminated with mould. He came back from the holiday to find some mould accidentally growing on the petri dish, but realized that the bacteria *near the mould* were dying. He soon identified that the mould produced a self-defence chemical that could kill bacteria. He isolated the mould and identified it as Penicillium Genus, and the rest is history.

Spencer Silver, who is famous for his discovery of unique M-3 adhesive Notepads, *post-it,* said, "If I had thought about it, I would not have done the experiment. The literature was full of examples that said you cannot do this." This is an example where a lesser than desired result, a 'messy' result, became useful in some *other* way.

Let us understand that new ideas very often get thrown up as *new* connections between *existing* dots; some of which occur by accident and some with multiple trials and errors. In fact, *in kitchen almost all our new creations meander through mess.* When I add much more liquid than required for a batter by mistake, I add some other ingredients, originally not intended, like semolina, or oats, rice flour etc., to fix the consistency and turn out some altogether new pancakes.

By the way, even if we are living in a world now, in which being 'organized' is the *sine qua none* for 'success', market buzzing with solutions to eradicate 'mess' in workspace as also home space, it is an absolute necessity to cut through this cacophony and ask ourselves, "Is it really possible to *fully* organise our lives? And is it even truly required?"

A small pause would let us listen to our own answer: No, on both counts. *It is neither possible, nor desirable beyond a point.* As we have already seen above, some chaos in life is a must. I dare say, do allow some mess, some chaos in your life. Many reasons. The simple quintessential reason is: *since life is full of uncertainties*, too much of organisation (knowing your exact goals, planning strategies, and rigidly executing action plans losing sight of new developments etc.) would impair your ability to be agile and adaptive as per changing realities. It may end up wasting your valuable time and at worst, may completely topple your apple cart. When future cannot be predicted with 100% certitude, it is only a myth to claim that organisation and planning can be done 100%. More importantly, you lose *spontaneity* if you always look for a state of being organised and that severely impairs your resilience to deal with uncertainties. And what is life, after all? A process of moving from uncertainties to uncertainties! One would be naïve to hold that they have a perfectly predictable personal life, a perfectly predictable work life, or a perfectly predictable social life, and they have been able to plan and organise everything accordingly.

I would rather maintain that *our life acquires real meaning from Mess and our ability to handle or optimise it!*

Are you an organisation-freak? Time to sit up, and ponder. Is having everything spic and span and completely organised worth what all goes into achieving this position, and a huge lot more just to maintain that? I have seen in my own life, and of course, in working styles of most of the greatest inventors and discoverers. Literally, but for the mess they had allowed into their working space as also working styles, at times inadvertently without thinking or planning, some of the greatest discoveries/inventions/innovations would perhaps not have happened.

So, relax! Next time you see that paper not filed into where it was supposed to be, do not beat yourself. Take out, read it again instead of hurrying with a guilty mind to place it in its pre-determined order on your filing system. There is a possibility that, in the intervening time, something else has come up, that might bear some important connection to this and hence can be addressed now in a fresh or more effective manner in the light of this piece of past information on hand, which, had it been filed away, would not have struck you in every likelihood. This has often been my own experience in my professional life.

Creativity and innovations are about stepping into and exploring in the zone of the unknown and chaos; while organization and planning is about being within the domain of the known. Creativity often springs out of ... no, not a very organised environment, but a slightly messy one which facilitates *random connections* for a new theory to be experimented and validated.

I am not advocating a messy mess – i.e., a significant or complete lack of organization, or no planning leaving every outcome to chance, nor absence of strategizing for achieving important goals. All I am trying to get across is: do not buy each and every idea that the market keeps on bombarding. Think and apply yourself; then decide whether you would like to buy what is being sold in the name of organising. The number of experts/consultants selling you the ideas of getting organised for life-changing benefits and devices supposed to help you 'organise' everything has grown mind-blowingly over past few decades, only because *we catch a fad too soon* without applying our mind and unknowingly help create and sustain these vested interest groups, giving them huge profits *at our cost*.

Amazing how our humble homely kitchen provides such a profound perspective on even the value of an optimum mess! So, worry less on mess. ☺

12. Developing Quality Consciousness

A balloon soars high because of what is inside it, not because of its design.

Ultimately, it is the quality of the content, that matters. No amount of attractive packaging and presentation, without quality of content, is going to sell your products, beyond a certain base point.

While having dine-outs in expensive restaurants, premier hotels, food festivals etc. what instantaneously attracts us is the *look* of the dish; actual taste and flavours come much later as we sub-consciously start forming an opinion about that dish just from its look and presentation. No wonder, professional Chefs observe great care and meticulousness in *garnishing and plating*. But ultimately, what wins positive feedback? What wins a *repeat* customer for the food? The *quality*! Its taste, flavour, and health quotient, not the presentation.

Even the regular home makers, while serving food on special occasions, or to special guests, do go for some garnishing of the dishes for an enhanced presentability. But that's it, and no further. You present a bad dish nicely, it might get tasted first, but would immediately be rejected. *The ultimate win-ability lies in the quality of the content.* Appealing presentation gives it an *add-on*, not original value. *As you take charge of the kitchen, very soon this lesson gets hammered into your mind!*

Nothing wrong with paying attention to make a dish look appealing, so long as we are also alive to the fact that enhancing the look may attract initially, but what stays back with the people is the quality of the food in terms of taste, texture and healthiness. That alone is going to influence their choice for that dish in future.

Cooking teaches us very soon that we must perfect the taste and quality of the dish first and foremost, and then if warranted for the occasion, go for presentation with garnishing. *This teaches us an invaluable lesson: for effective management and leadership, premium must always be put on intrinsic quality and content in all deliverables.* A clear understanding dawns on us that packaging is also important as a marketing ploy, but *only after* ensuring quality of what is getting packaged. *Another insight* we also pick up from homely kitchen is on *when not to bother about packaging at all.* While serving our homely daily meals, no breath be wasted on garnishing that does not add to taste as the family members already know what to expect from a homely daily meal. In corporate world also, there are areas where no-frill services do better if only quality of service is guaranteed matching customer expectations on the core service alone. And there are areas where a little bit of extra add-on influences customer preference.

13. Value of 'being just good enough' at times

Well, don't be too quick to trash my idea, if I say, "It is okay to be just good enough, at times." You won't like this statement if you are in a top leadership position, or a student of formal management training. Because, in formal training, it is drilled deep into your head that you must perform at your peak always. Strictly speaking, 'performance' has twin aspects: input (our efforts) on one side, and output/outcome on the other. Both. Lack on any side would not give a *peak performance*. You can't say you 'performed' great, without a great outcome, even if you had put in your best. Similarly, you can't say you performed great, although the outcome appears to be impressive, if you have not given your best. Because, in the latter case, your performance falls short of your potential and the possible outcome, had you given your best.

Undoubtedly, I agree that we must put in our best efforts always. Meaning, must try my best in *given* circumstances. But that need not necessarily be my true peak performance. *What constitutes my best foot at a particular point of time in a particular context is something we must have complete clarity on. It is about* my *inputs and efforts* given an operating environment – i.e., putting in 100% of what is *within* my complete control at the material time. Not about *obsession with best output and results, which are not entirely within my control at any point indeed, due to operational dynamics. If you believe that you must always deliver at peak level only, and when* you end up with a good enough result, *you get depressed. That is perfectionism which kills.*

I appreciate why Management would typically look at 'good' as the biggest enemy of 'best'. Mostly, their apprehension is right: being content with 'good' is likely to bring in a sense of *complacency* and might keep us settled in a circle of *mediocrity* - thus holding us back from reaching our full potential.

Yes, if we get into a *habit* of being satisfied with a good enough job every time, everywhere, it does promote a culture of mediocrity, which must be avoided.

But as with many other beliefs and outlook in life, even the above apprehension is ignoring the importance of 'context.'

Performance does not peak in certain circumstances, not because of complacency factor, but because of many other reasons not entirely due to the performer. For example:

i. *Status of the Performer.*

For the beginners and learners in any field/task, whether they are *excelling* in that job from day 1 (which in fact no one can) is not the real issue to be monitored. The parameters to focus on are whether they are, i. learning sincerely, ii. doing a good enough job as appropriate to their level of training, and iii. moving in the right direction demonstrating a commitment to learn and an attitude to pursue excellence (i.e., learning from mistakes and bettering performance continuously). Premium and incentive must be put on *learning* at this stage. This is not a time to bring in pressure for perfection. That will rather kill their incentive to learn. Just as expecting a gourmet dish from a beginner in kitchen is a killer pressure, whereas complimenting on a *good enough dish is a morale-booster for a new cook.*

ii. *Nature of a particular job and its importance in the whole scheme of things to do.*

There are certain jobs, especially *maintenance jobs*, which must be done regularly, well enough, but need not necessarily be in the best way as the 'best' way involves high investments in terms of time and other resources, whose opportunity cost may be much higher. For example, sweeping, mopping, dusting of house and household stuff. I bet, no one would claim that these jobs are being done by the maid, or you yourself, every day in the best possible manner. *What is important to be ensured is regularity!* That it is done every day – the exposed area getting full attention first and other places, decorative pieces getting cleaned at interval of days; and the corners and backsides etc. – i.e., places and stuff gathering dust but not in public view, get deep-cleaned at slightly longer intervals from *hygiene* point of view. It is simply NOT Possible for ordinary people of ordinary means who also must attend to a thousand other tasks and professions to do the cleaning jobs perfectly or get it done 100% through others every single day. So, in such cases, don't even aspire to be a perfectionist, or you will end up doing this maintenance job 24X7X365 at the cost of your other survival and growth-related jobs. A *good-enough job* in this field *with regularity*, although not exemplifying a peak performance, is of great value.

Kitchen illustrates on the above perspective too well. *Every time a meal from a homely kitchen need not be a gourmet meal!* Nor it be cooked with expectation of getting a 'fabulous' tag. It does not definitely mean that you cook without caring for how it turns out – badly done, inedible, or too bad. NO! *It simply means that we must learn to appreciate the value of 'good enough,' instead of seeking perfection every single time in every single thing.* That is for sure a setup for failure! You create continuous intense pressure for performance, much higher and much heavier than the optimum creative tension, which silently kills your motivation, ability, and agility, instead of allowing you to experiment, fail, improve, or create newness.

This is a very evident lesson from kitchen that we must carry forward to our day-to-day life, and learn to value 'satisfaction' – the balanced middle path in-between ecstasy of what we think is a 'perfect' score and frustration due to what we think is an 'utter failure.' Life is like a pendulum, swinging between two extremes, and dwelling longer on the in-between course. Happiness and sadness, similarly are two extremes and recognizing that satisfaction lies in between would rather keep our motivation alive to continue finding happiness in many things without getting stuck at the other end of sadness.

What a beautiful life lesson!

iii. *Importance of 'timing' of certain jobs*

Like cooking. Food is a time-bound necessity to survive. Unless provided on time, its value gets diluted, or lost. Would you prefer to wait for a slow-cooked delicacy when you are starving, you are already very late for, say, lunch/dinner? I swear, you would just grab at something that is instantly available, or prepared in a few minutes, like say a simple sandwich. Here is a case in point when even just a good enough dish is preferred to a perfect one. *There are many situations in kitchen when we find value in being 'good enough' if that helps us ensure food on time.* There are times when mothers are unwell physically, and due to unavoidable reasons, they still remain in charge of providing food to the family. Would you expect them to perform at their peak during such an exigency? Would not just a lentil rice on time be a better option than making the family go without food?

In fact, cooking being a hugely repetitive task, although we must be sincere in turning up the best with the available resources and requirements, we must also allow not only for 'good- enoughs', but also for mess-ups. Not intentional, though. There is another reason that we must understand why each dish in homely kitchen cannot be a gourmet meal, even if we are no less able than a Professional Chef to cook like a Pro every single time. And that is: at home, we are required to hit a common ground keeping in view the 'requirements' of all members (age/health prescriptions, timings, tastes, and preferences) on one hand, and availability of resources (ingredients, time, budget, meals already made in near past etc.) on the other. In such a situation, while gourmet meals are possible at intervals, good enough meals on a regular basis actually deserve commendation. Appreciating the good enough would keep us alive to the best that is possible. *In celebrating the ordinary, the good enough, the ok and through this the balance in life, we develop a true sense of acceptance, and open up to peace and true happiness.* You may not get a gourmet meal to eat every time; but you are keeping healthy with your humble meals and enjoying a better life. Do appreciate that. Moreover, do you think, you would really like to eat gourmet meal every time, every day? Do that, and you would know how soon and how strongly the law of diminishing marginal utility sets in for your taste buds, apart from the health hazards!

Indeed, most often, being 'good enough' on a longer and broader plane is the real achievement; not perfectionism. Yes, perfection is something to be pursued, with clear knowledge that it is never attainable, because life is not perfect, nor are we; and its essence lies in learning from mistakes on one hand and exploring for progressive excellence on the other hand.

'Good enough' is a milestone on the road towards progressive excellence, and ultimately that matters.

14. Value of Excellence and the trap of Perfectionism

Accepting 'good enough' is beneficial as a starting point, as also is an anti-dote to demotivation and/or burn-out, mostly in the initial stage. As already discussed, it also has its merit in some special circumstances wherein perfect *timing*, rather than excellent quality is more critical in the larger scheme of things. Things done perfectly, but not on time when it is required badly, loses its relevance. Waiting for the perfect resources and the perfect know-how to do something perfectly is a useless pursuit even if it delivers the exactly desired result *after its relevance is gone*. So, the key lies in deciphering *what need be done, along with when and how in the overall context*, and *acceptable* level of quality in that job should be decided accordingly.

But if we accept it long enough without genuine efforts to achieve progressive excellence in anything we do, 'good enough' can become the greatest enemy of our 'great' work. When making your young children get over the resistance to cook (so that they enter the kitchen to learn cooking) is the goal, you would not expect them to turn out a great *hakka noodle*, but would encourage them just to make a good enough *instant noodle*, from ready-to-make packets available in the market, like say, Top Ramen/ Maggie! From a hesitant novice, even this could be an acceptable level of quality. *But don't let him stop there- that is the principle we are talking about in value of excellence.* Whatever be our current level of skill, we must always try to reach for excellence progressively.

Not being a perfectionist is certainly not about being satisfied with shabby or average jobs. Or not making your best efforts every next time, as your 'best' is also a shifting post. That is, not *pursuing* excellence! Not being a perfectionist only means, we embark on a journey of progressive excellence-with imperfections first, and then gradually, but steadily improve our performance with consistent efforts so that excellence starts speaking. It may still be short of 'perfection', but should be way ahead of 'just good enough'. And continuously improving to next level. *Excellence is always a journey*, and a result of high intentions, sincerest efforts, and intelligent execution.

In fact, behind a fulfilling life, lies invariably an *attitude and pursuit* to autograph everything we engage in with excellence.

Perfectionism is indeed a trap; it might get you stuck in a paralysis of analysis and an unending wait for the perfect conditions to start something, indecisiveness, and immobility; while a value of excellence makes you try harder and harder every next time to continuously better your performance. This is possible once you start with clarity on the real meaning of 'just being good, at times' initially. Your pursuit to improve continues till it is perfected in terms of your 'own best potential', which in turn is not a static parameter either, as it continuously evolves by interplaying with emerging and dynamic 'other' parameters – both in terms of environment as well as people around.

So 'excellence' is also an evolving benchmark that need be pursued relentlessly.

A pursuit of excellence drives you to continuously review: Is your current 'good' actually 'good enough' against progressively shifting benchmarks? If not (which usually is the case), what more or different can be done? It is only in this specific context we can say, what is said by many a great Management Gurus, that 'Good is often the enemy of Great'

(Jim Collins), if you do not continuously introspect, evaluate your current level and try sincerely for upgrading yourself on a continuous basis. A conscious, continuous movement from good to excellent is in fact the essence of effectiveness and a sense of fulfilment.

I am sure, it needs no elaboration here how we very soon learn this value and lesson from kitchen in view of many things already discussed so far, and also from what we are going to discuss in later segments. Especially, how kitchen drives infinite improvisations, innovations, and creativity in recipes/presentations with finite number of ingredients shines enough light on how it imbibes in us an urge to pursue the value of excellence.

Excelling is not about reaching a finish line; rather it is the thrill and inner drive that we experience when we seek and explore ways to give our best, find out newer learning opportunities, discover newer potentials within ourselves, and the journey continues. This kind of a journey is very discernible in our growth process in kitchen, too.

15. Sometimes, Packaging also matters

Quality of content is the first thing that matters. Undoubtedly! Our homely Kitchen teaches it without fail. But it also shows us how, many a times, notwithstanding the great quality inside, we need to work on its appearance, i.e., presentation or packaging also, to make it *inviting* in the first place, so that your target folk would be attracted to the exterior to check out what is inside.

In homely kitchen, just a neat, simple, clean serving may be adequate most of the time. And when a gourmet dish gets cooked in the homely kitchen, as they do many a times, a simple but attractive garnishing to flaunt the appearance of the dish may become the needed value-addition to make it inviting. However, in a professional kitchen, presentation, i.e., *plating*, is immensely important along with taste and innovation. Think of why people go to a fine dining outside home in the first place. Food quality is important; but what one looks for is a fine dine '*experience*'- a complete package that contains quality food plated exotically and served to you in a beautiful ambience, wherein you can relax, get a break, spend time (mostly with significant others) and enjoy your food both visually as well as with an excited palate.

To give an example, supposed Biriyani is cooked at home. As YUMMY, or may be more, as any biriyani available in any famous restaurant. At home, mother would serve this usually by mixing the whole dish, accompanied with, say, a cleanly served kachumbar or salad, that traditionally goes with it. But the same thing in a hotel would come with a beautiful plating, with bits of barista, mint, whole spices (which are already used in the dish) nicely sprinkled on top; rice portion being served only lightly mixed to bring out separate colours used prominently, so that you would have some colour palate of white, orange, red, green etc. in rice and the other components like chicken/mutton/vegetables nicely spread or stacked on the biriyani rice. You mix and eat. Accompanied by side dishes like salad, kachumbar served in a stylish way. Well, the taste may be same or worse than mother's biriyani. But the whole package ensures a more relishing experience.

This *'expectation of diners'* can be easily understood by mothers in kitchen through extrapolation, and they instinctively know when presentation is worthwhile, and when it is not. They are brilliant enough to know to spend some extra breath when they have to *'market'* something against the known taste and preferences of their family members for a good reason, like health considerations, or no-option 'rainy days' etc. Observe, how mothers make unwilling children eat vegetables. Healthy but not-so-relished vegetables like bottle gourd, brinjals, green vegetables etc. Bitter vegetables like bitter gourd, fresh fenugreek leaves! *What mothers constantly try is to 'package' these a bit appealingly playing with colours, and looks, or hide these inside some other inviting recipes* like cake, pizza, pan cakes, pulao, koftas, stuffed vegetables etc. Yes, think about lauki raita, karela chips, brinjal in pizza...... ☺

Thus, mothers also learn this value of packaging as a marketing skill from kitchen experience, side by side with the lesson on quality.

All workplaces/business/profession ultimately revolve around marketing of some sort of product or services or ideas. Needless to say, if the employees are alive to the value of quality as well as packaging, they can better serve the organizational interests. Someone with such orientation imbibed from kitchen does not need any more training on this.

16. Waste Consciousness, Value of Redemption and Value of Discarding

Oh, my my! If you are a mother like me, you would not even waste *heat* in the kitchen, what to speak of other stuff! When I dry roast whole spices, I switch off gas quite before they are roasted to the extent needed, and keep stirring them on the hot pan till I get my aroma; then transfer elsewhere for cooling before grinding. In the process, I reduce the use of gas and achieve my purpose without wasting precious gas (very important for sustainability – the first R – Reduce!) Similarly, home chefs (let me call mothers in kitchens as home chefs -they are no less than Pros) also do another thing on a regular basis. Beyond boiling point, they never cook any gravy on high flame, as they know that once the boiling point is reached, cooking happens perfectly even at lower heat. This *saves a lot of precious gas, a scarce source of the most important resource in cooking - heat.*

Another very routine happening in Indian kitchens. Observe mothers/ cooks while making roti (whole-wheat flat bread). They would do rolling out and roasting on tawa almost parallelly, not one after another. As they place the first rolled-out roti on tawa(griddle) for roasting, they start rolling out the second one, so that by the time the first one is done, the second one is ready to go on the tawa. On one hand, this ensures that freshly rolled out ones go on the tawa. On the other hand, it *saves much time* in completion of making multiple rotis, as compared to rolling out all rotis first and then roasting one by one. That way, it also might make the roti dry. Most likely, some curry must be getting done on a second burner, as they prepare rotis. *Multi-tasking the right way to save time, an uber-important resource for everything in life!* We will talk about multi-tasking in greater detail later.

There are multiple ways in which mothers in kitchen *store and save ingredients and resources* from going waste, that we have already talked about. In stock management in kitchen, of both green groceries as well as dry ingredients and spices, they subconsciously follow a principle of FIFO (First In First Out). Why? *To avoid wastage.*

Point is: *Kitchen develops a unique sensitivity towards the need to conserve energy, save time, save money etc.* It is said, every rupee saved is one rupee earned. Every unit of resource saved is one unit of that resource acquired. *Every unit of wastage avoided is one unit of some resource gained, that too, at no extra cost.* In the context of corporate clientele also, this rule is eminently applicable: Averting loss of one existing client is equivalent to acquiring one more client at no cost.

Yes, waste consciousness develops pretty soon in kitchen and runs deep in mothers. It all starts from a single simple reason: when you cook yourself continuously, you realise how much of tireless efforts as well as cost on resources go into daily cooking, and hence, you would automatically tend to *respect* your resources, and avoid wastage. By all means! Gradually, of course, you pick up more and more reasons for converting wastages to newer uses through innovation and creativity. And this *consciousness* about avoiding wastages by *reducing* consumption and *reusing* in other ways prompts them to behave with this attitude in all walks of life.

The most important lessons they learn in kitchen is how our first attempt should be to salvage, and discard must be the last option only if something is completely irredeemable.

Observe how they deal with partially imperfect vegetables - an aubergine infested with a bit of insect or some mark of spoil, a piece of raw papaya/pumpkin with signs of thin rotting sides, or green beans having slight rotten portions etc. At times, this may be simply due to transit blows, not necessarily due to insects. What they do is: if it is possible to get rid of the affected portion *without risking the edibility of the rest,* then they just amputate the portion around the waste along with a generous margin of good portion to avoid any infection from the rotten portion to go into food and use the rest part which is perfectly alright and can be cooked without causing any health hazard. Here, they have not only discarded the already wasted portion, but also an otherwise good portion as a measure of abundant precaution. At the same time, they have not wasted the whole, and ensured use of what can be used without danger. Similarly, take for example some of the thick-peel vegetables like raw banana, beetroots, carrots etc. After storing in the fridge for a few days especially in hot climate like in India, you might have noticed how the skin of raw banana turns almost darkish (may be because of its iron properties). But peel it, you will find the interior good and safe for consumption. Discarding it would amount to its wastage only. Carrots and beetroots can be stored in fridge for many days, without losing their useability; the peel might get a little dry and crumply. Peeling becomes a little difficult, but interior stays fine, not to be wasted. Of course, to avoid even this stage, many mothers peel carrots and beetroots when fresh, and then store in air-tight containers in fridge.

In almost all parts of our country, there are some local dishes which are made using the peels of vegetables! Peels of Potatoes, green raw plantains, ridge gourds, bottle gourds etc., instead of being discarded and wasted, are used to make very innovative and tasty fries, fritters, or chutney. Height of waste-consciousness, ha ha! In the process, nutrition also does not get wasted as in many fruits and vegetables, the peels contain high level of nutrients.

Thus, mothers in kitchen learn not only 'when to discard,' but also 'what and how much to'; *as well as* 'what NOT to discard'.

Similarly, they also learn 'when to discard the whole thing'. They don't bat an eyelid to discard the whole thing when they anticipate the slightest danger. They can differentiate between rotting due to transit blows and rotting of a spoilt vegetable due to infection/infestation or otherwise which is not cook-worthy. Similarly, while preparing pure ghee (clarified butter), they know for right quality of ghee, it is better to cook the butter till the residue (*khuruma*) turns dark brown and just discard that burnt stuff, instead of cooking less to salvage the *khuruma* and use that in fillings for sweet items/ pancakes. Here optimising is not the goal, perfection of ghee is.

Burnt curry? Yes, mothers know that these simply cannot be salvaged. If you add new ingredients to it hoping to reduce its burnt smell, you will only end up wasting more. This smell just sticks around whatever way you might try to redeem the curry. So better, just throw into the dustbin, and prepare curry afresh. Another example: at times, some watery vegetables like, say, ridge gourd, bottle gourd, even aubergine, absorb moisture in fridge if kept for a little longer, or if the refrigeration is not happening properly. Initially, I used to peel and check if the interior looks alright, then cook. But after one or two experiments, I knew it is better to simply discard these if the skin shows clearly that water has seeped into it, as somehow their taste becomes horrible even after cooking with a lot of other condiments. The second time, I had tried making Jahni Posto (ridge gourd sautéed with a spice paste of poppy seeds – a very expensive ingredient) and because of a weird taste of the ridge gourd, I had to waste the entire lot. I learnt my lesson! In Economics and Finance, there is a dictum that says, *don't put good money after bad money* (as not only the bad money sinks, it will also drag the good money to sink after it). *Mothers learn this important lesson from their kitchen experience.*

Moreover, mothers learn to see the value of not discarding whenever they are bitten by the creativity bug! Instead of just throwing small amounts of left-overs, cooked/uncooked (like curry, dal, cooked rice, batters etc.), they develop the knack of utilising them by creating some other new recipe in combination with other ingredients. When I see that some of uthappam (the typical Indian black gram and rice pan cake) batter becomes surplus, I just add some more water, semolina, oats, may be some rice flour, vegetables, onion, ginger, green chilli, fresh coriander, salt etc., and make a fresh batter for a new variant of uthappam. Making rolls with fillings using left over rice, dal, curries is a fun time with mothers specially to experiment with small children.

My daughter does not like to have the edges of bread slices in any bread dish. So instead of wasting, I trim the sides, give them a quick dry grind in a blender to have nice and fresh bread crumbs. And use this in many ways, especially adding to tikki (cutlet) mixture of various kinds. Or, use it for the crispy coat, if deep frying fritters/crispies. Or even convert it into another yummy dish by adding some other rest-over. The other day, I did bread rolly-polly for my daughter, and was left with the edges. I had a little bit of boiled rajma (kidney beans) in the fridge, which could have gone into some mixed dal may be. I mixed up the fresh bread crumbs and rajma to prepare a new dish which really turned out great to be eaten straight. What I did was:

Heat some olive oil. Sauté chopped garlic till a bit fragrant. Add some black pepper powder mid-way. Then add chopped onion, ginger, green chilli, and a bit of tomato and sauté together a bit till onion just changes colour. Stir in the boiled rajma, rest of salt to taste for the whole dish and sauté on low to medium flame for one minute. Add fresh bread crumbs and a sprinkle of some meat masala/curry powder or garam masala. Mix and sauté well. Finish with some fresh mint and fresh coriander.

This was yummy and good enough for a breakfast dish. But again, I gave it a twist – mashed the mix and made pan-fried cutlets. Then I made butter-toasted sandwiches stuffed with this cutlet, sliced cucumber, sliced onion, sliced tomato, and a sprinkle of black salt. It was divine. Yes, it is how waste consciousness drives creativity in kitchen.

Many such cases come up in course of regular cooking which help mothers to sharpen their understanding of the values of both discarding and not discarding, as also the difference between wastage and discarding. And, they get creative.

Basically, *this infuses in them a quality, or, attitude of not out-rightly rejecting anything or anyone at the first sight of some flaw.* It comes to them naturally to explore how to *salvage or redeem* something first; if it does not work out, then only, reject it.

So, the lesson learnt is: Don't waste anything before thinking *in-the-box* for already known alternative uses, or creatively thinking *out-of-box* for experimenting with new combinations.

Thus, our homely kitchen infuses in mothers a strong sense of waste consciousness, which in turn, gives them the wisdom to recognise a. what is bad irreversibly or a potential danger to health, and hence must be discarded, and b. what can be redeemed with a bit of creativity. *Mothers get an experiential learning on this profound lesson in kitchen.* Amazing! Waste-consciousness for them must lead to re-using/re-cycling/redeeming whatever can be, side by side with ruthless discarding of something not redeemable or not healthy. Rightly so!

Value of Redemption

Although we have already talked about it, I would like to be a little more detailed on this aspect, as *the ability to redeem and reclaim, not only your resources, but also your people is one of the top-notch qualities of a true leader. Essentially, people are your greatest resource.*

Redeeming something going to be wasted is an art and a huge skill that is of immense value not only in the kitchen, but also in life. In fact, in life, no one is all black or all white. Everyone is a shade of grey – a combination of both black and white and in-between. As a manager, leader, or merely a part of a family and social groups, we must try our best to help everyone in our team/circle bring out their best. This will never happen, if we always demonstrate a mentality of rejecting people for some flaw/negativity in them. *Just as we first try to redeem cooking ingredients likely to be wasted in kitchen, we must similarly try to redeem and reclaim our people first, before giving up on them.*

A sense of waste-consciousness not only emerges from a value of avoiding wastages, it also mirrors an '*Attitude Not to Give up*' on anything! Think about why/how such a dislike for wasting something in the kitchen arises in the first place. A deeper introspection will make us understand that it is because we would not like to give up on something into which we have already put in so much of efforts already, or we have already expended so much on. The one who cooks regularly appreciates the *value* and *price* of what has already been sourced or cooked; so, would always try instinctively to use/salvage it first, before throwing into the dustbin as a last resort. *There lies a great perspective!*

Is this not a great lesson in managing people and situations in our personal and professional lives too? In real life corporate environments, we do not always get people of our choice to build our team. Rather, people are thrust upon us and we are supposed to do team-building and deliver the results through them. Is it possible to keep demanding to our higher-ups to change specific employees for new ones? I.e., is it feasible to *discard* people always if they are not up to our expectations? Or should we try our best to *redeem* them through motivation and training, and *reclaim* them as our worthy team members?

To sum up, waste consciousness makes us see value in both 'Redemption' and 'Discarding';

i. Redeem if feasible; do not just discard at the first sight of flaw
ii. Discard, if required; do not waste more going after the irredeemable
iii. Develop the wisdom to differentiate between wastage and discarding

At a higher level, the ability to discard what is beyond redemption also helps in inculcating an elevated *spiritual ability to let go* of past negativities. At the same time, while carrying forward this lesson to life situations wherein we must deal with other *human beings*, we can differentiate between the two facts - that human beings are not vegetables, and that while vegetables cannot change their state of being, human beings can. Suitable application, therefore, with/without tweaking, of the lessons learnt from kitchen comes naturally to mothers, because their sense of observation/mindfulness gets sharpened as they work relentlessly in kitchen day-in and day-out.

By the way, there is one more important perspective that comes out clearly from our humble kitchen. That is: the difference between waste-consciousness and miserliness. It may not be out of context to share an interesting story here that I have grown up listening to.

Kubera, the Hindu mythological God of Wealth, was once seen picking up rice grains lying on some village road, one by one. Perhaps, the grains had fallen off through holes in the container sacks while transporting on the bullock-carts. The villager who witnessed this got dumb-founded, and asked, "Lord Kubera! You are the owner of massive wealth. These few grains lying on the road should mean nothing to you compared to what you already possess. Why are you so bothered about this that you are personally picking up each grain fallen off from the sacks?" Kubera did not reply and went on picking the rest of the grains. After a few days, the village got lashed with copious rains and there was water-logging and mud over all village roads linking to outside. The village got cut-off as carts could not ply on them because of their wheels getting stuck in the mud. Supplies in the village started drying up. Somehow, villagers were unable to do anything about the roads. Kubera understood the predicament. He got many cart-loads of grains from his own godown, and spilled them over the muddy roads till the roads got paved with grains and bullock carts could be driven on them without getting stuck. When the same person saw this, he could not stop asking Kubera again, "Lord, last time only a few grains were lying on the roads which you painstakingly picked up to avoid their wastage. But now, you are not hesitant to waste so much of grains just to pave the roads. Why?" Kubera answered this time. "Oh, Dear One! foodgrains are too precious to be wasted. In the last instant, it was a pure *wastage* due to carelessness while transporting. So, I had to stop the wastage. But now, we have a situation and help must reach the cut-off villagers as soon as possible to save them from hunger, and no other ways of tackling the issue of muddy roads are available. I had brought these grains to distribute amongst the hungry villagers. But the carts are getting stuck in the mud. So, I used the grains to pave the roads. I have much more grains and now that the carts can run smoothly on these roads, I can quickly bring more grains to reach the needy villagers. "

How lucidly the story hammers a great message: DON'T WASTE; USE!

When you avoid wastage, it is waste-consciousness, not miserliness. At the same time, when you use your resources as much as required, when there is a genuine need and higher purpose for doing so (even if it is a waste in the sense of not being available anymore for its original use), it is benevolence.

17. Green Consciousness

Ponder a bit, and it becomes clear that *waste consciousness, in fact, is a vital part of Green Consciousness for survival of our planet,* too. An idea that has seized the global thinking since a few decades only, after gradually realizing how fast we are destroying our own earth and its sustainability by our reckless over-use, wastages, and contamination of precious, scarce, non-renewable natural resources! Worth repeating: *waste consciousness in the world of food and kitchen emerges primarily from two angles: an appreciation of the value of resources, and an appreciation of the cost (in terms of money, time, labour, i.e., its cost as well as opportunity cost) of procuring/replenishing/storing/using these resources for creating food items.*

Reflect again on what we have just discussed in respect of high degree of waste consciousness in mothers. Over time, this becomes their second nature – to reduce usage, to re-use creatively, to store for longer duration creatively, to prevent wastages and leakages of resources, wherever feasible. And they carry this attitude forward to every sphere. May sound silly, but look at the ways mothers *re-use* everything until its last point of utility! In typical Indian homes, worn out clothes that cannot be donated get re-used as mops till finally they get discarded 😊 In the gone-by era, this was especially true of our mothers and grandmothers, and matriarchs in regular charge of food. They were not aware of the fancy terms we use now-a-days (Rs of sustainability, green acts, green warriors, green corporates etc. etc.). These terms are now-a-days buzz words to spread awareness on the need for stopping reckless usage or wastage of scarce non-renewable natural/manufactured resources, like water, fossil fuel, electricity, clean air etc., those drive our so-called modern material developments.

'Sustainability', that we are so much concerned about these days with climate changes due to many reasons associated with our urban/ technologically advanced life styles that indiscriminately consume scarce, non-renewable natural resources, *starts with respecting the value of our resources, reducing usages to must-use purposes and avoiding wastages.* One such resource is water. Do you know, how much positive impact it can have if only we, the billions of people living on this planet, are genuinely alive to this and do our little bits in saving water, starting with in our kitchens?

Action lies at multi-levels, undoubtedly. Let us leave the macro-level deliberations, strategies, policies, laws, and implementations to the bigger shots. But what about each one of us – at the micro level? *Am I doing my bit? We, as individuals, must also play an equally significant role at the micro level through our conduct in our day-to-day lives. In fact, I would say, ours is a far bigger role than meets the eyes!*

There are umpteen small little things that we can do as individuals to make our drop of personal contribution count in the ocean of action required to address the "green" issues. *Kitchen acts as a very good starting point, at least in respect of precious water, cooking gas and use of polythene.*

Here goes my check-list in the context of kitchen alone, that many green conscious mothers try to act on: (And the idea is: every unit of scarce resources saved/reused/recycled is equivalent to that much resources created!)

1. Stop the leaking tap, if any.
2. Ask your maid not to leave the tap running while she soaps utensils and to open the tap only when she needs it for occasional rinsing before cleaning, and for final rinsing. That saves a lot of water, as I know from personal experience. Further, check on if all the time the tap is set to run at full force. You don't need running water *at full force* for every use in the kitchen sink. Monitor that too.

(Observe her/your own style of washing utensils closely and you will find where to conserve and reuse. You will be surprised to see how much water is actually saved if the dirty utensils are first dipped in just a small vessel full of water, then cleaned with detergent and then only washed well under running tap.)

3. Do not discard the water used for washing anything *without detergent* (like for washing chopped vegetables, dals, rice etc. in the kitchen). Re-use it for watering your potted plants. You may also use this water for keeping the soiled utensils moist before cleaning.
4. Do not waste the RO filter-discarded water while filling its storage. As we know, RO filters discard huge amount of water, almost 60% of what it processes for purification! This water is good to go for watering the plants, even for 1st or 2nd washing of grains and vegetables to clear dirt, whereafter those can be washed well with regular tap water.
5. Do not discard vegetable peels – make your own compost manure and use it to enhance soil quality in your potted plants/kitchen garden.
6. Use Pressure Cooker as much as possible in cooking (of course, keeping its nutrient loss aspect in mind). For example, instead of putting washed dal into Cooker straight away, you may soak it for an hour and then pressure cook with enough water for it to boil; it will reduce both nutrient loss and cooking time in cooker; and hence reduce cooking gas consumption.
7. Consciously reduce use of cooking gas, which comes from highly scarce and non-renewable natural resource like fossil fuel. At least, cook covered and bring gas to sim after a dish reaches boiling point. It can reduce gas consumption quite significantly. Similarly, while cooking rice, you need not cook on gas till rice is fully done. If, for instance, full cooking would have taken 20 mins, then just par-boil up to 75-80% for 10-12 mins and switch off gas, leaving the par-boiled rice covered in the hot boiling water for about 15 mins depending upon the quality of rice. Then drain out. This way, you save gas considerably. There are umpteen similar practices that mothers adopt to cook with less gas, less resources.

8. Use cloth bags for shopping grocery and vegetables. Use kitchen napkins and towels of cloth and washable materials instead of too much use of paper napkins/towels in the kitchen or while eating. This will contribute to saving trees ultimately!
9. Watch out for the fans and lights left switched on after the maid completes mopping the floor. Switch off immediately when the floor dries up. If not checked habitually, on many occasions, you will find your fans on full speed even hours after your maid leaves.

Etc.

Mothers have this tendency to convert their small world of kitchen and food to a *'green zone'* without advertisement or without consciously naming it so. Because, kitchen silently but consistently shapes them *to be mindful* about every little act, and its consequences, and imbibes in them a *respect for resources* (scarce or otherwise) and *respect for Nature* that is the ultimate source of their resources. Recall our discussions on how mothers save, plug leakages, and re-use whatever and whenever possible using their creativity– a habit made from kitchen work.

A mindset that needs be carried forward to all spheres of life! Amazing how kitchen facilitates this.

18. Time Management

It goes without saying, 'TIME' is the most precious resource of our lives – utterly limited vis-a-vis the host of tasks and responsibilities that must be attended to. Naturally, each of us, no matter where we are, whether knowingly or subconsciously, keeps doing what formal Management Study terms as "Time Management" in some way or other. Some do it consciously and efficiently, while some others do it without proper *mindfulness* and end up overwhelmed/ineffective, or failing/unfulfilled.

Even a lay person slightly conscious of the need for time management would roughly do the following in their own informal ways:

– Identify tasks to be attended to during the current time period (A good planner would look at a slightly longer time period like, say a week or more, all the time keeping an eye on the far-off bigger goals, instead of just today and tomorrow.)

- Estimate time needed for already pending tasks on hand plus these new tasks.
- Re-run a check for priority based on importance and urgency.
- Schedule prioritized tasks and execute them first.

But those who are more mindful and systematic, who understand early that time is required for everything, yet time cannot be 'manufactured' and must be 'managed' optimally, go a step forward and *consciously keep processing the* 4 Ws – What, When, How and Who – that form the backbone of any effective time management plan.

To zero-in on '*What*', we have to list out all our tasks and rank them according to priority based on their purpose, i.e., based on another W-*why* do I want to do them in the first place. *We have already seen how purpose-orientation gets imbibed in mothers through kitchen*. So also, the skills of prioritising. Having known what all they have to cook for the day, they do that in order of priority, though that might involve some multi-tasking also. But they would see to it that from tiffin to dinner, all get ready on time. Same in workplace and life in general. When we are aware of *What* - our bigger goals aligned to our ultimate purpose, and the daily tasks and action points for achieving them (the smaller goals)- we *ration/allot our time* as per their priority and contribution to our bigger goals.

This is where '*When*' comes into our decision-making on time management – what to do when! This also captures *how*, in the sense that we decide how much time to allot to what activity in our daily schedule. Every activity need not be a one-day project. Rather, we have many tasks/goals that need daily inputs, or inputs at regular/irregular intervals over a period. When you exercise for weight loss as a priority, you must allot time for it daily, that too at a time like morning or evening, when your body is in requisite readiness – not anytime during the day, or once at irregular intervals. Similarly, in kitchen, you allot time for different dishes depending upon when they are needed, not randomly. Moreover, when preparing certain special items, say like kebab etc. that must be marinated much earlier, mothers plan accordingly and do the preparatory work beforehand ensuring neither over-rest nor under-rest.

Since time is severely limited, and you are only one individual, even if you are a rare super-efficient human being, some things will still remain pending for lack of time, if not for anything else. So here comes *a very significant aspect of 'How' of Time Management – delegation and outsourcing.* To manage your limited time most effectively, you must develop the skills and learn the principles of delegation, or if needed outsourcing, to free up some of your valuable time for more important engagements by passing down some of your *passable* tasks and responsibilities to reliable and appropriate others.

It is of paramount importance to assess the 'Who' in your time management plan for effective delegation, that takes burden of work off you without undermining the quality of outcomes. We shall discuss in greater detail on delegation later in this book and how kitchen very soon makes you learn the need for it, as well as its fundamental principles in terms of what, when, who, how, together with the need for supervision. Delegation is a critical part of time management, especially in organisational set ups, and quite similar principles apply to delegation in kitchen management as well as workplace management.

In the context of overall time management in life, it is also important to keep checking the who we keep interacting with, whether you receive enhancing energy from them, or they are mere *energy-vampires.* If the latter, your time management plan must contain strategies to minimise interactions with such people. They drain your energy and simply kill your precious time. Look at mothers. *When they are in kitchen,* how they focus on cooking, pushing away distractions/unwanted people at least during that time stretch.

Lesson is: if you have allotted your precious time for something important on your priority list, focus on that alone during that time period. So, *focus* is also another significant aspect of time management. Managing time effectively requires your great attention on the job-on-hand. A newer jargon called *'Time boxing'* has come up which simply means boxing out periods of time to work on distinct tasks each day without allowing distractions. Nothing dramatically different from what all have already been advocated regarding allotting time and time periods to tasks as per their priority and attending to them accordingly with self-discipline and focus, and without unwarranted distractions.

Managing *Time windows*, already available as well as suddenly opening due to unplanned circumstances, forms another great part of time management although it sounds insignificant. We will talk about it in detail in multi-tasking segment later. *Kitchen is a great place to pick up insights on this.* Just to give a small example: while cooking a meal of multiple dishes, you don't finish each dish to take up another. As you put one dish, say rice, to cook, you start preparing for another during the *time window that is available* to you before rice is fully done and you need to drain it. Or say, you have put marinated chicken in the oven for slow cooking. You don't wait till it gets over to start the other main dish to go with it. You work on the other after putting the chicken in the oven, so that the main dish also gets ready simultaneously.

Time windows can also open suddenly. Once you have the urge for effective time management, you would not let even a suddenly opening time window pass by unutilised. Recently, I had ordered some groceries online and the delivery slot that I chose was 7-10 am. It was an inadvertent mistake on my part to choose the same, as this is exactly during this period that I need to go out of flat sometimes for certain works, plus I take my bath every day during this time slot. I was alone at home that day, and so, had to remain home-bound to receive the delivery, postponing bath, and other outside works for the day to post-delivery. Now I had that much extra morning time. So, I just amended my schedule a bit, ate my breakfast before bath instead of my usual habit to take it post-bath, started cooking some dishes for lunch till the person came. That saved some time from the time originally allotted for cooking lunch, during which I cleared some other pending work. So, my precious time was not wasted. Most of us do this. But imagine if we are mindful about such practices, how much better we can manage our time!

Effective time management, however, requires some sort of *self-audits* on how we spend our day to help us build awareness, alignment, and accountability. Goes without saying, this is nothing but a form of planning and review that we have already talked about. Unless I am conscious about what I had prioritized for doing vs. what I actually ended up doing, there is no point in planning and allotting time for that. *So, another major lesson is: keep reviewing -keep a track of how you are spending your time daily, and bring in self-discipline if allowing time-wasters!*

As is obvious, all the above – the 4 Ws – need a thorough planning and preparedness. Recollect how well kitchen teaches lessons on these very skills. We have already discussed that in fair detail earlier.

All the values and habits, imbibed from our humble kitchen -e.g., showing up, just making a start, setting goals, planning and preparedness, putting in place some sort of structure and routine to be followed with discipline and needed flexibility in keeping with their spirit, inculcating overall self-discipline etc. are all examples of *tools of time management* also and eventually help us manage our time better.

Further, in kitchen, time is of essence – you cannot leave something on fire for an eternity, neither can you take something off fire before it is done. You must develop a keen sense of how much time to allot to your cooking processes. Plus, a mother does not do cooking alone. She must take care of a whole lot of other things simultaneously: laundry, cleanliness, children's needs, guests, looking after other family members, own needs, so on and so forth. *How she manages her time, aligning everything important can be an eye-opener for lessons in time management.*

The rigours of balancing work, home and professional lives cannot be handled without effective time management. *Time passed by is time lost for ever.* No doubt, therefore, Time Management is an utmost critical aspect of management irrespective of the area you are operating in – personal or professional, or social, whatever! We have already seen how regular kitchen management gives us these insights on time management very soon and very convincingly.

To gain a deeper perspective, we would take two examples that are widely popular in Management courses on Time Management, and check out how in kitchen, we act as per these principles even without knowing these formal management theories. One who is mindful picks up these lessons and carries them forward to workplaces - management training or no training.

One famous example, that elaborates on *how* of time management, is the illustration on how to fill the maximum space of an empty glass jar with large rocks, pebbles, granules, sand, and water. To plan your day, imagine your day as a large empty jar. Imagine your tasks which are big, important, and urgent as large rocks, tasks which are small, urgent, and important as pebbles, numerous miscellaneous tiny tasks as granules, routine tasks as sand and sudden tasks as water. So *how and in what sequence* should you fill the jar with different elements so that the maximum of elements finally get space inside the jar? The best and most optimum way to fill the jar is as under:

- First prioritise the tasks within their own groups -large rocks, pebbles, granules, sands, water.
- To begin with, take *some* large rocks in order of your priority and put them in the jar
- Then take a handful of pebbles, and put them in. Shake the jar a bit to let them fit well.
- Next, add a handful of granules, and shake the jar a bit for them to occupy as much empty spaces in between as possible.
- Then drop in handfuls of sand and jiggle so that sand fills up all the small gaps.
- If you still have some 'water' that must go in, then now pour it till it seeps in fully.

This way, you can fill the jar to the maximum without any wastage of space and ensure that maximum possible elements, which are important, urgent, mandatory, and sudden also get space in the jar. In other words, over a time period, you will be able to make space for and attend to all things important and necessary, as per their priority. You would neither get overwhelmed with the burden of too much to do, nor end up neglecting any important issues. Contrast this with a scenario where you go on attending to routine, small but urgent issues as a habit. You would find your jar (working day) full very soon without time for the large, more important issues. It would keep you perennially busy, without desired productivity.

Here, the large rocks are your important and urgent tasks. Each day, you must first make space for some of them in your daily schedule – *some big tasks every day*. If you keep them to the end, after filling sand, pebble, granule etc., there will be no space left for them. And if you go on filling the jar with large rocks only, you would still be left with many more rocks outside the jar, plus all of pebbles, granules, sand (routine, small but also necessary on a day-to-day basis tasks) on one hand. And on the other hand, you would be left with empty, wasted spaces between rocks inside the jar. Thus, no optimisation on any aspect.

The second example is the *Urgent-Important Matrix*, brilliantly explained in Steven Covey's book "The 7 Habits of Highly Effective People". This also advocates a similar approach as above.

	URGENT	NOT URGENT
Important	I	III
Not Important	II	IV

It says, our time management should be aligned to Quadrant I in the short term, but Quadrant III in the long run. Consciously, on a daily basis, we must take up issues which are both important and urgent (Q I), instead of spending all our time and energy on clearing urgent but not so important issues (Q II), or not-important & not-urgent issues (Q IV). Often, Q II and Q IV appear overloaded, but these tasks are easier, or instantly gratifying to deal with, generating a false sense of busyness and productivity; and thus, we are tempted to attend to these instead of Q1 and Q3, which are more challenging. Moreover, we must make space in our schedules for Q III - important issues from a long run point of view, which may not be urgent right now, but over time, would also become urgent if not attended to steadily from now itself.

If we analyse our schedules, we will be shocked to see how we play around Q II and IV, and by not paying attention, how we keep on pushing items under III to I and create stress and ineffectiveness for ourselves and everyone around.

By now we have discussed many significant things about kitchen and the world of food. Just reflect a bit on how kitchen management on a long-term basis involves implementation of these time management principles even without formal knowledge of these management principles.

In the limited context of kitchen, goals are very clear, and mostly fall in Q I and Q II. There is no option for not meeting those goals. Long term goal (or purpose) is to ensure nourishment and health for family (Q III), which gets built into every small goal every day. Short term goals are: to ensure 3-4 *healthy* complete meals a day with *regularity*. So, every day, there must be a breakfast, a lunch, and a dinner at least. That too, ON TIME. And all the meals must be healthy, i.e., balanced in nutrients, tasty and made hygienically. There are a bunch of other conditions about meals that we have mentioned in the beginning, like diversity, catering to special needs of individual members, within budget, social obligations, entertaining guests etc. So, all these are small routine goals, but most significantly, must be achieved around set timings – so both important and urgent (Q I). Another long-term goal might be to acquire top-class proficiency in culinary skills and spread happiness among all. This also gets built into daily cooking through mothers' conscious efforts at trying out new recipes. In kitchen management, Q III gets built into Q I and Q II on a daily basis. Accordingly, all mothers manage their time – prioritising what to make when and how and by whom -personally or through hired hand or outsource. Mostly, mothers operate in Q I and sometimes in Q II, but very rarely left with time to operate in Q IV.

I dare say, if you cannot pick up time management skills from regularly managing kitchen, you run a scanty chance of learning it from elsewhere!

19. Sense of Proportion and Balance

Cooking is a game of playing with various ingredients. *But most importantly, it is about striking the right balance in ingredients, textures, tastes, flavours, nutrients, and cooking techniques by understanding the required proportions, complementarity, processes involved, AND ensuring these.*

Each dish to work well must have ingredients in *right* proportions. Even the best of curry can be killed with an overdose of salt. Further, a *meal* (a combination of dishes on a plate, called Thali in many parts of India) *to be complete in a real sense must have dishes covering as many as possible of the 6 tastes,* called *sad-rasa* in Ayurveda, viz. salty, sweet, tangy, spicy, bitter, and astringent,; *texture-wise varieties* to keep the palate interested and excited like something soft, crunchy, crispy, chewy, gooey, mouth-filling, some moistness or gravy; *flavour-wise variations*, and some *combination of basic nutrients* like protein, carbohydrate, some fat, minerals, vitamins, fibre etc. *And in ensuring all these, the art and science lie in interplay of everything important and varied in right balance and proportion.*

No wonder, mothers see to it that, their menus for, if not every meal, at least the three major meals for the day *together* contain all these in a balanced way. I am sure, no one would like to have *only* protein, though this is the most vital nutrient, in every meal during the day, or for days together. Similarly, usually no one would like to have just one taste in a meal even if it is your most favourite taste; the palate soon gets bored due to the law of diminishing marginal utility. Only a single texture of food, or single flavour coming out of all dishes on your plate, even if feels great the first time, would be very uninviting and unsatisfying. Hench the watch word is balance in diversity.

The techniques of cooking are similarly many and must change according to what is cooking. While boiling, steaming, poaching are very *healthy* techniques, no one would like to have only, say, boiled elements on their plate all the time. So, not only the most appropriate technique must be used (e.g., for simple rice, boiling is the best technique, while grilling is the most appropriate thing for say, kebabs and pizzas), dishes should also be so chosen as to have different techniques of cooking. Cooking all dishes with a single technique, say boiling, or roasting, or grilling, or poaching, or sautéing or deep-frying does not work in the kitchen. Similarly, *complementarity* of ingredients/dishes (*what goes with what*) is also necessary to bring in balance in taste and flavours. You don't put a cup of hot coffee along with an ice-cream and expect both to be taken together. You don't put bitter gourd in mutton curry in the name of improvisation. 😊 You don't serve a delicious biriyani with a bowl of dalma (though tasty individually). You serve kachumbar, that goes with biriyani!

Thus, our daily food always calls for balance and proportion, along with complementarity and mothers cooking regularly pick up this sense very well. Let us see, how it develops.

First of all, you must *know each ingredient* – its inherent and unique qualities like its flavour, taste, texture, cooking time, needed heat, how much to use, when to use in the course of cooking a dish, compatibility and complementarity for combining with other ingredients etc. Having known these aspects, you must judiciously choose your basket of ingredients for a particular recipe and their quantity, ensuring a proper proportion so that there is a balance in taste, consistency, and nutrition. Ultimately, cooking is an art that predominantly requires a great sense of proportion and balance, which in turn calls for knowledge about everything you are going to use, along with a clear understanding of the process, i.e., where exactly an ingredient is going to be introduced into the dish while cooking.

The good news is: kitchen very soon makes one develop this sense, and helps sharpen it over time with ease. Almost intuitively. Just like you get a knack of something by doing repetitively. Take for example, salt in a curry. No 1. Do you put it indiscriminately? No. You may err a few times initially and spoil the dish. But soon you *learn to err on a lower side* so that you can adjust at the end. Plus, soon you also learn the right quantity of seasoning ingredients like salt, sugar, and other spices to balance the taste of the dish. Disasters wait to happen the moment ingredients are used disproportionately. For cooking rice in pressure cooker, a usual proportion of 1:2 is maintained in quantity of rice and water. Depending upon quality of rice and exact consistency you desire, this proportion may vary slightly. But if you put water disproportionately, imagine what would happen to your rice eventually. Similarly, it is interesting to observe how adding a specific ingredient at different stages of the process of cooking, or in different forms (like ground, chopped, crushed etc.) changes the dish. So, *a thorough understanding of the process involved in a recipe* also helps in developing a sense of balance and proportion for the best result.

Let us talk about team work in workplaces. How important it is to strike a balance there too in every aspect to manage your team effectively! *For effective team building, it is a must that you 'know' your team members individually* – especially their strengths, weaknesses, general character, and value pre-dispositions, what usually motivates them etc. In cooking, you must know your ingredients well to make combinations with great results. Similarly, you must know your people well to lead your team maintaining proper harmony in team dynamics. We shall talk more about cooking and Team Building separately.

Our sense of proportion and balance is also a must in dealing with every situation in life – managing self as well as others. For example, a crisis in workplace situation cannot be effectively dealt with only through anxiety or strict discipline, or complete lenience. Certain amount of anxiety, which can act as a creative impetus for solution is fine. Certain amount of order and discipline in action is also called for. Certain amounts of leniency, calmness, tolerance, empathy, understanding, compassion for the weak or erring parties may also be needed. *In situations that a leader faces on a regular basis, a great sense of proportion and balance in demonstrating emotions and feelings is called for to successfully navigate through both routine days and crises*. People in leadership roles, who also happen to have learnt this lesson from kitchen, realise its importance too well, and usually handle all sorts of situations and people in a balanced way.

So is also the case in virtually every sphere of life. In our day-to-day life, it is about proportions and balance between various *roles* that we play, various *feelings and emotions*, various *competing goals,* and *interests.* Kitchen teaches us clearly why and how we must know our 'ingredients that we use in every step of living' (viz. our own emotions and feelings, our strengths, our weaknesses, our knowledge and perception about others' personality traits, their strengths, and weaknesses etc.) and keep introducing the right ingredients in right proportion at the right stages in the process to make the most out of any situation.

How fulfilling and worthwhile our life is will depend on our ability to balance all these!

It won't be out of context to quote Aristotle, who maintains, "Virtue is the golden mean between two vices. The one of excess and the other of deficiency." Which implies BALANCE! He says, we must find a balance between the two in everything. For example, courage is a virtue between two vices at the extreme-cowardice and rashness. Effective people have found the golden Mean and have the will power and long-term vision not to succumb to any extremes. So easy to find the parallels in kitchen. Would you like to eat something too salty, too sweet, too tangy, too spicy, too hot, too cold ...? No, every good cook strikes a balance amongst everything they use and create. We can well imagine what level of effectiveness persons in leadership roles can bring into their functioning styles, if they have a great sense of balance.

Know thy *ingredients* (people, resources, emotions) and strike a balance in their use and proportions! A very practical lesson from our humble kitchen, indeed.

20. Innovation and Creativity

I think, even the worst denigrator of cooking job would agree to the fact that it involves a lot of innovation and creativity. *The sheer fact that unlimited varieties of recipes are made across the globe, across regions and cultures, from finite number of ingredients is simply undeniable evidence of how much creativity goes into a modest, yet endless job like cooking.*

As soon as you start taking charge of your kitchen, something starts coming to you almost magically over a very short period. And that is *improvisation* – which is nothing other than innovations in small or incremental ways.

Especially when you face the challenge of bringing in diversity into your daily menus, you get the motivation and drive for being innovative and creative. No family likes to have the same menu, the same recipes every day. As the one in charge of providing meals to your family, you tend to, or are compelled to, *invest your mind* in preparing menus in such a way as not to repeat dishes quickly. Further, you are also not expected to cook the same ingredients the same way every time. In that case, both the makers and the eaters would get bored in no time. Thus, *need for diversity effectively sets you up for creativity in kitchen,* not only in food preparation, but also in umpteen other areas, like technique of cooking, use of cookware and tools, space management and storage, cleanliness, finding sources of procurement, and what not. *It eventually helps you develop an attitude of exploration and experimentation, that lies at the crux of creativity in any field!*

Let me give a small example of being creative in areas, other than recipes, relating to kitchen. In instant recipes when ingredient like Eno (fruit salt) is added for raising the batter for soft and spongy Idli/pancakes, the rule is to cook/steam the whole such batter *quickly after adding Eno*. If you keep it without steaming/cooking for long, instead of rising, the final product would rather become hard. So, when making a larger batch than my regular steamer with 12 moulds can take care of, to serve many people at the same time, I use some innovative arrangements for steaming by combining deep bottomed vessels (kadai), perforated stand that comes in Pressure cookers, cake tins for filling up with batter and a perfect-sized lid to cover the kadai. And all get steamed at one go on 2/3 burners! If I am still left with some Eno mixed batter, I use the microwave, too. Would it have been prudent to buy 2-3 sets of Steamers, or is it wiser to use your already available cookware in some innovative/creative combinations? So, this also exemplifies how you are virtually *pushed* to use your creativity in kitchen very frequently, apart from the obvious need for creativity in recipes and platter combinations.

Quick and simple improvisations also start when a few of the ingredients of the original recipe are not readily available at home, or there are bits of certain perishable/left over stuff that must be used before they get wasted. *So, dealing with situations of 'lack' and need to avoid wastages in kitchen often stimulate our inherent ability to be creative.* And so is this in all other workspaces in life. Once you realise consciously how your creativity steers you through all kinds of 'situations' in your humble homely kitchen, you would never give up in other situations outside kitchen too. *Creativity becomes a habit with you.*

As they say, *necessity is the mother of invention.* An undisputable fact! When the necessity arises, you learn to do without many things that you thought earlier as indispensable. Similarly, when you *value* everything properly and are keen *not to waste*, your creativity gets a kick.

And of course, once you taste the excitement of creating newness, even in the smallest, insignificant ways in a non-descript place called kitchen, you are bound to develop a keen interest in experimenting new recipes, new combinations of flavours and ingredients, new techniques of cooking! Many of us eventually find our passion in it!

Yes, it happens very commonly. Many women, in their youth while in their parental home, leading a carefree life must have faced comments from elders, "She is not taking any interest in cooking. What will she do after marriage?" (A manifestation of our centuries-old patriarchal mindset that has stereotyped women's roles⊠). But it would be astonishing to check back on these same women post-marriage after a few years. You would most likely find many of them having transformed into passionate cooks/chefs.

Challenges have this stunning power to arouse your *dormant innate capabilities* to face and solve even seemingly unsurmountable obstacles, what to talk of small, little problems here and there! Yes, it may feel unpleasant to face initially, but when you buckle up and work through them, you bring about real change in your work competence and your lives, making you a better worker as also a better human being. *Taking a challenge head on becomes your attitude towards life in general, no matter where you are.* Is it not a great trait to cultivate? Our humble homely kitchen can be that starting point to push you to discover your own streaks of creativity.

Little steps out-of-box, but taken regularly, matter ultimately for a cumulative impact on attitudes. Kitchen chores mostly being quite repetitive, provide such opportunities to go out-of-box again and again to sustain interest in them.

Earlier, I had made a simple reference to how waste-consciousness drives creativity in kitchen. I had talked about my child's distaste for the edges of bread slices, whatever may be the bread-based dish. That leaves me with great quantities of bread edges on a regular basis. Let me take the same situation to explain how it drives my creativity stepping *out-of-box* along with finding uses *in-the-box*. I personally love the taste of these brown crusts, and so do many others. Normally, I use up the bread edges by converting them to breadcrumbs, which is used up in deep frying/panfrying chops/cutlets/fritters. But for mothers like me who are mindful of the health quotient of food on plate for the family also, deep frying does not happen frequently, and as a result, not much breadcrumb is needed on a regular basis. The second common use could be to add the fresh breadcrumbs to the moist mix for any type of regular *pan-fried* cutlets/chops, like vegetable chop, fish chop, potato cutlet etc. The third option could be to chop the edges into small pieces and deep fry to have croutons for topping soups. Again, soup is not a frequent dish in our climatic condition in India. So, apart from using in the normal 3-4 ways (*in-the-box* solutions), as per my need, I have improvised its use in some other ways too, so that I can relish it.

- As I like its taste, I simply eat it in place of bread. I toast the broken edges from the bread slices on a pan/griddle, sprinkling oil/butter, till nicely crispy. I simply eat this like toasted bread slices with whatever I would like to have – egg omelette/scrambled egg/poached egg/paneer bhurji etc. This way, I consume the edges fresh mostly without having to store in fridge. Even if I must store in fridge, that is not an issue.

- At times, I even convert this to a yummy sweet breakfast by simply adding milk, sugar/banana, cardamom powder. No toasting even. A simple healthy, yummy dish for some!

- At times, I play around a bit more. Heat oil on a griddle/pan. Pour in regular omelette mix. Keep flame on sim. Spread the toasted edges on top; cover with grated cheese and a sprinkle of mixed herbs plus pepper powder. May be, a few strips of bell pepper and tomato. Cover and cook on sim till cheese melts and gives a binding to the pancake. Enjoy your Cheesy-Egg-Bread Pizza with a bit of tomato sauce on top.

So, the point is: our humble kitchen stirs up our innate creativity even just out of our waste-consciousness, or boredom of repetitiveness in use of any ingredient. There are usually many occasions, on which a small quantity of cooked rice gets left over. This is perhaps one source, from which I have experimented with many recipes, which have turned out very yummy and wholesome in one-pot.

Once, I had experimented with an improvised version of Russian Chicken cutlet. The mix fell a little short, and I could keep only a small cutlet for myself. A situation of lack. What immediately came to mind was to turn that into a stuffing for bread/pav sandwich. I chopped some red and green bell peppers, some onion, garlic, ginger and green chilli, and a bit of tomato – all into super tiny dices. Fried them in butter. Added the cutlet, breaking and mixing it in the pan, a dash of whole spices powder, and bringing everything together. This not only increased the quantity of the mix to be enough for stuffing one large sandwich, it also added much flavour and vegetables to the original version which already contained beans, carrots, and shredded chicken. Made a super delicious stuffed sandwich and enjoyed.

There are hundreds of such examples in my personal journey of culinary skills over last close to 4 decades. And I am sure, many of us, whether working or not, must be sharing similar experiences.

Once after watching great Ads on Instant Masala Oats, I got a few packets from the market to check out. Honestly, I did not like the taste or texture: neither did my family. But it immediately struck me to experiment masala oats in a different way using regular oatmeal. I dry roasted oatmeal flakes. Boiled enough water adding lots of vegetables like carrots, bell papers, beans, green peas, and tomato, onion, and fresh coriander stems– all finely diced, salt to taste and *Sambhar Masala* (a typically South Indian spice mix that is liked by one and all). As the vegetables were 70% done, I added dry-roasted oats. Cooked till done keeping a rolly-polly consistency. Flavoured with lots of chopped fresh coriander leaves. Believe me, it was way tastier than the ready-made one. Later, I found that whatever vegetables you may or may not use, but don't skip three things-tomato, onion and fresh coriander; those three ingredients complement sambhar masala a great deal. Still later, I experimented with adding cheese (mozzarella cheese which we get easily in India). Lo and behold, it turned out super yummy, cheesy delicacy for my daughter! Meanwhile, I had also tried other regular curry powder mixes (available in market readily) and most of them worked in the recipe very well.

So, do observe the process of creativity – wandering through simple improvisations, in-box but different combo experiments, as well as out-of-box explorations. Creativity does not always lie in one "Aha" moment after series of experiments with out-of-the-blue ideas. Mostly it is about how differently, and in how many different ways you can join the existing dots.

The ability and skill to join the dots differently, and/or create new dots based on inference/insight/experimentation/extrapolation lie at the heart of all creativity in the kitchen. *And so is the case in every other sphere in life.*

And please always keep in mind that such ability to be creative originates and gets strengthened when one nurtures the trait of *learning* as a core value. *That is what our homely kitchen facilitates and pushes us towards – to explore and learn, learn, and learn.*

Moreover, since creativity does not allow us to stay bound to anything, it promotes our *spontaneity* on the sideline. Spontaneity not only makes our lives interesting, it also helps in coming up with *coping mechanisms* in any situation with ease and quickness.

Indeed, ultimately everything worthwhile that we can achieve requires us to keep staying on the learning curve.

The element of creativity that is already there in every person, gets stimulated in Kitchen as it is a great place to experiment with new recipes, create new ones, and/or improvise the existing ones. And as already mentioned, very often it is also need-driven. Because not only there is a need to cater to different preferences of different members who look up to you for their food, but also there is a constant need to bring in *diversity* to prevent boredom both for you (the creator) as well as others (the end users). Moreover, it is always easy and safe to experiment a new recipe on yourself before serving it to others, or on a small scale. *There is not much risk in experimenting in kitchen (at the worst, the dish gets wasted after teaching what does not work), so fear of failure and ridicule is also minimum.* Since we already know that the consequences of a failure of a recipe is not going to be 'catastrophic,' we are less afraid and more willing to try and experiment in kitchen.

When we start using our creativity in these small ways, but on a regular basis, we see for ourselves that it is possible to make a *habit of being creative*, and *creativity* need not sound as a hyperbole, or something unique found only in a few blessed/gifted ones – as is believed ordinarily.

The following are four very useful perspective/insights our kitchen experiences make us pick up easily:

i. *Everyone is already endowed with creativity.*
ii. *This can be tapped into as a matter of habit.*
iii. *Observing the processes keenly AND reflectively (spotting the 'dots' and how they are joined versus how differently they can be joined) leads to new ideas to experiment with.*
iv. *Allowing failure helps conquer the fear of failure that is perhaps the greatest obstacle on the way to experimentation.*

The 3rd insight (Observe the Processes) is in fact invaluable from a practical point of view as regards *how* to develop innovativeness and creativity in any field. Smart cooks would not always rigidly follow or try to memorize different *recipes as they are.* What they would notice mindfully is the processes involved – the combination of ingredients that work out great and those that do not, proportions for balancing different ingredients and flavours, the sequencing of incorporating various ingredients, the modes of heat control, the ideal time ranges for cooking different ingredients, the uniqueness of flavours etc. These are the building blocks of various recipes – the DOTs that are joined in different ways to create variety of dishes. Innovations and creativities lie in experimenting and exploring in what new or different ways these 'dots' can be joined.

So here in kitchen, we always keep riding on a curve of *learning* (existing recipes), *unlearning* (you don't stick to the recipe always), and *relearning* (create new recipes). *What a great learning platform our modest kitchen provides!*

In every sphere of life, it is seen that creativity need not necessarily involve all new knowledge. It comes about by working with the known in 'unknown yet' ways. Kitchen helps build one's *creative confidence* to a robust level through already mentioned insights. And it is this confidence, that drives them better in professional spheres to analyse and take productive risks for devising creative solutions undeterred by the fear of failure.

Is not creativity and innovation a highly required trait for a true leader in any field? More so, in today's world? Is not this also a basic requirement to reach our best potential in life? Look at how consistently this is cultivated and nurtured in a sustained manner in our homely kitchens. Mind-blowing!

In fact, innovativeness and creativity is THE jest of life - something that pervades across spectrum in our lives, both in our inner world, as well as outer world. The efforts to bring in *newness* into anything we do infuse *vibrancy and enthusiasm* in our inner world. And it brings about positive and constructive outcomes in our outer world, *enthusing us further.*

Let me add something here. Doctors usually advise aged people to do many routine things in different than their normal ways to avert problems like forgetfulness/dementia. For example, if you are a right-hander, then on some days brush your teeth with your left hand, eat holding the spoon in your left hand, take a different route to your frequented destinations, learn a new language etc. Basically, the advice is to *learn something new* getting out of your normal habits, your comfort zone. In kitchen, when we get injured/burnt, especially in our most used fingers/thumb/palms, *we instinctively get creative* and find out ways to manage our chores – cutting/chopping/washing/grinding (what not?) – with the other unhurt fingers/parts of body. Because we know, in most situations, we simply cannot *flee the kitchen midway* of cooking. Gradually, this *resilience gets ingrained in our personality and gets demonstrated in other walks of life, too.* Is this not something truly laudable?

Renewal and recreation of *Self* very often lies in finding new possibilities in the old circumstances. It need not always be about moving away to newer horizons. This is also being creative. Indeed, creativity is THE fulcrum of our progress and fulfilment in practically every sphere of life. And a grand role in developing this quality in us is played constantly by kitchen if you happen to be cooking regularly. Can't help mentioning at the cost of being repetitive!

21. Learning, Unlearning and Relearning

Let go to let in (tilt like a funnel)!

We have already seen that 'learning' is a core value. Let us be clear, it is not *what we have learnt*, but *the ability to learn continuously,* which is a core value; and the process of learning moves through three phases, viz. learning, unlearning, and relearning. True learning never stops or gets stagnant at one point.

The most difficult part of learning is, perhaps, unlearning. That is why I felt like deliberating separately on this in greater detail, though it goes without saying that learning- unlearning- relearning is embedded in the process of innovation and creativity, and we have already talked about that just before this.

New learnings to happen, old ideas and beliefs must be shed to create space for new ideas. *Let us take the example from our homely kitchen.* While filling an empty bottle with oil from an outside source (a can or a refill pack), a funnel is inserted through the neck of the bottle, *and tilted a bit*, so that some air escapes through its nozzle, allowing oil being poured in to get inside the bottle. Try pouring the oil into an erectly placed funnel, and you would find how difficult it is - because the so-called empty place inside the oil bottle is already filled with air. Unless that air is let out, no space gets created for the inflow of oil. *In case, you are a keen observer, you pick up this critical insight just from this one experience.* Kitchen keeps reminding us that, our mind is like the funnel through which new information, new knowledge, new insights are to flow into our inner world. Unless we tilt, or bend a little in humility, acknowledging that we need to *let go of something inside us to let in something new,* we would fail to learn in life.

Similarly, unless you give up your *ego,* or belief that you already know everything about something, you would never be able to learn anything new. So, humility and readiness to let go of own ideas, at least partially, is the key to learn, unlearn and relearn on a continuous basis. Destroying/discarding old habits and patterns of thinking and behaviour and welcoming change is the only way to keep on re-inventing your own self in this world, where change is the only thing constant.

To re-iterate, we must empty out the old contents at least partially and create space to let the new flow in.

If you maintain a kitchen garden, you would quickly appreciate the value of unlearning, i.e., undoing or discarding a part of what you have learnt/ accumulated. Herbs like holy basil, mint, curry leaves, wild coriander etc. that we grow in our kitchen garden usually *must* be *pruned* and branches/ leaves *plucked away* from time to time for them to renew themselves and grow. Holy basil plants need their terminal spikes with clusters of seeds to be snapped as soon as they show signs of maturing. Otherwise, they simple grow old and die. Take the example of even the aged plants which have almost stopped growing but not fully dead yet, and are sitting there in the same pot along with new saplings. What happens? The new young plants cannot grow properly as a big share of the nutrients from the soil is getting drawn by the aged one. Just *root out* the old one, and see how fast the new plants start growing. Moreover, not only Nature teaches us to periodically prune all plants and trees, it also teaches us to periodically clean off the *dead* leaves/branches/stem, so that any kind of 'dead wood' would not come in the way of new growth. Same happens with our previously learned ideas and habits, too. Unless we let go of some of them, which are no longer working as effectively as they used to, newer ideas cannot enter and take root. *The process of unlearning must run continuously, simultaneously with the process of learning, for re-learning to happen effectively.*

It is said, the shore of ignorance increases, the more we cover the shore of knowledge. The more you learn, the more you realise that there is yet a lot to be learnt, and hence you start learning to unlearn and relearn.

Unlearning is not about forgetting something you already know. It is about being open, willing, and able *to choose* an alternative solution/ approach/paradigm that is more effective for your purpose now. It is your ability to give up what is no longer true, or relevant or helpful, even though once they were so. Incremental building of knowledge and skills upon existing knowledge usually keeps on happening to keep pace with a changing world. But at times, there may be a point, where true effectiveness, or a new level of needed proficiency in the same old, or, changed context might call for a *paradigm shift,* requiring you to simply discard fully what you knew and was quite working for you so far, and adopt something new and different.

Unlearning is about a deep realisation that what got me here will not get me there. This leads to the openness and ability to completely discard something you *think* you know so that you can learn something that you *need* to know!

Yes, unlearning can be hard on all of us. After all, it takes us out of our *comfort zone* first – habits/routine/mental models of thinking and interpreting accumulated over time, with which we could work with ease. Secondly, there might be worries: the new ways might take more time to master even after learning. Thirdly, it may also be emotionally painful to admit to yourself that what you so confidently held on to as your sure-success formulae so far, are actually not so 100% and you did not even realise it for so long; or that these have simply become obsolete.

So, to unlearn, we must first be open to it, and then, from time to time, challenge our own ways critically. Especially, when signs of less than expected results keep showing up, or when we learn about some new pieces of information.

Challenge your mental maps and models.

We can now see clearly how improvisation in kitchen is a fine example of unlearning partially what you knew previously and re-learning something new.

Once we understand that learning-unlearning-relearning is a continuous process that must be followed to stay relevant to and match our ever-evolving world, we become agile and capable to adapt quickly and effectively, making most of the emerging situations. Is not this a huge requirement for management and leadership?

"The most important lessons lay not in what I needed to learn, but in what I first needed to unlearn."

Jim Collins in the book "Good to Great"

Our homely kitchen operations keep helping us immensely in this process.

22. Learning and Value of Failures

Learning from mistakes that led to a failure is a significant part of the learning process.

Failures are, in fact, a major part of success, as they at least teach us what does NOT work and must be done differently to succeed. Past errors are not blots or burdens; choose to wear them as badges of honour, as these are your real stepping stones to success.

There may be times when you end up messing up a dish, or delivering a less-than-your-best prepared dish, even though you might have done it fabulously many times in the past. Do not take anything for granted, nor have fear for the outcome. *Kitchen teaches us to treat every time as the first time and to focus.* A dish is a combined outcome of many elements- ingredients, proportions, cooking times, adding stages, heat regulations etc. Even a documented recipe may come out differently at different times. Accept it. It pays neither to be boastful if you are a great chef (or in any role), nor to be demotivated when a failure strikes. Be humble, embrace your mistake, look back at what/where you went wrong possibly, and be more careful in future.

Even the best of Chefs spoils the broth at times. Failures are as much a part of kitchen, as of any area in life. For everyone, in every sphere. These cannot be avoided completely, so must be *embraced* in a right manner.

Embracing mistakes and failures in a right way may involve all or some of its finer dimensions as under.

i. *Willingness to fail,* notwithstanding the fear of ridicule or rejection, is the other name of courage! Show courage, and you can experiment and explore and move ahead steadily on a learning curve till you succeed. Don't back off just because you failed.

ii. *Heed a lesson!* Often, we are told, *mistakes are not to be repeated.* A huge lesson, indeed. Essentially, '*we must not repeat our mistakes*' is not only a technique to experiment successfully, more than that it is a *mindset* that makes you 'heed a lesson'. On one hand, this mindset keeps you alert against committing the same mistakes repeatedly in the same manner; while on the other hand, it rather encourages you to practice and experiment further even at the risk of committing some new mistakes, or even the same mistakes at times, but by adopting different approaches every time. *It is about the approach to the mistake, not the specific mistake per se.*

iii. *Practice makes one perfect!* You should take a picture of your first-ever roti (round Indian flatbread from whole wheat flour dough)! 100% sure, it must have acquired some funny shape – not a neat round, and uneven thickness 😊 Will you stop rolling out roti because you committed a mistake in getting its shape? Or will you practice further knowing fully well that you are very likely to commit the same mistake of getting a funny shape for quite a few times till you get it right? Obviously, the latter. Point to understand here is: the mistake was not in the shape; it was in the process of rolling out. It was in the *lack of skill and practice. So here, you learn two vital lessons: a. practice makes one perfect, and b. understand where from the mistake is originally emanating, so that you can focus on mastering at that point.* THAT is learning from mistake.

In fact, I think, kitchen is one of the greatest workplaces where your entire learning process is intricately embedded with mistakes-learnings-more explorations-more mistakes-more learnings, and so goes it on and on.

iv. *Nature of mistakes that must NOT be repeated.* As a newbie to kitchen, you must have accidentally touched the hot stove, or a hot vessel on fire. Happens in a hurry/lack of mindfulness. But this is a mistake that is ill-affordable to be repeated, simply because it is *hazardous.* You must learn from this mistake committed once and create an auto-mode coping system to reach for a tong/grip/towel as you go for a hot thing next time. There are umpteen examples of this nature in kitchen (handling hot liquids, putting things into hot oil, dealing closely with hot steam, chopping things very fine with an extra sharp knife etc. etc.) *All these incidents in which you get hurt physically teach you to be habitually careful about them.* Thus, here again, it is about a mindset. This mindset of exercising care and caution every time you deal with hazardous processes, when gets imbibed in your character, makes you similarly mindful even while dealing with words and actions that are hazardous to feelings and emotions, your own as well as of others. Is it a small lesson from kitchen?

Let us take another example of mistakes that must be avoided the second time because it leads to wastages or damages, which could have been averted. Preparation of clarified butter(ghee) requires you to strain and pour into the storing bottle, which is usually a *glass* bottle. The first time, I straight away put the strainer on the glass bottle, and strained the hot liquid ghee from the pan into it. The glass bottle did not break as it was very thick and toughened. I had done this *unmindfully*, although I know that at times, glass utensils crack if very hot stuff is put into them. Thus, though I knew a lesson, I did not apply it and just by chance, suffered no loss. Next time, I poured similarly, directly from hot pan from the stove, into another glass jar, but it cracked. This was a fancy jar, and though slightly thick, perhaps it was not of toughened glass. I was so sad to lose one of my favourite nice looking glass jars from a famous brand! Plus, of course the ghee made so painstakingly!

But I learnt my lesson and that is important. Next time onwards, I first strain the hot liquid ghee into a steel pot, allow it to cool down a bit, and then only pour the lukewarm liquid into storage glass bottles. *Every blunder has at least one lesson on what does NOT work, which, if noticed correctly, is no mean a lesson from a failure.*

Thus, kitchen teaches us to learn from mistakes and failures; experiment further despite some mistakes *for creativity*, but not to repeat mistakes that involve serious injuries/damages to self or any other person or property, which are not worth anything.

Thus, apart from instilling in us a mindset to heed a lesson, kitchen also imparts a still bigger learning: WHICH mistakes are NOT to be repeated, and for WHICH ones we must rather develop a willingness to repeat a few more times till we get the knack of getting it right.

Quite funny, but true. Mistakes are more terrifying *before* they are committed than afterwards. Most of us do not even try out a new thing out of fear of failure. That tends to eventually stunt our growth. But

Kitchen teaches us that *mistake per se is not a failure. Mistake is very often merely a mis-take on the real reason behind a failure.* Failure could be because of lack of adequate knowledge, lack of correct appreciation of issues involved, lack of correct approach, lack of critical support systems, lack of needed skill and competence, lack of needed focus/dedication/discipline etc. Mistake *per se,* is merely a result of one or more of those lacks. Correct those lacks, instead of giving up out of fear or frustration of failure.

v. By the sideline, such experiences of failure also bring out *the sense of humour* in mothers. Very often, when we fail, we also receive negative feedback. But soon enough, mothers learn to take some feedback from others with *a pinch of salt, or learn to simply laugh it away. Who would not have laughed good-humouredly at the funny mistakes they themselves committed as a novice in the kitchen?* For example, at the funny shape of the first few Rotis, or a half-burnt curry, or a messed up dosa/pan cake, or a half-baked cake, or a half-cooked kebab? They know this kind of mess-ups happen initially, so they take them with a sense of humour when others commit similar mistakes, without criticising them, or to make the atmosphere lighter and friendly for further learning. Let me tell you, I personally put this personality trait, *a great sense of humour*, on the list of top leadership qualities, without which, I believe, no leader can manage or lead people in a challenging workspace which already would be full of tensions and stress and pressure.

To reiterate, mistake is a *mis-take* – you acted based on some presumptions you truly believed are correct, or due to lack of required knowledge and practice. So, no guilt angle must be allowed within. Moreover, it becomes so reassuring, when you see that sky actually did not fall down because you made a mistake. It leads to strengthening your ability to face your fears still better in future. And ability and willingness to fail is perhaps the first and foremost prerequisite to explore, and be creative! There are umpteen examples to validate the wisdom that courage and perseverance will reward you eventually with great success, only if you take your lessons from mistakes and failures seriously, and take your actions/ideals forward with a sense of justice and well-being for all.

23. Followership

Seek Out – Leadership starts from good followership.

When you enter the kitchen as a novice, do you take a plunge to experiment from the scratch on your own, without knowing anything at all? No. You bring in some basic knowledge and insights that you might have acquired earlier from watching your mothers and matriarchs in kitchen. As you start with your kitchen responsibilities, you do talk to your mother or other experienced people known to you. You do go through books, blogs, recipe books, watch YouTube videos etc. You do initially *seek out* advices, and look for guidance from many sources available to you, use your own common sense and knowledge, and start acting. You do not waste your energy on *'reinventing the wheel'*. Following others' advices for, say, basic infrastructure for cooking, recipe for basic everyday staples like rice, roti, paratha, dal, bhaji etc. makes sense. You just ask others and follow their advice. This does not *bind* you *not to start exploring new things on your own*. You eventually do that over time. Moreover, even after becoming a seasoned cook, you don't stop following. The greatest Chefs, the mothers and amazing cooks rather continue to 'follow' newer recipes from any source they can tap, experiment, and further improvise if need be. Great Leaders continue as great 'followers', which is the real secret behind their ever-expanding vision and competence. And as you follow, you also gradually realise how behind meaningful followership, there are, in fact, two *key abilities* that you get to strengthen:

- an ability to *network*, and
- an ability to decipher who/what to rely on, and who/what to reject unapologetically

Are not these two abilities critical for effective leadership as well as a meaningful life, too?

Point is: kitchen responsibility teaches you in no time on how to seek out, how to ask for others' advices and how to follow, *without feeling ashamed of the same*. I am sure, even a person with a huge ego of I-Know-it-All would keep that ego aside in the initial phase at least and become a willing follower if given the responsibility of managing a kitchen on long term basis. A novice but good follower eventually blossoms into a great

Chef - a leader in that space, when cooking becomes a passion for them and they go on learning from every source available to them-including following other great Chefs.

Though it may sound contradictory, a good leader is always a good follower. 'Leadership' and 'Followership' are the two sides of the same coin, viz. *teamplay,* to make a positive difference to the people and environment; to achieve worthy *shared* goals. If 'a person in a leadership role' stays stuck to one position in spirit (leader or follower), they could end up becoming either an autocratic/dictatorial leader who fails to reap the benefits of the talents of others and could become a tyrant in overconfidence; or a weak, obeisant follower *in spirit* though sitting in a leadership position without courage to stand up for just causes, or lead effectively carrying all in the team along, or making actual contribution to the team efforts.

Quintessentially, a leader starts as a good follower, and keeps following *simultaneously with* leading from the front!

Issue is: we usually focus more on the semantic than on the spirit, or soul of any term that we talk about. Let us take, 'good follower'. We make a huge mistake while understanding "good" in the context of followership. For most of us, 'good follower' only means a subordinate *obeying* what the leader says, and just following their commands. A huge disservice is done this way to the leaders themselves, as no one under the sun is infallible. The leaders are human too and do have many human shortcomings and flaws of their own, which are bound to affect their decision making at some point or other. In this context, if a follower, despite understanding the flaws in any command/decision, blindly implements, or obeys the leader without question, that would amount to sheer acquiescence, not good followership. You, as a follower, become a party to the wrong outcomes, and guilty of wilfully NOT protecting the larger interests in the right manner. Remember, the *shared* goal is a responsibility of *everyone* in a team, not just the team leader. *Followership must be understood as allegiance to a shared goal, a larger interest, the organisation, and not to any specific person on the chair.* Allegiance must be towards the Chair and position, not towards one who sits on that chair. If the one who is sitting on the chair is straying away from the shared goal, it is the moral and ethical duty of a good follower to question or stop that.

If you are the one who manages the kitchen, and in your profession, you are in a leadership role, most likely you would carry forward your lesson on followership to your management style and would be able to draw out the best from your team members, by being a follower of their ideas, too and picking up the worthy ones from your point of view. This way, you synergise your team efforts in a more optimal manner.

Something more significant happens when you yourself are a good follower. As a 'good' follower, you do not blindly follow your leader, but expect some values, principles and competence in your leader for carrying the team to achieve the organisational goals. This, in turn, makes you alive to similar expectations of those who follow *you*. You understand that expectations of professionalism and ethical conduct run both ways. If I expect my followers to be punctual, I must be punctual myself.

The best part is: Followership and its value for better leadership instils a sense of humility.

Humility in its true sense is a manifestation of strength of character that emanates from respect for others, and not from downplaying your own strength and abilities.

Kitchen in its own subtle ways throws up all these perspectives for us to pick up.

24. Learning by doing

Once you are in charge of kitchen, you very soon realise that there is no escape from doing, and to do, you must learn how to do, and to learn that, you must *actually do it*.

Learning by doing!

Mere knowledge without ability to apply is not going to sail you through this responsibility. You have to firm up learning by putting to action whatever you have learnt from other sources. *This is a great lesson from kitchen that you carry forward to all other spheres in life – act on the field and learn the nuances.* No matter how much knowledge you gather from all sources, you won't *get it right* unless you *apply* that *on your own,* at times *under guidance,* and check out for yourself how actually it works out. In fact, we all know the supreme importance of *doing,* i.e., ACTION. Even a grand *idea* fails to work if we do not actually *work* on it. Kitchen keeps on reiterating this, lest we forget.

A significant part of learning ultimately happens only by doing it yourself, that too, repeatedly. In kitchen, one does not take time to pick up this important lesson.

Look at the corporate workspace. Something like *on-the-job training* is a must during probation for new entrants in perhaps every organisation. If you have learnt your lesson well from kitchen on the importance of learning by doing, you, as a trainee, would make the most out of this learning opportunity instead of wasting it. On the other side, if you, as a Team Head, get such new entrants entrusted to you for on-the-job training, you would attach genuine importance to their laid down schedule for such training. In the organisation I worked with, there is a wonderful institutionalised practice of training new entrants by combining theoretical job knowledge through courses at training centres, with on-the-job training in critical operation-related training inputs under suitable guidance of operational functionaries at front-line operating units. I had observed that some Operational Heads become too happy when they are assigned some such officers-on-probation, as they treat them as extra-hands and start misusing them to clear arrears, or manage desks in place of regular staff, instead of allowing them to work on seats as per their training schedule. On the other side, I have also observed similar lackadaisical attitude for the on-the-job training schedule on the part of the trainees themselves. Instead of treating these seriously as learning opportunities that would add to their own management effectiveness going forward, they utilise these as stop-gap arrangements to prepare for other services or examinations! Both are kinds of wasted opportunities. Let me put on record, I, as someone wiser with lessons from kitchen (😊), neither took my training schedule lightly, nor did I, as Branch Head later, ever resorted to the undesirable practices of treating trainees as extra-hands. As a probationer, I used to plead with my Branch Manager to allot to every desk I needed to work on as per laid down schedule, while assisting them simultaneously with other works by walking an extra mile. Further, as a Branch Head, I had given each trainee complete opportunity to learn by handling the specific jobs, that too, ensuring proper guidance and mentoring.

Undoubtedly, kitchen is a workplace which brings out the importance of how learning can happen very quickly and most effectively in on-the-job mode. This is also true of most other workplaces, including management. You learn managerial effectiveness the best, by actually handling managerial responsibilities and assignments. Yes, learning happens in many other ways, too. But *hands-on learning* has its own great importance in every walk of life. Whether you are required to handle the area personally as a front-line employee, or required to manage the operations as a senior manager through your team, you must have basic job knowledge. In fact, you cannot be effective in managing anything if you lack knowledge on its basics. And basics are usually learnt by direct engagements - learning by doing.

What a great insight from our humble kitchen! Once you realise this importance of hands-on learning, you would never be wary of doing jobs below your supposed hierarchy in any organisational set up, or elsewhere, if needed for the purpose of your own learning.

25. Mentoring and Knowledge Management

Being mentored by someone wiser and more experienced always improves your pace and quality of learning. No wonder, mentoring is an important and often-used concept in Management and Leadership. All formal organisations try to institutionalise this practice in several ways. Mentors are usually senior and more experienced, who not only guide you directly, but also ensure a battery of guides from other team members, to help you learn management/leadership principles by example alongside learning basics of job knowledge through institutional training and on-the-job training. There is a fad (almost!) to advertise and declare every Organisation as a Knowledge Organisation since a few decades. As all know, a Knowledge Organisation, pays serious attention not only 'to grow their own timber' – implying investing in and executing a robust training system for their personnel from start to finish of their careers, but also to laying down procedures and processes, so that knowledge remains *documented and gets shared* in-house (also outside, as appropriate). Idea behind such documentation and sharing all the critical knowledge is that *knowledge* stays with the organisation, i.e., *is not lost with the retirement or unavailability of the specific knowledgeable person(s)* for reasons whatsoever.

Now let us see how this also keeps happening in our humble kitchen all the time. Any keen observer can easily pick up these insights and carry forward to their workplaces, even without laid down instructions. For, it is always beneficial to keep essential knowledge documented, without any harmful side effect.

First, you seek out from other sources on recipes and techniques of cooking. Then, you actually prepare a few recipes. Ordinarily, you have someone nearby or at a call's distance these days to guide you in case you need. In fact, in most of the Indian families, mothers (in general, we can say matriarchs) start teaching their children (especially daughters, unfortunately due to stereotyping of role responsibilities) how to cook at least some basic dishes under direct guidance and instructions. *That is the start of mentoring in kitchen.* Recipes are handed down by word-of-mouth generation by generation, everyone most likely adding their special touches in due course. I am sanguine, this is the first-hand experience of every one who learnt cooking at home. Mothers are available always for further mentoring as the children grow up and start managing their own food at hostel/home – marriage or no marriage. Some wiser and more grounded women also do this with their sons/brothers/husband/father – out of a conviction that *cooking is a life skill* and has no gender, and hence everyone must know this at least to survive in emergencies.

How knowledge management happens in Kitchen is also very simple and continuous. I am sure, every novice in cooking has a tendency to *write down recipes in diaries/Notebooks* in their own ways. Gradually, that becomes a habit. Check out every family. There must be Notebooks and Diaries with many recipes that get passed down over generations. At least 2-3 generations now a days with improved preservation techniques of documents. I have my mom's recipe notebook, and I do try out a few at times; although over time, I might have improvised upon many. *The point is: knowledge is documented even in the context of a homely kitchen. Add to that, the trend of publishing thousands of Recipe Books, Food Blogs, hosting TV shows, and YouTube videos on FOOD!* If that is not a robust knowledge documenting and sharing process, then what is!

Just as in kitchen, mentoring in every sphere is about *sharing* our learnings from longer life experiences as we hand-hold our youngers and juniors. For the mentored, it is about respecting and learning from the *practical wisdom* of their elders and seniors who have, may be just because of their longer age and exposures, already learnt valuable lessons from life experiences rich in challenges, mistakes and success.

So, the point I wish to bring out is: Managing Kitchen can also help you to pick up this insight on *how extremely important it is to document and share knowledge for others and for the posterity, instead of letting it die, or get lost along with you departing.* Once you develop a conviction about this, you will do your best to put in place needed structures and practices in your workplaces too. You won't be waiting for instructions from above! And when in top leadership positions, you would surely look into this area in your organisation and arrange to *institutionalise* these practices through suitable laid down instructions and structures to implement/monitor them.

26. Basics never get redundant

Basics are basics, and they never lose their relevance altogether. And it is so in all spheres, because that is where the foundation gets laid, and that is wherefrom you can take off.

Innovations and creativity are all fine. But there are elements, dishes, techniques, and processes that are basic to specific cuisines and food habits. *Kitchen makes us alive to this fact* that these basics must be left as they are without too much of tinkering with them. Yes, in some cases, you may experiment at times. But if you fail, you must go back to the basics.

For example, in any balanced meal, there must be a *staple.* It might differ in different regions and cultures. But it is better to stick to these staples as per your own regional specifics, instead of playing around it too much by substituting them with what you think can give the same food value. In many parts of India, especially eastern and southern parts, rice is *the* main staple food for lunch. It is better to stick to this item in a lunch menu, along with some more basic dishes to go with rice like some dal, or legumes or kadhi, and bring in your creativity and surprises to taste buds through the other accompanying side dishes. There again, you must ensure the compatibility of tastes of all dishes in the meal, so that they do not shock or confuse your palate in a negative way. Imagine how you would react if you are served with, say a pizza accompanied by a dal tadka, fish fry and a green salad! Weird and horrendous! So, *compatibility of tastes is another basic element* that you must always ensure, instead of making weird menu plans in the name of fusion or creativity.

Goes without saying, *nutrition is also a basic* that must be ensured in whatever you eat. One inviolable basic rule that must be adhered to while deciding on meals is that *not only the food be nutritious every time, the combination of food that we eat over one full day at least must have all the nutrients needed for a healthy body in a balanced manner and in sufficient measure.* Only protein one day and only fat one day will not do. Apart from ingredients, cooking techniques also impact nutrition and we must treat *some cooking techniques for certain specific recipes as absolutely basic* that must not be compromised. The best and most nutritious technique to cook rice is to boil rice in enough water and drain the excess water after cooking, that ensures unhealthy starch portion to get out. You can pressure cook, microwave cook, steam cook rice, too. But that is not worth it as you pay a cost both in terms of nutrition and taste. Similarly, boiled vegetables seasoned with something simple must be done by *boiling* the vegetables, not by pressure-cooking. Tandoori items need be done in tandoors for authentic taste. Etc.

Compatibility of ingredients is another basic element in cooking and must be ensured. In one reality show on cooking, I remember, one contestant made coffee Shrikhand, which was a plain disaster, as curd and coffee just didn't go together! Yes, some experimentations to check out compatibility of ingredients is okay, only if you get back to basics once you fail.

Pl recall our discussions on importance of balance and proportions in food. These are all *basics of cooking,* and you cannot play around these. Their importance in food would always remain relevant, howsoever professional, or creative you get!

As regards *process* also, for many recipes, there is a very basic standard process. For example, if you are onto preparing Indianised Chinese dishes like Chilli anything (Chilli Chicken, Chilli Paneer, Chilli Mushroom, Chilli

Potato etc.), or fried rice, noodles, veg stir-fry etc. etc., the process is very basic and almost the same in most recipes. In fact, I have made yum Chilli Potol (pointed gourd) and Chilli Kunduri (Coccinia) following similar procedure, which you can say is my experimentation with a different major ingredient, the *basic process* remaining the same.

Like our world of food, when we talk about managerial effectiveness, leadership, and living a meaningful life in general, we also must understand that there are some *basic values and basic codes of conduct*, in our personal and professional spaces which would always stay relevant, and hence must be adhered to. Do return to basics asap, if you stray away, before setting off an irreversible chain of serious damages. So, what are these basics? We all know. Integrity, honesty, sincerity, self-discipline, co-operation, humility, empathy, compassion, gratitude......... and so on. We cannot afford to stray away from these *basic human values*. In case of our business models, there will always be some *core* business, e.g., in banking, accepting deposits and offering loans constitute the most basic and core business. It is fine to go for allied and diversified, at times even fancy, business lines to enhance our market presence and brand image, but *only after we ensure quality customer service in our basic/core business lines.* Customer delight and add-on services deliver only in those circumstances, not at the cost of basics.

Again, a great insight from our homely humble kitchen! It opens our eyes to the fact that basics constitute the foundation upon which you can build up, and from where you can take off. So, never run down or neglect the basics.

27. The Science and Art of Multitasking

Come on! Kitchen is THE place for multitasking. Observe how mothers work. As something is cooking, preparation like chopping, washing, grinding for other items keep getting done simultaneously. You have put something in oven? Oh, you know how long you are not going to even check it out, or how long exactly you leave it to get perfectly baked, grilled, or roasted. Will you just sit tight and wait for that time to get over, instead of attending to other chores fully or partially as possible?

Or say, you are preparing some curry on gas stove; you have already cooked its spice paste for gravy with all the attention needed, added other main ingredients; added water or stock for gravy and already brought it to one full boil. Now is the time to reduce heat and cook it covered on low heat for, say, a good 10-15 mins. Many traditional Indian curries are done this way. So? Won't you utilize this time for other tasks, keeping in mind to check out the curry occasionally? *That is, you ensure high mental presence for the curry coupled with not-too-far physical presence from the kitchen.*

Well, we all do that, i.e., multi-task as tiny empty time windows keep appearing while doing some tasks. Even other small household chores not related to kitchen, like say drying the clothes cleaned in washing machine, attending to the child playing with toys, or helping the child with arranging the school bag, etc. etc. go on simultaneously, along with checking out intermittently on what is cooking. *So, if you say, "Don't multitask; it affects productivity" - mothers would give real dirty looks!*

The Science and Art of Multitasking as I understand:

Take up any scientific research on multitasking; and you will be convinced that it is actually a silent killer of productivity, and hence, better avoided. Science says, focusing on one task is much more productive as *our mind can't do two things simultaneously, but does tasks sequentially.* Research shows, switching between tasks involve *time cost* to correct the control settings of mind for the task-switches. And although switch-costs may be relatively insignificant on any one occasion, sometimes just a few tenths of a second per switch, they can add up to large amounts when people switch repeatedly back and forth between tasks. Thus, multitasking may seem efficient on the surface but may actually take more time in the end and involve more errors. Science says so.

Interestingly, Science is ordinarily not wrong. But our understanding, interpretation and application thereof can be! Once we correct that, we would see how multi-tasking, in fact, must happen not only in kitchen, but in many different spheres of life, albeit *in right circumstances and in right ways.*

Kitchen helps us pick up these very fundamental lessons on multi-tasking which can be carried forward to other workspaces.

Yes, multi-tasking of certain kinds of activities hampers productivity, as can be gleaned from our own experience. It happens when the switches are amongst multiple left-brain-oriented tasks, i.e., serious/complex tasks involving heavy cognitive demands. Can you productively switch back and forth between solving two complicated mathematical sums simultaneously? NO. Or say, writing a research paper on one subject, and making an analysis of the findings from an experiment on some other subject matter? No. Each of these tasks makes heavy cognitive demands from the same parts of our brain, and hence each need be done separately with full attention. Multi-tasking is obviously going to be unproductive in this case.

Multitasking is also harmful when we are working on some *time-slot* allotted for any specific *top priority* task as per our daily plan; yet we go off our plan and multi-task adding sundry unplanned/unimportant jobs to the urgent/important jobs on hand. For example, engaging in social media while on an urgent time-bound task. So, when multi-tasking adds to harmful *distractions*, it must be avoided/kept to the minimum. It helps to do some planning of each day with a schedule for how you would like your day to go, listing your top priority tasks for the day and allotting time slots to them. Once done, we must follow this plan as far as possible keeping unproductive distractions away.

Science is again correct, when it says that our mind does things *sequentially, not simultaneously*. When we say 'multitasking' in the context of ordinary humans (not computing systems), we are also saying the same thing, i.e., we do things not simultaneously, but sequentially. And hence, multi-tasking to be possible and productive, we must have *specific kinds* of tasks *combined* whose *sequencing* can be *'rapid'* with *negligible switch cost*.

Multitasking, as we loosely refer to, eventually means combining a few tasks to be done in *'rapid'* sequencing, within an overall small time period, moving back and forth between any two tasks in the combo quickly. This is what I mean by this term in our day-to-day lives. Multi-tasking happens in rapid sequencing, not simultaneously. We never claim we are doing things exactly simultaneously. *So what matters is which tasks we combine and what are the switch costs involved.* The real use of all the scientific research findings on multitasking must lead to our understanding of not why multitasking should be avoided, but understanding *how* we should attempt multitasking that is beneficial and more productive. What kind of tasks can be done in very rapid sequencing with no/almost negligible switch-costs.

If we observe carefully, we would be stunned to discover how much pressure we keep on fighting every day in real life, both at home as well as in workplaces, to deal with multiple tasks within tight timelines – some of the tasks/projects requiring our attention almost around the same time. In actual life situations, we can't just run away from this fact and start doing everything in leisurely/convenient sequence on the pretext of getting the highest productivity. In life, we must prioritise all demands on us and assess what *quality of outcome* would serve our purpose. The priority in *some* cases may be 'optimization' within the *available* timeline with the *available* resources, and not necessarily 'maximisation' of result by creating the needed perfect conditions for the best result. Interestingly, many of our small and daily tasks would fall in this category. Food is important; but do you have to have *the best* every time? You would rather have simple food, but *on time* as per your habit (optimisation of outcome from consumption of food), than waiting for gourmet dishes every time and missing meals. Yes, in some cases productivity or quality of outcome can simply not be compromised, and multitasking may even ruin the game. Just avoid combining these with other tasks just for the sake of multi-tasking even if feasible. Like, you are cooking an elaborate exquisite dish that needs constant attention. Then focus on that; why divert mind to other tasks? I tell you, even simple pan-fried kebabs which usually take only a few minutes to get nicely roasted need your *undivided* attention for those few minutes. Don't multi-task during those 2-3 mins. The point is: we must develop the knack of deciding when multitasking is feasible and beneficial; and when not.

This is especially why I would like to discuss in some detail here about the *Art* of Multitasking, based on a clear understanding of the *Science* behind it, that we have already discussed. And I owe this to my kitchen drills.

It will make us introspect why, when, and how we should resort to multitasking productively instead of just rubbishing it as an unproductive way of functioning. *Multi-tasking, per se, is not always a bane. It is a skill, and in our day-to-day lives, there is a place for this skill.* As already explained, what we are referring to as multitasking is a way of doing things in sequence, but in *very rapid* sequence switching back and forth to the same task within an overall time period.

So, for effective multi-tasking, we need be clear about:

1. which tasks to combine.
2. How their time spans can be sequenced/overlapped within an overall time period taken by one of the tasks chosen.
3. How to ensure *strategic presence* for all the tasks although attending to one only at any point of time.
4. How to avoid drawing on the same resource for more than one task within the overall time span.

It is about managing *tiny time windows* while attending to multiple small tasks in a co-ordinated manner.

There can't be a better illustrative example than our humble kitchen to comprehend this aspect.

Let me first give examples of a few simple cases.

When I cook in the kitchen, usually I play songs on YouTube and sing along as I cook. Or, put some audio/video with long spiritual discourse and listen to that as I cook. Please note that I don't *watch* the associated videos. I feel nice as singing is my passion and I am also a keen listener of spiritual discourses. Meanwhile, if I have clothes to wash, I just put them in the washing machine and it gets done as I am busy in other chores in the kitchen or elsewhere. Point is: if I am in the kitchen, that does not mean, I attend to only kitchen related chores. Rather, I utilise the available time windows to be done with 2-3 other things parallelly, so long as it does not really disturb me in cooking. Multitasking works here, as *different faculties* are being used for these 3 different tasks (viz. cooking, singing, listening) AND all these are 'simple' tasks not involving deep application of mind at the same time.

Another example, the other day, I had got some nice bunch of Pumpkin creeper branches, tender and juicy. I love it when cooked with fish or prawn especially. But the only issue is, making it ready for the dish is a time-consuming job. You need to peel off the thin layer of outer skin using knife and your fingernails, that really takes patience and time. So usually, I combine this task of cleaning these creeper branches with something else that does not require my hand. That day, as I was getting ready to do this, first I put rice for cooking on gas burner on high flame. I knew, it will need my attention for lowering the flame only after say, 5-6 mins once it comes to a boiling point. After that, I have at least 10-12 more minutes before rice gets cooked fully needing me to drain out the excess water from cooked rice. On another burner, I put the dalma to cook in a pressure cooker. I knew, I just have to switch it off once the whistle comes. So, two dishes on gas that do not need my doing anything else other than just being a little mindful about the timing. Earlier, I had saved a nice YouTube video on a collection of classical raga based Hindi movie songs. I love music- a singer myself.

Now, I put that video on. Since it was the audio that I was interested in, not the video, I started skinning my pumpkin branches as I listened to the songs. I paused the video; drained rice water when rice was ready. In about 25-30 mins, I was done with my rice, dal, pumpkin stalks, and listening to many nice numbers on the video, and finished my dalma which was ready for tempering and finishing elements by then.

So basically, I did 4 things together – rice, dal, listening to songs and cleaning the creeper. In fact, I was also doing a 5th thing – I was also singing along! Not only I enjoyed doing what I was doing because of my singing, I also used my time most optimally, most productively. Did I bungle up any of the tasks due to multi-tasking? No. But had I chosen to, say type something on my computer as I was cleaning the creeper branches, that obviously would not have been possible – my fingers are needed for both tasks. Similarly, if I choose to listen to some music for learning the tune and memorising the lyrics, I would not combine that with drafting something on my laptop. That would be sure to work at cross-purposes. But if I simply put on the music and work on my computer, that is not going to be distractive. As already mentioned earlier, the key to beneficial multi-tasking lies in combining tasks involving separate faculties that do not work at cross-purposes.

Thus, we get to develop in a kitchen the basic insights on productive multi-tasking as a skill, if we keenly observe how we actually work on the ground.

Let me now give the example of my morning routine for the first say 30-35 mins in the kitchen every day, between 6 am to 6.30/6.35 am. – a self-explanatory example of multitasking with numerous simple jobs within a short time frame.

These are the things I typically do every day after I am done with my morning ablutions. And I do this within 30-35 minutes, after which something else is lined up, which cannot be done along with these.

- Arrange the soiled utensils to one side of the kitchen sink to make place for a small bucket for collecting discarded RO water
- Drink a glass of normal water
- Drink ½ a glass of warm (a little hot) water
- Fill 5-7 water bottles from the storage of my RO Water Filter (with RO filtered water)
- Fill the storage of filter
- Collect the discarded water from the RO purifier by placing a small bucket in the kitchen sink
- (While filtering water, RO purifier discards 60% and releases only 40% purified water to its storage! A massive wastage of precious water happens if we do not use this discarded water for some other purpose. So, I collect this discarded water in small buckets placed in the kitchen sink into which this gets discharged and use this to water my potted plants in two balconies. Wastage of precious water, I think, is a criminal negligence.)
- Water the potted plants (so that when one bucket is filling, I can empty out the other and keep it ready to replace the first one.)
- Prepare morning tea, usually with some herb/flavouring ingredient like ginger/mint leaves/tulsi leaves/black pepper powder etc., allowing a good 15-20 mins for boiling milk with water and herbs, before adding tea.
- Collect the cream/*malai (sara)* from milk boiled on the previous day and stored in fridge. Store the cream in fridge to use later for preparing ghee (clarified butter).
- Transfer this milk from the vessel in which it was boiled the previous day to another smaller pot for storing in fridge and give this vessel for cleaning by the maid who comes by 6.30 am.
- Once in 2-3 days, split milk and prepare chhena (cottage cheese) from milk.

- Empty out dried cleaned utensils from the previous day afternoon from the utensil rack and arrange them in drawers/earmarked modules, so that maid can use this rack after doing the utensils.
- And of course, have tea.
- On some days, I also make ghee, or do the preparatory work like chopping some vegetables for breakfast item etc.

Sounds like a whole lot of tasks! Not really! Each of them is truly tiny, can be done in ultra-tiny parts, which can be sequenced and done in various different orders depending upon the exact situation every day. (OMG! It may sound far-fetched, but the truth is, this kind of flexibility and doing things in different ways also enhances neuroplasticity to some extent. No wonder, women generally have less cases of memory loss with age, and also live longer, as compared to men.)

The trick in how I do all these chores within 30-35 mins, lies in not finishing one task after another, but combining a bit from here and a bit from there, depending upon the tiny time windows available, while utilizing the longest timeframe required for one of these tasks, i.e., making tea. *I do this in any order*; it does not really matter as I am within my longest time span (for tea) in any case. *But definitely in rapid sequence.* My mind is not overburdened with switching between these kinds of tasks, as they do not make cognitive demands – involve just simple motor and muscle functions only and presence at/around the same space. So, productivity does not get affected.

Do observe yourself. Now a days, who does not know the art of checking smartphones even as one is busy with something else? Yes, beyond a limit, it leads to Attention Deficiency Syndrome. But keep it within healthy limits for managing *tiny time windows*, or for a needed break; and you would know, it can work for you beneficially without really distracting from the main job on hand. This is also multi-tasking.

The purpose of elaborating so much on this point is that I can make you observe the basic tenets of beneficial multi-tasking.

i. *Tasks combined for 'multitasking' are so chosen as at least one of the tasks needs a slightly long time-span for completion AND does not need be supervised constantly.* Other tasks are to have smaller time-spans. After adding water, when the gravy of a curry is ready to cook on sim for a good 12-15 minutes, you can switch to some other task in the kitchen or nearby, as *a time window emerges at that point from cooking curry*, which can be used to do some other tiny work.

ii. *Tasks combined must not require your physical presence at separate distant places.* Either they need your presence at the same place (here-kitchen), or just nearby places (balconies in my case). What is required is *a strategic presence should be possible covering the places where you need to do the multi-tasks.*

iii. *Most importantly, combined tasks must not have same kind of cognitive demands.* You cannot, for example, multi-task with your hands while dry roasting semolina, for the simple reason that it requires constant stirring (motor work with hand) and frequent adjusting of heat by changing gas-switch position between medium to low (full focus). If you start doing anything else along with this task, you are sure to end up with partially/fully burnt granules of semolina that would spoil the taste of the entire lot, if used for any dish! Yes, you can do thinking, as that requires mental work, not motor work; and once you become an expert in kitchen, things like constant stirring etc., go into auto mode needing less focus.

iv. *Switches between tasks must not require time-taking* mental mode re-adjustments. You can't write an article on some topic and say, read a book on a distinctly different topic, at the same time, rapidly switching between the two! You would be actually doing none of the two then, as your mind gets confused as to what to absorb. Plus, the switching between such tasks eats away precious time in getting into the required mental frame again and again to do that task.

In fact, observe any kitchen. Ordinarily, no kitchen functions with a single stove/gas burner. Usually we have 3-4 burners, out of which, a mother would typically keep at least 2 or 3 burners engaged at the same time. Their skill lies in figuring out 'tiny time windows' from 'sequencing' possibilities of the various steps of recipes for different dishes, that can be managed together within a *larger* time window.

So here lies the catch. Multi-tasking may or may not be effective depending upon the combination of tasks you choose to do simultaneously. Besides, multi-tasking, per se, is not the culprit or reason for lack of focus. Lack of focus happens only when we try doing different things requiring the same resources at the same time by being available at different places.

As you multitask intelligently, you also sharpen another skill, your *sense of observation*, which is one of our basic skills required to do anything more effectively. Picking up insights by using or extrapolating those as per need to handle any situation better.

Once we pick up this skill of multi-tasking with complete understanding of science behind it, it is sure to help us in optimizing, not only in the kitchen, but also in our workplace, as also other walks of life. In office, time management can happen through intelligent multi-tasking. Multi-tasking is not always an anathema to focus and success, as we have seen by now. Simultaneously, it makes us alive to the need for *co-ordination* while doing/managing many things.

Further, it teaches you to always *apply your mind*, no matter what you are doing. Usually there is a tendency on part of the majority of us, to blindly accept something if told by an 'Expert", or, there are multiple studies showing some particular findings. While we must respect these sources of information, it does not mean we stop *applying our mind* to verify these *in the context* of our own specific situations. Some may work, some may not, As regards multi-tasking, notwithstanding what the studies say, we do resort to it *intuitively* in kitchen and cooking; as also in many other cases in life. For the simple reason that we don't have all the time in the day to attend to only these tasks. That is a harsh reality; and that's why so much emphasis on time management! So instead of outright rubbishing of multitasking as a productivity-killer, it is important to learn the *Art* of doing it as a tool of effective time management, with a keen sense of intelligent observation as you work on something to spot those multiple tiny second-minute-long time windows WITHIN THE TOTAL TIME FRAME REQUIRED TO FINISH THE MAIN TASK, so that you can gainfully utilize these breaks for attending to some other tasks needing your attention around the same time.

28. Sustaining Motivation, Inner Drive and Enthusiasm

Like many other positive feelings, motivation/inner drive/enthusiasm is better understood when it is *lacking*. So, we would start from there and then try to elucidate how kitchen teaches us *how to stay motivated on a sustained basis*.

As a mother who cooks for the family, have you ever noticed how you *don't feel like* cooking elaborately or preparing delicacies for yourself when no one else is around to share that food? It is very rarely out of laziness. More often than not, it is a case of *lack of motivation*. You don't have the eagerness to cook delicious food that is not going to be shared and enjoyed by your loved ones.

A huge lesson there. Even if we remain content and self-motivated in our own company for many other things (and that is a great quality), it does not work well in the context of food. The world of *Food* is soul-less without sharing! It is a common experience that when we are cooking for others – our family and friends- we find ourselves highly charged and motivated to cook a great spread of delicacies. When we are alone, food becomes a mere necessity just to satiate our hunger and ensure some basic nutrition. We end up cooking very basic meals, avoiding the elaborate. Why? The motivation dries up. I admit, we all have a human tendency to show off our competence and calibre to others, which acts as a great driving force for doing anything in a much better way when others are going to 'see' it. But it is also true that it involves another great human tendency, basic to all human beings. And that is, *an inner urge to contribute and share, to do good to others and find happiness in others' happiness; to spread joy!* With a warm and pulsating heart, we pick up this great lesson from kitchen that *happiness shared is happiness doubled.* The pleasure and satisfaction that you may get from cooking a delicacy only for yourself, gets significantly enhanced when you prepare that for others, too, and SHARE.

No wonder, even average cooks suddenly feel motivated, and try harder when they have to feed others.

Thus, one of the initial lessons on motivation you pick up soon from kitchen is:

Always put a premium on others, and think primarily on how to contribute to their happiness and well-being!

Once that becomes a deeply ingrained trait in your character, you would be amazed to discover that you have found one of the most potent keys to *sustained* motivation in every important sphere of work. A word of caution, here. When I say, put premium on others, it does not mean you must do that in a self-effacing mode of sacrifice at the cost of your own basic survival and growth. Nor that should be a result of your own unhealthy tendencies to *seek validation from others all the time.* We shall deliberate more on this later when we talk about the lesson on joy of sacrifice.

Sustained motivation always is a play of its twin sides – feeling motivation and combating demotivation- side by side for net positive impact on performance. On one hand, of course we have the affirmative action that motivates self and/or others. On the other hand, we have the 'don'ts,' i.e., the actions that de-motivate or demoralise, and hence must be avoided. In fact, de-motivating someone, or getting de-moralised yourself, is way easier and much more impactful than motivating, and hence, we must be ever vigilant specially in respect of the demoralising factors. Any understanding of motivation is incomplete and any action to motivate loses impact, unless we address the issues of demotivating factors simultaneously with taking positive action to boost motivation. This realisation also dawns quickly in kitchen -another potent lesson from kitchen. How? We will see as we proceed.

Our humble kitchen teaches us that the anti-dote to demotivation is *appreciation*, both in terms of *understanding* what goes into any work, as also *encouragement to* the person who puts in so much efforts into that work.

Be appreciative!

Kitchen, in its own unique ways, makes us realise how crucial it is to *appreciate*! That is the *golden rule of motivation.*

Ability to look for the good in everyone and every situation! Being appreciative of others' efforts and initiatives, irrespective of their success or failure in achieving any *specific* outcome. Acknowledging good work to encourage people. Putting your own best foot forward to inspire and motivate others to give their best. These are very important qualities of true leaders and effective managers, that need no elaboration. It does not take long for those operating regularly in the humble homely kitchens to understand this and imbibe these qualities, *for they know how it feels when others do not notice, nor acknowledge nor appreciate their great efforts.* It takes hard work for hours of pre-cooking processes and cooking itself, but only a few minutes to consume. Only people of great understanding and empathy can assess and appreciate it; not the majority.

So, the next significant lesson that we also learn being in charge of food and kitchen is: *'Appreciate your own efforts first'*. Self-pat! You have to motivate yourself first to be able to motivate and inspire others.

Because whether others understand it or not, you yourself know well your own circumstances in toto and what you have put in. If you cannot appreciate your own efforts, put in so painstakingly, why expect from others? Further, without at least self-appreciation, it might get very difficult gradually to sustain your motivation level in the absence of appreciation of your work from others. What happens to your purpose driven goals, then? Successful performance requires us to stay motivated in our job, no matter what life throws at us. *So, motivation must start from self-motivation through self-appreciation for sustaining own enthusiasm and inner drive, and then carrying this habit of appreciation to motivate others with empathy.*

These experiences also apply in other situations in life. Even if you overtly don't look for others' praise and recognition for your work, you do feel happy, encouraged, and morally boosted when others appreciate you and your work. It is human nature, and there is a deeper angle to it. When others appreciate us for our work, we can see *their belief in us*, and we tend not to belie their belief in us by trying our best to rise to their expectations every next time. *We tend to prove them right in believing in our competence, in trusting in our trust-worthiness.* And if you feel unnoticed and unacknowledged by others continuously, then even the most self-motivated persons do stand a chance of falling a prey to demoralisation (unless you have attained that highly elevated spiritual state of being a *'Sthitapragyna', a stoic* – 100% unaffected by pain or pleasure/failure or success!)

If 'believe in yourself' is the first fundamental rule for self-motivation and self-confidence, 'believe in the belief of others in you and prove them right' is the second, which must be practiced, in turn, by yourself as 'believe in others' as a third rule to motivate and boost others. When you yourself feel motivated if others believe in you, you realise you must do the same thing in respect of others-*believe in them.*

Kitchen makes us get these perspectives immensely well.

Cooking, that too, *regular cooking* for others is a tedious job, to say the least. May well be called a drudgery. Those who do it themselves, or even directly manage the kitchen affairs, *day-in and day-out* can understand well how much tenacity goes into it. Sadly, their work being a regular routine activity, mothers do not even receive appreciation from others as often as they deserve. Sometimes, it is even worse: many homemakers are asked "What do you do the whole day?" Think about it! Not only they are not appreciated for their huge contribution towards the nurturing and growth of the family members, but also their contribution is often either slighted/undervalued, or simply not acknowledged! Most mothers, I am sanguine, must indeed be going through great emotional pain that comes with *being simply taken for granted.*

A strange thing happens when one feels *deep* pain – it changes the person; either to a better or a bitter one.

The beauty of homely kitchen is: it converts the pain into lessons on *Dos and Don'ts* that change you into a better person. How? It always makes them refer to the *purpose* behind why a 'mother' would cook for the family in the first place! *Having known how it feels not to be acknowledged or appreciated, they are more likely to develop the ability to empathise with others, appreciate their efforts and initiatives in doing any work even when they fail.* Because in kitchen, you learn to look at *success* in terms of what you have invested into it, not the result alone. Every failure here is a lesson on what does not work and you fail only if you repeat those, or you don't explore a different way. On the other side, long experience in kitchen teaches the 3 most important 'R's in 'DON'Ts' to mothers – Reward, Recognition and Reciprocation! As they go on toiling day in and day out for the wellness of the family, mothers learn soon enough NOT to expect these 3 Rs. Their contribution ceases to be *conditional upon* these three Rs. In other words, sincerity towards the purpose, (and hence, a strong sense of responsibility towards their role and jobs), becomes a second nature of mothers. Imagine, when such characteristic traits get carried forward to professional sphere, what an asset such a person would be to the organisation!

I can tell from personal experience, how the face of my mother lights up when I say "Huun... it's yum!" after tasting a dish that she has prepared. Same happens with me, when my children (or anyone else) appreciate my preparations. Appreciation from others does leave you more motivated. And there is nothing wrong in it *so long as you do not 'seek' it all the time.* If it is coming to you, just respect and accept it gracefully.

This is how, alongside the habit of being appreciative for others, a significant other ability also gets cultivated in mothers. *The ability to rise above the immediate demotivating factors and see the greater purpose in what you are doing; the ability to put things to context!* Even if your current job is dubbed as small and inconsequential by some others, you learn to see the bigger context in your mundane kitchen routines and find cogent reasons to be self-appreciative enough to keep going.

Yes, it is not worth giving your all to something that does not matter at the end. Mundane routines indeed call upon you *to keep evaluating* what you are doing on an ongoing basis:

i. if whatever you are doing currently has a larger purpose, even if it looks small now;
ii. if it conflicts with something else that has a still larger purpose, which you can do with excellence if you better focus;
iii. If answer to ii is yes, then if you can shift your better attention to ii without fully neglecting your current job's responsibilities by resorting to delegation and outsourcing.

Example: Cooking. If answer to (i) is yes, you are most likely going to continue giving your best, even if others say it is a small job giving you only busy-ness, not real business. If the answers to both (i) and (ii) are yes, then you will start introspecting: "Am I using (i) as a pretext to avoid the more important (ii)? If yes, you will more likely pause and find out other options that can take care of the purpose behind (i), like hiring a cook etc. and free yourself partially or fully to focus on (ii). If answer to

(ii) is No, in the sense that you have no other professional commitments, and also full-time home-making in itself is a very demanding and fully engaging job for you *at the moment*, then you shall not be perturbed, and would treat your current job as your most precious occupation to give your best.

So, kitchen is an amazing school to teach us all the nuances of how to comprehend and appreciate *purposeful action*. Goes without saying, *motivation for purposeful action tends to be self-propelling.*

Kitchen also teaches well *how to take negative feedback in a positive way*. In fancy terms, we can say, kitchen teaches mothers how to boost *resilience* through cognitive re-appraisal of negative events. Cognitive reappraisal reinterprets an adverse event, often going deeper into root causes, to see it as a challenge as well as an opportunity, and thus *reframes* events from a negative to a positive, from a problem to a possibility for positive outcomes.

This is a hugely significant factor that impacts anyone's motivation level. Spiritual state of being, too!

Let us see how kitchen facilitates this in apparently very small ways.

Tastes and preferences of individual family members differ – at times greatly to our surprise. Differences can be at many levels and of many kinds of preferences/abhorrence for various seasonings, spices and flavours, vegetables, non-vegetarian ingredients etc. So, many a times, *this* could be the reason behind you drawing flak on this or that dish from one odd member, while others find that dish fine. At times, there could be some family member(s) who is/are more critical *in nature* and that's the simple reason why they might not acknowledge even if they like it, or just comment in a dismissive way. So, you as a regular provider of the family pot, gradually develop the knack of understanding why the negative or not-so-positive comments are coming your way, and would learn to ignore these, or better/change the food suitably next time, if you feel you need to. *You don't react merely*. Is it not a great life lesson, too?

Similarly, it is also true that at times your dish does not actually turn up nice and tasty, though palatable. The waste conscious you would not also like to throw it into dustbin. You may not even have time to cook an alternative. So, what do you do? You serve, and while your family does eat it, they give their honest comments, which obviously will not be very positive. As regular cooks and caregivers, we learn to take all these negative feedback in our stride, as *constructive criticism*, with *grace*. Even when we ourselves are satisfied with the taste and quality of our creations, yet we get negative feedback, we still show grace in taking it in our stride although we don't really deserve criticism *as per us*. Mothers managing kitchen regularly imbibe this great trait of GRACE without perhaps realising and that gets demonstrated in their behaviour elsewhere too.

The point is: not that the maker (cook) does not know how the dish has actually turned out, but feedback from the eater always keeps the flame of motivation glowing at all times. When others forget to comment, one does feel a little down – that tinge of disappointment of not having been noticed, or having been taken for granted! *In this process, kitchen teaches how important it is to give feedback – both appreciative and honest at times even if negative.* Yes, as mothers who are usually taken for granted, we understand how important feedback could be because of its lack in our own lives. We also understand that feedback to be constructive, no. 1. there must be an acknowledgement of your effort in the first place; no. 2. as far as feasible, what went wrong need be mentioned precisely, instead of a blanket rubbishing; no. 3. *if possible*, suggestions be given on how it can be made right/better, instead of just pointing out the shortcomings.

Imagine, how useful these insights can be when carried forward to workplace and acted upon from your own side!

In fact, I wish to make a statement that is universally valid in every context. That is: when we understand and feel something in our bones, and accordingly hold some expectations about code of conduct, or values and attitude, from others, not for vested interest, but in a larger interest, we become alive to the fact that we must first demonstrate exactly those qualities to get them reciprocated by others. *Setting appropriate personal example by leaders is a key driver of motivation level of their people.*

Coming back, *feedback is not always about the quality or taste of the dish, or about motivating; quite often, it is more about the relationship.* Any bond would eventually languish if the *importance of the person on the other side* is not acknowledged and appreciated. So, there may be times, when that appreciation must come, even if the product is not so great, to mark the importance you attach to the value of the other person for you in the relationship.

For a manager in an organisational set up, it may prove disastrous to ignore the presence of some key players whose absence gets conspicuous. And so is in life situations. If you do not *appreciate the value of people* in important relationships, constantly and continuously, it may not be long before you lose them for ever.

So be appreciative, always, if you want to be effective as a leader carrying your people along!

Inner Drive

Another dimension not to be missed at all is how kitchen teaches us about *inner drive*. We have already talked about earlier why and how self-appreciation is important. Mothers or persons on regular task of bringing food to the table for near and dear ones are *driven from within,* as they understand why they are into this task even if so mundane and not rightly appreciated (the purpose of it all) and their role in the overall welfare of their loved ones. So, even though they feel sad at times for no one acknowledging their work and contribution, they still carry on undaunted driven from within. They *experience* what it means when it is said that *the greatest reward of anything well done is having done it well.* That is inner satisfaction! Where there is inner satisfaction, no outsider can dim your sparkle, or kill your drive.

Effective leaders not only motivate their team members through appreciation, honest feedback for betterment, setting own example to inspire etc., they also help them build their own inner drive. Leaders take keen interest in making their teammates feel alive to that great experience of self-satisfaction that inundates every soul after doing something well and worthwhile. Once a member starts observing their own feelings this way, motivation for good work becomes self-propelling. And that is inner drive. Job knowledge, skills, talents, education, intelligence – all are highly important, but drive is critical. Remarkable individuals, whether a leader or a follower, are driven by something deeper and more personal than just the desire to do a good job.

Is it not truly wonderful how our humble kitchen drives home such great lessons so easily and so understandably?

Besides self-motivation, sustaining *motivation of your people also* becomes very crucial when a leader has to manage delivery within strict *deadlines*. We shall talk about it separately in the next point. Before that, let us take up *enthusiasm*, as the inner drive to stay sustained, we must remain continuously enthusiastic about doing what we are doing and stay hungry to find out better and newer ways of doing things.

Enthusiasm

Nothing great ever got achieved without enthusiasm. (Emerson)

Enthusiasm lies at the core of all success as *consistent action* does not happen without it. Without it, you will continuously find excuses/alibies/reasons/scapegoats for blaming. Well, we all know and even understand this. Yet, we find it easier said than done. In any project, sooner or later, we get upset with turns of events that simply discourage us no end. So, in order to maintain a healthy level of enthusiasm at all times, *we may first try and understand why or how we get discouraged in the first place,* so that we can get the antidotes. If we work on our mindset at those points of blockages and leakages, then, we can stay in a generally enthusiastic state of mind always.

- Lack of Consistent Action. At times, although we start something with a lot of enthusiasm and commitment, it soon loses steam simply because we find it hard to stay course with *consistent action*. Anything worthwhile needs a lot of hard work on a regular basis before it starts showing results. Sustaining the ability to work consistently on a continuous basis requires a robust self-discipline, which must be consciously developed with *habitual practice driven by purpose at the inner level*. So, the only anti-dote to this is: *self-discipline*! We have already discussed it in the very beginning how kitchen pushes us to learn this lesson.
- At times, we do put in consistent action, but it starts taking its toll on our human body-mind machinery by way of making us feel *fatigued*. It is very natural and must not send us on any guilt-trip for not being a Superman/Superwoman. We must accept it as a natural consequence of acting tirelessly without break. So, understand that you simply need a break or some rest. That is the sole antidote for fatigue.
- In real life, we don't get to do just one thing at a time. Sometimes, multiple projects might be competing for our focused attention,

or we might be coming up against multiple trivial things as unwanted distractions, that slow down our progress against intended/planned progress. Repeated setbacks to planned progress due to big or small obstacles leave us somewhat discouraged. We feel like giving up. The anti-dote is to buckle up again telling yourself "8 times you fall, 9 times you get up!" Make a review of all work and working dimensions, relook at and revise priorities, clear off the unnecessary.

– Sometimes, despite best of efforts, we do not achieve as planned. May be for various cogent reasons, but we do end up with a feeling of failure. If taken to heart, this could become a terrible roadblock to enthusiasm, i.e., frustration. You might get so discouraged that you may lose self-confidence to try it or anything new again. The antidote is to try again, analysing where you could have done better last time, telling yourself that failure is a part of the journey towards success. Re-focus on your original purpose, check back on your failed attempt, and pick up your lessons with a determination not to repeat the same mistakes. Do things differently afresh.

– Sometimes, not an actual failure, but *fear* of failure and *anticipated* ridicule can discourage us totally to initiate any action or take up any project. Fear of failure is deadly as it virtually freezes us in inaction. No action, no risk, no failure! But as it is said, ships are not meant to be on anchor all the time; they must sail, face storms if they come and pass through them to reach their destination. Similarly, no one grows without overcoming the risk of failure. Fear of failure is a solid roadblock, that can only be cleared with the help of optimism. Mind has to be trained, *not* to anticipate failure, but to expect success. One may employ any trick that works for themselves. Some draw their eternal optimism from their unflinching belief in the Supreme Power who ultimately steers everything good and worthy. So why fear when HE is in command? Some believe in themselves without any trace of doubt in their own capabilities and competence, and manifest tremendous self-confidence. They usually do not succumb to fear of failure easily. They do feel fear while starting something new and arduous; but they do it *nevertheless*. Thus, the only antidote to fear of failure is to overcome it with courage or trust in the Supreme. No alternative.

- Lack of preparedness in terms of knowledge, skills and resources required for the project often leaves you discouraged. It may be either that you have failed to foresee, plan, and acquire; or these have not been made available to you by those responsible for it. The antidote lies only in correcting the position, instead of abandoning the task out of discouragement.
- Lack of appreciation on accomplishments in the past. At times, despite accomplishments and success, you have an experience of not having your expectations regarding a pat/a raise/a promotion met in the past. That might discourage you from taking up new tasks enthusiastically. But you ought to understand that this is a personality issue of the 'other', not of you, and you must learn to have the *key to your own mental state* in your hands, by not letting others' action affect you negatively. The anti-dote is to find self-satisfaction in a good job done.

In short, motivation, inner drive, enthusiasm – all are intertwined and, in a sense, manifest together in terms of your complete 'engagement' in any task or project. If you are motivated, you feel both enthused and driven from within to do your best and keep challenging your skills for continuous improvement. If you feel enthusiastic about doing something, it keeps you motivated and driven from within to do that the best way possible. Similarly, if you are driven from within, you will sustain the motivation and enthusiasm for your tasks, no matter what. Kitchen keeps throwing us into umpteen situations to pick up these great insights and learn to stay motivated ourselves, as also to motivate and inspire others through exemplary personal qualities.

29. Management of Deadlines and Motivation

When I say deadlines, it is not only about strict timelines, but also includes any serious challenge which is not normal, and if not faced rightly, might snowball into a crisis.

Very often, we don't look at the routine timelines in kitchen as 'deadlines', although, in essence, they *are* deadlines for the most part. You don't have the whole day to serve the breakfast to your child before she leaves for the school, or your other members before they leave for their office/workspace, or say your super old parents before they are served all the meals and snacks as per the schedule. But since an inescapable routine, mothers go on managing these on time with self-discipline and self-motivation; and no one even notices.

Parallels abound in the professional workspaces.

Managing challenging deadlines is an inescapable part of leading in the corporate world. In fact, it does create immense pressure for the leaders themselves, but how they handle this pressure is key to whether they are effective leaders or not. *Some leaders pass the pressure down the line mindlessly, while some others, who know how to carry their people along, pass on this pressure in a very thought-through process guarding against demotivation or frustration in the team.* I find very gainful insights from kitchen management in this context, as that, too, involves numerous deadlines on a daily basis.

The first important insight from kitchen in this context, of course, relates to *'purpose'* and we have already discussed how motivation easily flows from purpose, passion, and love. Similar is the case in workplaces. If you are passionate about your work, and you can *transmit* that passion to your team through clear communication of purpose, vision, goals, and can make them see *what is there in it for them*, then motivation for meeting challenging deadlines does not fall short.

The second critical insight is on *'heat'*, i.e., *the 'pressure' dimensions* that any leader must know how to handle (how much is enough; when/how to apply; and on whom to apply), just as in kitchen we manage heat for different ingredients and different dishes to make them *rightly* cooked.

As we all know, and must have been told hundreds of times, *the most critical job of a leader, or say a boss, is to get the work done by their team.* And so, it is also necessary, along with things like motivating, incentivising etc., *to put pressure, spell out expectations and be tough on performance as per deadlines.* While most in leadership positions find it easier to get the people to work (or so they think) through the policy of *'stick' and 'fire'*, *i.e., tactics of pressurising,* the true leaders understand what is the *optimum level of pressure* that need be exerted to keep the fire burning in the belly *(achievement motivation sustained through creative tension)* of the team members, beyond which some members might break down.

Someone who has regular experience in cooking understands with clarity what the above means. Because a cook develops a *knack* to know exactly *how much heat* is required *at what stages* of the recipe *to rightly cook* the ingredients; neither overcook, nor burn, nor undercook the dish! This understanding mainly flows from the knowledge of the unique nature of each ingredient as also the steps of the process in recipe. This experience, when carried forward to work situations outside, proves immensely handy to handle your people and get the work done by them. When a leader knows his people as individuals along with their professional competence levels, and the nuances of the project on hand, they would know how to fuel a creative tension in each to perform.

The third insight that develops from working with high heat in kitchen is also supremely important. Just like a mother in the kitchen, these leaders know what and when to put something on *'full flame' (putting maximum pressure),* and what to do in case the situation suddenly goes wrong (*bringing the situation back under control if something misfires*). They also know what and when to put on sim (on low heat, i.e., under low pressure) for a longer time, or it will create a mess.

To give some specific examples, let us take water and milk, whose properties cooks are well aware of. *'Know thy ingredients' in kitchen is nothing but 'know thy people' in workplaces.* We will talk about this later in greater detail.

A mother knows, if she needs to bring water to a boil, she would put it on high flame; mostly with a lid for faster boiling. But if it is milk, she must not boil it on high flame *with a lid*; or else, it will be uncontrollable once the boiling point is hit. She also knows that at the first sign of steam escaping, she must take out the lid even if water is boiling, add say rice or whatever is to be cooked, and control heat to lesser modes. Once boiling, *high heat is just a wastage of precious cooking fuel. All it needs to keep boiling* is *minimum heat*. But in case of milk, it is always better to leave it on *sim*, do your other tasks and come back when milk is done. If your vessel is large enough as compared to the quantity of milk, you need not even check it out on sim till you switch off; the swell and fall would stay within the vessel without any spill-over.

Similarly, leaders must know what *quality* of team members, or projects, they are dealing with; whether high pressure need be put right from the start and managed thereafter, or continuous training and motivation along with just enough pressure to retain the creative tension will do. When team members are generally knowledgeable, committed, and motivated, continuous but small doses of heat (guidance, supervision, reminder of deadlines, small motivators like pat on the back, some pressure to deliver etc.) can do the trick. But when the team members are not homogeneous, some lacking in commitment/competence, some hard nuts to crack.... Well, then they have to be put on *high heat* (necessary pressure regarding desired level of performance, guidance, frequent monitoring, supervision, frequent reminder on deadlines, consequences of non-delivery, pat on the back etc., combined together) from the start itself. Later when you as a leader are convinced that the project and team are on track, you may reduce 'heat'.

As a beginner, I used to think that if I put the milk on high flame and stand right over there, I would be able to save time by getting it to boil quickly and save spill-overs, too. To my dismay, very soon I found out, in kitchen, you simply cannot stand at one place sticking your eyes on one thing for even 3-4 mins at a stretch, without doing anything else. Whether you plan to or not, you will end up turning your head away a bit, or move away a few inches, and the disaster would strike exactly at that moment if something like milk is on high flame. Milk spilling over your stove and platform! Not only you lose milk, you add some more work, of cleaning! It is only after this happened to me a few times, despite being very alert, that I learnt my specific lessons:

i. Use *high flame* from the start and right through, only if you can be present right there all through and handle it. It is not advisable in some cases when the substance can expand/inflate uncontrollably beyond a point.

Carried forward to the workplace, this lesson deters us from using too much of pressure on the team for any job. There are some bosses who pressurise their staff excessively right from the beginning and what is worse, continue that throughout without taking stock of the real position regarding staff engagement, ground dynamics on levels of skill and training, and actual progress being made (i.e., without staying right there to watch over). Very likely, this kind of monitoring fails to either motivate the team members or to achieve the best results; at times even triggering an overt staff discontentment, and a conflict situation; productivity going for a toss.

As a corollary to this lesson, I gradually learnt that it is better to put milk on sim for boiling taking its own time. Between saving time and saving milk from spilling over and getting wasted, the second is surely a preferred option. What is more significant is: this way I need not stay there to watch over milk, and can do several other things during that time. I can always come back to check out. Usually, once the milk starts boiling, it gives out a typical smell. I come back around that time.

In a workplace similarly, if you trust that you have quality team members who don't really need to be constantly monitored, then it pays to apply and maintain minimum needed heat/pressure, albeit with adequate supervision, as needed. This brings forth better delivery as your visible trust in your people, without a constant stick chasing them, makes them live up to your expectations despite the difficulties and challenges. *So, do know your people and repose trust in them.* Trust begets trust.

Moreover, in kitchen, we must have observed how bitter juice comes out when we squeeze a lemon too much. Similarly, even an elastic/expandable thing like rubber band snaps if over-stretched beyond a point. So, the message comes loud and clear from kitchen through many types of examples that *too much of anything is good for nothing- not even pressure.*

ii. *Immediately control the situation in case something still goes wrong, by dealing with issues at the root level, not at the level of external symptoms alone.*

Suppose, for some reason, you were distracted for a second though standing right there, and the boiling milk is on the verge of spilling over, or already spilling has started. *How to do quick damage control?* Some immediately start blowing air into the swelling milk so that the spurt stops. But this is not really an effective way to control the spurt, which would still continue with the heat on. *To immediately stop the rising, we must immediately stop the reason behind it at the root: the high heat.* So, the first thing to do is to SWITCH OFF the source of heat, the stove. *A very small thing, but a huge lesson.* We will see how cooking helps in Team building, especially in incendiary situations in a later segment.

iii. *The 3rd great perspective I have developed from kitchen in the context of keeping the flock motivated and managing stress constructively, is to allow failures,* initially, and at appropriate junctures, subject to quick re-learning, even in situations with challenging deadlines.

It is said, set a challenging deadline, but never set an impossible one. When you set a deadline, though you should be firm with its compliance, that should not mean you allow no one to fail.

In planning and review, we have seen how for managing food, we do plan with deadlines (as food *on time* poses almost non-negotiable deadlines for a mother/caregiver daily), but we always keep a margin for failure in terms of menu at least. Similarly, we have understood in creativity segment the immense value of allowing failures in helping ourselves as also others to get more creative.

When you are not allowed to fail, extreme stress is created, and one loses out on optimum utilisation of time and skills. But once you know that it is not ok to have laxity in efforts, but ok to fail at times despite efforts, you perform better. Less stress, more productivity. And to your surprise, even if you fail, you fail by not a very significant margin. So, to keep the team motivation at an optimum level, even when deadlines are hanging over your head like the proverbial sword of Democles, let your people feel comfortable without putting excessive pressure for performance during the period when work is on. Let them never feel weighed down with a thought of nil margin for little bits of mistakes and failures. Believe me, this leads to lesser mistakes and higher productivity.

As a leader, keeping these insights from kitchen in mind, helps a lot. Coupled with other positive action like proper training, guidance, and supervision with a clear message regarding quality delivery on time and incentives for performance, and some visible disincentives for non-performance, these lessons can carry you a long way in keeping your people motivated even in challenging situations, performing at their peak. Goes without saying, the personal example you set during these tough times must never smack opposite of what you are preaching to your team.

The kitchen experience, when carried forward to work situations outside, proves immensely handy to handle your people and get the work done by them with *a right mixture of carrots, sticks and fire. This* is a soft skill, that is learnable and must be learnt by all irrespective of their sphere of work, and kitchen is a grand place to give you all the insights you need to develop this knack of dealing with challenges.

30. The Toolkit: Value your mixed bag

It is interesting to note how simple routine functions in the kitchen relating to *usage and upkeep of our kitchen tools,* can give us profound insights on always remaining relevant, as also why to value diversity in groups.

In a routine mode, we always sharpen our knives the moment they show early signs of bluntness. In fact, we do not even wait till they turn blunt. *It is a common practice to get all the knives in our kit sharpened periodically.*

Just as a kitchen knife becomes blunt after use if not sharpened every now and then, and so, is rendered unusable, our skills and competencies also stop being of much use, or obsolete (blunt) if not 'sharpened' continuously through more and more learning and usage. No wonder, *'Always keep sharpening your Knives'* is a very common edict, often said, even in formal Management Courses to emphasise on the critical importance of continuously staying updated and upgraded on part of every individual, and more so for a person aspiring *to lead in any field.*

It is also said, *a dull knife is far more dangerous than a sharp one.*

In management studies, it is taught that if we have 5 hours to chop a tree, we should better spend 4 hours on sharpening the axe! For effectiveness.

Why?

Because with *blunt* and *obsolete* tools and resources, we take a disproportionately long time to do the job, that too, ending up with a shoddy one. At times, these are not only less productive, but also dangerous.

As you get going in the kitchen, it takes not much time to observe and understand, may be after a few slips, that the knife we use must always be kept sharp. Yes, it goes blunt with frequent use, or perhaps rusted with long disuse. Blunt knives not only make our job shoddy, they can, in fact, become far more dangerous, and risky at times than the sharp ones.

Picture this: You are attempting to finely slice something round, say an onion, with a blunt knife. Since it is not cutting cleanly through the onion, you are having to apply more pressure. Suddenly, the onion slips/slides out from underneath your fingers, the knife goes off-trajectory, and all the pressure you were putting on that *safe (?)* dull knife is now redirected suddenly at your finger, or palm or other body part! So, a blunt knife is in fact dangerous in this particular case. But had it been a sharp knife, you would have put your fingers holding it at safe margin; the knife would have sliced the onion cleanly without any issue, without any extra pressure. Yes, accidents still happen; but you can attribute that to, may be bad luck, or whatever, but not *the tool* that you have personally taken care to select for use.

Carried forward to people management, the above would always keep you alert against letting your people stay dull and unenthusiastic. Instead, you would always invest in keeping them 'sharp'; i.e., up-skilled and motivated.

Not only it is important to keep the tools in best possible usable condition, but we must also use our tools intelligently.

For example, we must always keep our knives sharp, but at the same time, we must remember that *we don't have to use our sharpest knife for everything*. The first part is about being in *ever readiness*. The second part is about *right application*. You are ready with all weapons does not mean you will employ all at the first opportunity.

We need not use our sharpest knife for everything, especially when we know that there is a possibility of contact with flesh, and that even a slight contact can really hurt/cut deeply. In such cases, do go for a much less sharp knife- even a blunt one at times. *Most of the times, if you notice, using a combination of tools, even of the same category, works much more effectively*. For example, personally, I use at least 2-3 different knives for one session of chopping. Depends on what kind of vegetables or stuff I am chopping; what shape and *fineness* I need, and how sharp or edgy my knives are. If I want to just lightly shave off the peel of say, potols (stripe gourds), I prefer using a slightly blunt knife. If I have to chop something really fine mince-like, first I slice slightly slowly with a very sharp knife; then I use a Chef's heavy knife reasonably sharp to cut through and chop really fast, taking absolute care to ensure that my thumb or other fingers stay near to hold the portion being chopped finely, BUT at a safe distance from the target fall of the knife, AND keep on moving back my fingers swiftly keeping pace with the mincing act in progress. Chopping fast with a very sharp or comb-edged knife can really spell disaster for your fingers, I swear, if you are not mindful.

Similarly, picture this: You are shaving off the skin of drumsticks, or taking off the side ridges of beans/flat beans (simba). All you need the knife for is to give a slight cut at the head or tail, and just pull off the peels/ ridges, during which most likely your thumb will come in contact with the edge of the knife. Try using a less-sharp knife, and you will observe how easy and risk free it is. For chopping however, you should mostly use a properly sharp knife.

And yes, always go by what works for you personally! This also resonates with what you should do in your professional space as a leader. Your leadership style must be authentic, so that it works for you. Being a copycat will not last for long.

This teaches us that *we must observe utmost care and stay mindful while using the sharpest minds amongst our team members*. You have to treat and use your tools in your workspace including your people by *mapping* what you want to get done and what/who is the most appropriate for that purpose, as also should utilise them intelligently and sensitively.

There is another very interesting side of using sharp tools in kitchen. It demonstrates *the power of habit!* Observe, how the expert cooks/Chefs chop vegetables very fine at great speed with sharp knives. A little miss, and catastrophe would strike. But these experts usually manage it so well, even as they would be talking, giving instructions etc.! Means, they are able to do this tricky job even without paying complete attention to it.

How come? *With relentless practice, it becomes habitual with them, and even 'attention' becomes a habit and comes to them in auto-mode.* It is the power of habit, that their brains no longer have to think specifically on the attention required for the task every single time. Imagine, if habit can do this in such situations otherwise requiring your focussed attention, how impactful it is in case of our normal behaviour patterns? A very practical lesson from kitchen: *practice makes one perfect, and habit is powerful!*

So, do observe these chopping processes keenly. Do observe how we use different tools in the kitchen for different jobs. How we use different kinds of cookware-vessels/serving tools/cutlery - for different purposes. A ladle for serving some liquid/semi liquid stuff, as against a spatula to serve something flat. A bowl to serve soup and a plate to serve rice. A whisker to mix finely, while a spoon just to mix up. A grinder for a smooth wet paste, but a manual mortar and pestle for crushing coarsely. A tawa/griddle for a nice, crispy dosa, but a pan for a fluffy omelette. Etc. etc. *We use our mixed toolkit as per the appropriateness of each tool for a specific job.*

And of course, we always do the upkeep of our kitchen tools in right ways, *which are different for different materials.* For example, we put a steel vessel into dishwasher for cleaning, but manually clean plastic utensils. We use a soft cleaning sponge to scrub a non-stick pan, but a steel wool to clean a mixed-alloy kadai with stains.

All these have valuable lessons for your workplaces, too.

- *It is good to have a mixed bag.* Already we do have our Teams with members as diverse as our tools in the kitchen. Nowhere it is possible to have people together who are always and for everything on the same page. Impossible! So, instead of being wary of such diversity around us in our workplaces and personal lives, thinking of it as a *problem*, we should welcome it and look for the *opportunities* to make the best combinations for different tasks and reap the benefit of synergies in terms of greater efficiency in management and delivery.
- The MANTRA is: *Handle with care*! Sharp knife - go slow; heavy knife - fast but with complete mindfulness; less sharp - go relaxedly etc. etc. While working with and through different types of human beings in our Team, we have to be careful about

their individual traits, temperaments, strengths and weaknesses so that neither you yourself trip, nor you let them trip, due to mishandlings.

- *To be able to be careful, we must know the unique qualities*, the sharpness, or otherwise of the knives/tools we are using. Similarly, we must first know our people individually, as individuals, not just as our employees, and try to discern how 'sharp' they are intellectually, emotionally, or skill-wise as we work with/through them as Team members. Our antennae must always be up for this. That is *sensitivity* which results in *empathy*. This is why, it is emphasized in Leadership and Management courses, again and again: Know Thy People. Just as in kitchen, it is: Know thy ingredients; Know thy tools and keep them serviced.

Kitchen brings us to a position where we *accept* that in work situations, we do not even need all our Team members to be extremely sharp, of highest skills and expertise in the field for specific projects. *Eventually, in real situations, every team is a mix of variedly endowed members.* As a leader, we must inculcate the ability to synergise different abilities and skills for optimum team performance, using every member as per their qualities and team requirements. There could be times, when you need just *followers*, who would execute parts of your plan without trust issues/ much questioning- for which even the 'less sharp', but dependable ones would be fine. And there could be times, when you would need some of your members to act on field like your front line of *leaders – applying their own mind* to the emerging dynamics of the situation, and acting within the broad framework of directives, or even have the guts to go outside-the-box, for a right cause. Pick up your 'sharper' ones, who are good followers, *plus* have leadership traits for such jobs. Never claim to yourself that you know your people fully. Train, nurture and give them responsibilities as opportunities to prove their mettle before you.

(And yes, just as in kitchen you have a Plan B, while experimenting with something new, always have a Plan B, C etc. in place in terms of support/switch while *trying out* people for higher responsibilities)

So, value your mixed bag of people, always. Take good care of them so that they stay updated and useful at all times.

31. Use it, or lose it!

Kitchen shows us how 'upkeep' of tools also requires it to be *used on a regular basis*. Just storing and forgetting something is wasteful.

If you don't use it, you lose it! So goes the saying; and it is true in most cases. The bane of *disuse!* Even a stretchable thing like rubber band, when stored for a long time, simply snaps when you try to tie something using this. Iron tools in kitchen, get rusted if not used for a long time. Iron, cast-iron, or mixed alloy-based cook-wares like woks/griddles/pans need a continuous use and *seasoning with oil* in a particular way for staying smooth/non-sticky. All cooking ingredients also have a *shelf life*, and if not used by then, lose their usability. Look around, examples abound to validate this.

Disuse leads to losing your usefulness. *This is especially true of our mind and all its significant activities – cognitive, intellectual, and imaginative.* Talents, gifts, personal qualities, intelligence, discrimination power, decision making abilities – *everything that matters to us must be put to continuous use to stay active and useful.* Yes, this is on the same page as the dictum 'keep sharpening your knives', but with an extra step: *Use-Upgrade-Use,* and the process must go on.

Don't sit over what you are privileged to have now and here.

Great lessons there from our humble kitchen.

32. Delegation and Outsourcing

Kitchen management, which ordinarily starts for most of us managing our own small kitchen, becomes a bigger and bigger responsibility as time passes and our family grows in number. So, sooner or later, you also start knowing intuitively *the need for delegation* of some of these tasks, so that you don't get overstretched/overwhelmed to a point that you fail to attend fully either to these daily tasks or to your other important responsibilities and missions in life. Alongside, you also pick up valuable *insights on the fundamentals of effective delegation: what to delegate, when to delegate, who to delegate and how to delegate.* And last but not the least, *how to effectively supervise* to get the desired results. Neither micromanage too much, nor pass down and forget. *Delegation requires you to always remember that it does not let you completely abdicate your duties/responsibility or escape accountability.* You are still the one accountable for the result - to yourself (if a chosen and accepted duty, especially in your personal life, like a mother's role as nurturer) or to your superiors/stakeholders (if an assigned role-based duty especially in a professional set up). By stressing on a leader's final responsibility and accountability for results, I do not advocate that leaders must take on the mantle of delivering critical tasks themselves. I only emphasise the importance of *assessing* the strengths and skills of your people for delegating the right tasks to the right persons.

Perhaps delegation in kitchen first happens unknowingly in the area of cleaning-overall maintenance of cleanliness in kitchen, doing the soiled utensils, cleaning the kitchen platform, arranging cleaned utensils etc. How common it is to hire a maid to do these along with other menial jobs, in labour surplus countries like India! Yes, without much thought apparently, *we identify these tasks as the right ones* which we can get done through others without much adverse results. That is, we *delegate this work* to hired hands who are already doing these jobs elsewhere (i.e., *the right persons* having minimum necessary skills for the jobs). But before delegating, sub-consciously you must have examined your situation: if you really need to delegate it because it is truly weighing you down; if by not doing it personally you are putting your family to some sort of risk of health hazards due to possible shoddy work by the hired hand; if financially you can afford it without a deep cut in your pocket; if freed from this task, your saved time has more useful/worthwhile other engagements, if it is a minimum relief for you that you would like to have etc. etc. That is, you are also *assessing the circumstances to ensure that it is right for delegation*, in the sense that delegation is possible and a better option for you for the desired result.

Slowly, you may move towards delegating small preparatory tasks in cooking like helping in preparing spices/pastes, chopping vegetables etc., while still retaining the main cooking job to yourself. *And a time might come, when you also start delegating the cooking job partially/fully to a hired hand, if satisfied with their skill level and dependability.* Of course, normally before that either you teach them your family recipes, or you are satisfied that they already possess enough culinary skills to meet your requirements well and would incidentally learn these as they go forward. That is, you know you need to simply *guide and supervise*, as required at some points. At times, they might be good enough to be just given the instructions, like the menu, the recipe, the quantum etc.; and at times, you might be required to directly supervise and keep checking at various points of time.

So, essentially, what is happening here? For delegation to be effective, you are *first delegating small, small tasks and gradually building up to challenging ones.* As you do so, you are also giving guidance and instructions *(i.e., right two-way communication is happening)*, and continuously checking out skill and commitment levels *(right supervision is also happening)* for performance, training, and suitability for further responsibility.

You get to know with experience, what can be delegated, and what simply cannot be delegated to hired hands. In some cases of working women with heavy professional commitments outside, time may be a huge reason for employing hired cooks, and delegating the entire responsibility for provision of food to the family to them. But the ultimate accountability and the need for supervision (may be, at the 11th hour) still remain with you, being the lady of the house (sorry, again a manifestation of patriarchal mindset). On special occasions, like when you are hosting a party, you may choose *not* to delegate 100% and prepare one/a few exotic dishes, or your signature dishes, yourself. *So, intuitively, you do gain insight that you cannot delegate 100% all the time, and must have clarity on what cannot be delegated.*

When grown-up children staying away from family visit home for a few days, mothers cook themselves the favourite dishes of the children instead of delegating to the hired cook, who might cook these as nicely. Mothers know, these few dishes are *not the right ones to delegate* at least during the stay of their children. Why? These dishes are uber-special with *emotional value* because children are nostalgic about the exact flavour and taste that they associate with their childhood memories of 'Ma ki haath ka khana', 'Ma ki haath ki khusboo' (made by mom / flavours of mom's hands)! Delegation is a No-No in such cases to retain the precious mother-child bonding; *circumstances here are not-right for delegation.*

For mothers of slightly grown-up children, it is a common practice to let the children do some dishes themselves. Very often, when the lunch and dinner stay with the mom, breakfast/snacks are made by enthusiastic children with a liking for 'trying out' recipes. It serves two great purposes: the children learn this life skill with interest and excitement, stirring up greater creativity in them; mothers get some free time off the usual kitchen job to do something else that interests them. This is also a mode of delegation that mothers learn in the kitchen: *do delegate when someone is interested, but be around if newbies, allow them to try and fail and learn again (significance of trust and reliance for delegation to work).*

There is another interesting way that mothers delegate. When the maid absents, or guests are to be entertained at home over a meal, mothers start distributing small tasks amongst the family members. Here also, they subconsciously follow the principles of effective delegation, and distribute tasks keeping in mind the skill/aptitude of the assignee (importance of *choosing the right task for the right person*).

These experiences in regular kitchen management give a fair idea on what should be the principles of effective delegation. You can get still clearer insights if you have the opportunity of working/managing kitchens in joint families, or working in professional kitchens, as in those kitchens, the workload is very heavy and unless carefully *distributed* amongst multiple hands, one person cannot manage singlehandedly. Unless you pick up these skills, you may discover yourself overwhelmed with all your responsibilities – not having enough time to complete everything always. Look at the managers in operations. Unless they effectively delegate, they will always find themselves missing this target or that.

In many formal Management trainings, they teach something called *The Five Rights of Delegation:*

- the Right task
- the Right circumstance
- the Right person
- the Right direction/communication

And

- the Right supervision.

Is it not interesting to notice from what we have already discussed how all these five principles of better delegation indeed get applied in kitchen management, though may not always be consciously?

Let us deliberate on these five *rights* a bit more, for the benefit of anyone interested in management/leadership, as this is a key area for them. No one, even the CEO of a company, can know everything to run an organisation. *Delegation is a must; but must be done in right manner.*

The Right Task

Delegation to be effective, we must first have a good sense of our overall project as a combination, or series, of small and medium tasks, involving various degrees of skills, competence, and urgency. Additionally in professional set up, confidentiality and 100% personal responsibility for doing certain things are also to be *factored in* while evaluating what tasks can be delegated to lower rungs and what cannot be. To give an example, in a small company, the leader of the team must be the one to personally call on very high value customers. This is something which is not a right task to be delegated to *any* 'representative' all the time.

Heads/Managers are required to write performance appraisal reports on subordinates. They must not delegate this to someone else who appears to them as very knowledgeable, unbiased, and reliable in this regard. No! This must be done by the managers personally, as it is their responsibility, and further no one can have a better view of a subordinate other than the Heads themselves, who get to watch the subordinates through various situations over a period. Delegation of this would only make the exercise devoid of the original purpose of *assessment by the Team Head*.

But there are umpteen varieties of tasks, that *can* be passed down to save your precious time for other priorities, without consequentially damaging your desired final outcomes. As we have discussed earlier, we have to develop a sense of optimality. *There may not always be a need for 'maximisation' or best result in every task done. Just as in kitchen, we do not have to cook and present every meal like a gourmet meal, in real life very often we deal with multiple tasks that are to be completed 'timely and fairly well-done' without needing the highest skills and productivity, for aligning with other major tasks.* It is okay if one does it decently, need not be spectacularly every time. There can be permissible margins for errors. *Such tasks can be delegated and effectively supervised* to guard against total blunders. *Just being good enough in these delegated tasks might serve the bigger purpose. In food, for example,* anyone with basic cooking skills can cook plain rice, dal, simple curries, and fries. So, if you need to free some of your time from cooking, and can afford a hired cook, who can do your cooking as per your needed *timings*, you should in fact delegate the preparatory jobs and these simple dishes to them. Perfect examples of 'right tasks' for delegation.

In office set up, let me give just one example. The head of the Operating Unit/Manager is responsible for the ultimate performance of the Team. Hence, DAK (the Incoming and Outgoing correspondence) is amongst the most crucial *management tools* to keep your eyes and ears open – to know what is actually happening in your operational field; how your team is playing it out; especially how your customers and other stakeholders are being served and what feedback/complaints keep coming from them. *Hence Mail/Correspondence is always seen as a direct responsibility of the Head.* But in large units, is it feasible to handle all inward and outward DAK personally and single-handedly? NO! You, as the manager, have to break it up into smaller tasks, find out members to delegate partially, while you must retain overall supervision and control over it, by following some facilitative procedure and making all in your team know (or at least perceive) that '*you know it all*'! Registered mail is supposed to be very important, as it is usually resorted to in important/critical communications which one wants to ensure receipt of and action at the other end. Further, since you/your unit acknowledges receipt thereof, there is an accountability angle. So, in many offices, delegation in fact is not allowed in opening registered mails. The Head personally tears the covers open and glances through the contents, then noting the total number of such covers received, delegates it to someone as per roster to enter the details ensuring all the dak received are documented and received by the dealing employees against their acknowledgement to ensure dealing with the matter therein. The Dak book then is routinely monitored for disposal. So here is a nice example of what portion of one task is *right* for delegation and what portion is not.

Thus, delegation process starts with *identifying the right tasks* for passing down. Anyone who consciously picks this lesson up from kitchen is likely to do a similar conscious scan in other areas of one's responsibilities.

The Right Circumstance

Even when you have ascertained which tasks or which portions of any task is right for delegating, you still have to assess if the circumstances are right for delegation. You know you can delegate some chores like chopping of vegetables, peeling of garlic cloves, making of roti etc. to the hired hand without risking the outcomes. But picture this: your maid has already done her morning shift and left, and will come only in the evening to make fresh roti and do the utensils. Now you receive a message that there is a sudden guest for early dinner. Your maid is not likely to come again during the day, or even earlier during the afternoon as she has some unavoidable work that she had informed you about. What do you do? Wait to delegate her share of work when she comes in the evening, or do a major portion on your own and finish before the guest arrives? Obviously, the latter would be the right choice. Here, right tasks are identified, but the circumstances do not favour delegation. Thus, *availability of the delegatee and/or availability of time to the chosen delegatee to do the assigned job must be our major elements of assessing the circumstances.*

Carried forward to work situations, this principle of always assessing the circumstances before delegating ensures that your delegation does not hinder the work instead of facilitating. You may have figured out right tasks, right people, but if, say, time is not on the side of those right people, or, if it is an emergency in which you have to pick up the mantle yourself, then let that be. Do not wait or depend on delegation.

We have already discussed above how mothers cook themselves the favourite dishes of their visiting children. We have also taken the example of why the leader must handle the high value cliental relations. In both cases, the parameter on which these tasks are rendered 'not -right' tasks to delegate is the *non-negotiable need for personal touch* in the circumstances.

The Right Person

Goes without saying, not everything can be delegated to everyone without assessing the delegatee's capability to do that task.

People have different levels of skills, experiences, commitment etc. Obviously, the task to be delegated calls for certain levels of skills and competence. Unless these match, how will delegation be fruitful?

So, a very basic principle of delegation is to find out the most appropriate of your team members, in terms of skills and commitment needed for the identified task.

Just as we have seen in kitchen, mothers delegate only after being satisfied about the skills of the hired cook, or own family members. Yes, training is a great step towards enhancing the skills levels of your people to make them right for delegation.

The Right Direction/Communication

In kitchen, till the hired cook is proficient in your kinds of dishes, even for a simple job like chopping, you do have to show them what exact sizes different vegetables might have to be chopped for specific dishes; ask them to chop a few pieces of a few vegetables to re-check if *she got it right or not*. Similarly, if delegating a dish with a slightly complex recipe, you clearly explain the recipe step by step and ask her to recap to ensure she has got it. You also supervise. For even a simple job like dish-washing when you have taken out and used your fine cutlery sets, you usually give your maid extra instructions on how to do them in special ways if needed/cautiously, instead of just piling them up thinking she does the cleaning every day, so will do on her own. *The lesson on importance of communication for delegation gets hammered in kitchen through many situations.*

Delegation does not give the desired result, may even become counter-productive, if the delegatee does not understand clearly what they are expected to do. *So, clear, concise, and unambiguous communication by the delegator is of paramount importance in the process of delegation.* Not only you must clearly spell out what is to be done, at times how exactly to be done, by what time to be done etc., must also be spelt out. *You, as the delegator, must also double-check, through two-way communication,* that the delegatee has understood/received the message correctly. Not only that, you must also make it clear to the delegatee what would be their responsibility/accountability for the result. One cannot just do a shoddy job of a delegated task and go entirely scot-free.

Where there is accountability, there has to be some authority that gets delegated along with the task. Clarity in communication plays a significant role in delegation of authority. As a leader, whenever you delegate a task, you need to make it clear what kind of authority you are passing on to them: whether you just want them to do exactly as you say; or you want them to do some research and report you back with recommendations for your instructions; or you want them to assume still higher responsibility and decide at their level how the task is to be done, and keep you posted; or you want them to act independently but produce the result! *In many instances, delegation fails due to lack of clear communication on details of task, expected level of authority to be exercised and expected results.*

The Right Supervision

Having delegated a task, would you just get busy with other stuff and take no stock of how the task is progressing till it is time to check out the result? Common sense says, NO! Depending upon the capabilities of the delegatee, the task complexity, as also the circumstances, you would supervise at certain stages and guide or provide necessary inputs and impetus to ensure quality result on time. The same happens in kitchen and similar process ensues in professional spaces. Delegation cannot be effective without supervision at right junctures. You as a delegator should neither micro-manage in the name of supervision, nor completely leave it till it is completed in the name of accountability of the delegatee for the result. As said earlier, delegation does not take away the ultimate accountability for the results from the delegator.

And *right junctures* will be different for different types of delegatees. For example, if you have delegated something to a new employee, or say, someone is doing some project for the first time, apart from training before going on the job, frequent supervision may be needed to guide and mentor on-the-job, before the project goes off-track. A little bit of micro-managing may be beneficial in such cases. But for experienced, skilled employees, your supervision would suffice just to ensure the timeline. In kitchen, when the matriarchs train the youngsters in cooking, they delegate, but under supervision. You might have to stand right beside your daughter rolling out her first few rotis, hand-holding, explaining, guiding, and supervising. But once she learns this well, would you micro manage in the name of supervision? Just a bit of 'how it is going', 'how many left to be done' etc. would suffice as supervision for task completion in time.

Supervision, thus, involves 'strategic presence' of the delegator around the delegated task. Neither too near to keep intervening/interfering unnecessarily while the delegatee is doing their job; nor too distant not to be available when your presence/expertise is required to keep the project on-track. In today's world of advanced telecommunications, what we are talking about is not physical distance of your presence, but also the 'felt' distance.

As a corollary, the principles of effective delegation also teach us why it is crucial for at least leaders at the middle and senior levels, who are primarily responsible for implementation and delivery, must also have some *basic job knowledge themselves* which is required for the team members at the front lines of delivery. What will you supervise if you are completely devoid of some knowledge on the basics of the specific delegated work?

<u>Coming to the real issues of delegation now. The Obstacles to delegation.</u>

Many of us, even after understanding that delegation of some parts of our tasks and responsibilities would indeed make us better and more effective, simply *cannot* delegate! Yes, some of us suffer from a strong tendency to hold on to our jobs. For a variety of reasons, we shall be talking about. Secondly, even if we delegate, it does not actually work that smoothly on the ground. Again, for certain reasons. These reasons can be bundled as obstacles to delegation.

i. At times, YOU are your greatest obstacle for delegating.

Your own Resistance

There are some people, who simply find it easier to do something on their own, rather than getting it done. In essence, it stems from lack of leadership quality to get things done through others. Such resistance may also manifest when you have a strong tendency to hold on to your jobs out of a ridiculous fear of losing your own importance in your circle. You suffer from a persistent/obsessive need to prove your mettle before significant others. Such people suffer from a limiting belief that delegation might reduce their authority and importance. They are also nervous about what if, the delegatee does a better job? Obviously, this is a great *weakness of character* and the only remedy lies in acknowledging this first and making conscious efforts to overcome this resistance.

Your own Excellence

There are some people, who personally possess an excellent level of skills required for certain, even most of the, jobs. *Highly efficient type people!* Some of them find it too difficult to *trust in other people's efficiency.*

Pause, and observe yourself if you generally find it difficult to delegate. Do the following types of thoughts cross your mind often?

"Oh! I can do it much better myself."

"My people are just not capable enough; they can't match the benchmark I would like to set."

"I can finish it with less botheration and in less time than it takes to explain what I want done, and then supervise."

"If they do wrong, I'll only be accountable."

"My people are risk-averse and avoid responsibility."

Etc.

These are symptomatic of your inability to delegate because of your *overconfidence in your own competence.*

Fact is: *this has essentially three angles: a trust issue, overconfidence in self, and yes, lack of leadership quality to get things done through others by suitably training and developing them for higher skills and competence.* This attitude of yours points to your weakness. If you have other equally or more important jobs to take care of, obviously delegation would only help you. Firstly, no one knows the best in everything. Secondly, even if you are the best in everything (an impossibility), you don't have all the *time* under the sun to do everything the best way singlehandedly. And in any case, real life puts so many asks on us that time is never sufficient to meet all of them. So, if delegation is possible, i.e., we have right tasks, right circumstances, and right people, then we must resort to it for better results by overcoming our own fears and prejudices about others. We must be alert not to make our own excellence become a hindrance in the way of beneficial delegation.

Many a times in kitchen, even if you have hired a cook, you don't *let her do* all the cooking. You end up cooking the more difficult, more time-consuming ones yourself, or micro-manage, out of *a lack of trust in her skills*. You feel, you are looked up to by your loved ones for the food, and so feel nervous anticipating how they would react if food gets messed up at the last moment. You are always ready to ride on a guilt trip. *The solution is two-fold:* 1st, get out of the guilt mania as if food is solely your responsibility (meaning you must *personally* do it all and cannot delegate or outsource at times). 2nd, if you are not confident about the skill level of the cook, start delegating small tasks first and gradually delegate bigger tasks and check her skill level. Train and check her learning capability. Culinary skills, and in fact most of the skills in this world, are learnable. Further, if you have the deep pocket, you can hire already certified cooks/chefs, and carve out time for your other meaningful missions.

[Yes, if you are highly proficient in any skill, have all the time, no other important work to suffer, doing on your own is financially a better option, and you enjoy doing the job too, then may be, doing it yourself without delegating is a wiser decision sometimes. But that comes under the ambit of assessing circumstances, not obstacle to right delegation. You are not delegating because the circumstances do not *warrant* it, not because you are not able to delegate, or you are resisting it. So have clarity on the reasons for not delegating.]

Your Own lack of Clarity on your project

At times, you are confused, or don't know what to delegate in the first place. While discussing right tasks for delegation, we have seen how important it is for the Head to be able to split up every job/project into series of smaller tasks. In cooking a dish, for example, there are clear steps for the recipe: you identify the ingredients, quantity required of each of them, clearly segregated preparatory work like chopping, grinding, crushing etc., then the step-by-step cooking procedure. Once you are clear on this, you know which bit of task exactly can be delegated to the hired hand. *Similarly, it is your own leadership failure if you cannot picture the whole process and segregate the smaller tasks right for delegation*. Remember, while delegating, you have to spell out clearly what is to be done with what results and responsibility levels. So here again the *only solution lies in* your own efforts to first gain clarity on what you want to achieve through what process. Clearly a leadership issue that you must face head on.

Basically, when you are unable to delegate, first introspect if YOU yourself are the obstacle, and overcome your own lacks.

ii. At times, issues of Trust and Reliance may be genuine.

Delegation does not mean blind trust in the capability of and reliability of the delegatee. At times, you might be heading a team with some members with less-than needed trust-worthiness. Guidance, training, mentoring can resolve issues related to skills and competence of your people. Even commitment levels of most people can get raised inspired by the personal example of the leader. *Yet, there may be some hard nuts to crack.* When you are even vaguely aware of the low commitment level of some persons, *or seen them being undependable in their current roles,* you might feel nervous about delegating tasks to them, not only because you're not sure of their capabilities, but also because *you know you cannot trust in their reliability.* Happens very often in the corporate world when you are just assigned a team from the higher ups without power to hire and fire.

But that does not spare you from your leadership responsibilities of achieving results through your allotted people. You cannot forget that people have been employed to get things done, and *you, as the leader, must make that happen.* So, here again *solution lies in* delegating small, simple jobs initially and then building up to more challenging ones, *but under close supervision* and continuously testing the person's skills and *attitude* before going further with them. Communicate clearly defined tasks/ functions with clearly defined responsibility *and accountability.* Further, create a stake of these employees visibly in their own development plan if they successfully handle the delegated tasks.

It is also important to note that *trust begets trust.* The more you delegate, the more the delegatee would be motivated, and inspired to rise up to your expectations. In fact, everyone needs to move up and find newness in jobs to stay motivated. Otherwise, boredom and frustration might set in. As you delegate *higher* responsibilities, your people automatically *feel trusted, get up-skilled,* and hence *stay motivated.*

iii. Delegation of the same *responsibility* to too many *people*

Yes, Kitchen teaches us *how too many cooks spoil the broth.* Mess ups happen when you let more than one person work on cooking the same one dish. The dish might get doubly salted, or without any salt as one thinks the other might not have, or might have, done a step. In workspaces too, at times delegation fails because you, as a top boss, delegate the *responsibility of the same task* to too many people, *especially through delegation of supervision* to too many people. *A typical situation is when the core task is meant to be executed by one, but there will be layers of supervisors to monitor status.* No wonder, more time is wasted in reporting *status* than on completing the task! Do not fall into this self-defeating style of delegation. It is more an obstacle than a facilitator of delegation.

Here, if you observe Joint family kitchens or professional kitchens, or how caterers engage people for heavy amount of cooking, you would understand what is the difference between delegating *tasks/functions* and delegating *responsibility*. Allocating the same job to many is almost a must when, say, quantity of what is to be cooked is huge, involving high quantities of preparatory work, like peeling, chopping, grinding etc. Such low-risk, low-skilled jobs can be delegated to many without spoiling the process. If you have 20 kg of potatoes to be used in the curry, obviously you will not engage one person to do all the peeling, chopping, and washing of all the potatoes; but delegate peeling to say 5-6 people, chopping to another set of say 6-7 people, even washing to say a different person, so that the three tasks run concurrently. It speeds up the preparatory portion. But you engage only one person (the main cook/chef) to cook the curry. You do not engage multiple cooks to make the curry either jointly or separately. Here, 'responsibility' for the cooked curry resides with one person- the main cook/chef. Yes, supervision of all processes is also mostly done by one person who has the ultimate responsibility for the result. In some cases, *more than one supervisor may be there, but the functions/tasks to be supervised by each are different.*

Thus, delegation of same *functions* to many might be effective in certain situations, but delegation of *supervision* over the same functions to many usually creates obstacles to effective delegation.

Kitchen, thus, teaches us to delegate whatever and whenever you find the *right fives*, whether in kitchen or in workspace, avoiding/overcoming the afore-mentioned barriers (which are more psychological than real.).

And guess what, if I have learnt the lessons on delegation well even from my humble kitchen, I am also clear on *what I expect from the people to whom I delegate responsibilities (e.g., the maids, the hired cooks in kitchen).*

This, in turn, makes me alive to the fact that *even my employer must be having similar expectations from me as an employee.* Imagine how kitchen turns me into an asset-like employee in an organisation – committed, responsible and productive.

I think, we have talked enough on delegation. Let us move on to outsourcing.

OUTSOURCING

As is clear from the term itself, outsourcing simply means you source something from outside. *Delegation is in-house,* i.e., you delegate to people within your house/company/organisation (even a hired cook comes to *your* house kitchen and cooks; you don't go outside). But *outsourcing is transferring a part of your tasks with responsibilities to some outside agent.*

In our world of food, outsourcing has become very common these days, especially when you are staying alone, or in a hostel/hotel/Paying Guest accommodation without provision of food, or kitchen facilities to cook personally. We *order food* for home delivery, or we physically go and *eat out.* Outsourcing of food in such cases becomes either a compulsion, or turns out to be more economical because maintaining a full-fledged kitchen might be much more expensive for a single person in terms of cost as well as time and energy. At times, such out-sourcing in food is also resorted to by families for a good break and some relief to the home maker.

We can pick up at least two critical insights on outsourcing from managing our humble kitchen and our world of food that can work well in organisation set ups. Those are: in office set ups, firstly, outsourcing must be evaluated in terms of whether it would prove reliable, AND secondly if it would be cost-effective.

You may observe, companies outsource tasks/responsibilities like cleaning of office premises, security guard services, general maintenance like electricity, generator, plumbing etc., to dedicated experienced and certified service providers/contractors/agencies, i.e., whose credentials are established and so *reliable in respect of quality of service.* This also turns out to be *economical* cost-wise. Cost of maintaining *permanent* staff for these menial/exclusive jobs, with all the various employee benefits in-service and post-retirement, coupled with the difficulties in firing them for non-performance, is usually much higher than outsourcing cost. Additionally, when you outsource, you can comfortably pass on a good share of *accountability* for quality performance through suitable *contracts* of engagement, failing which you can terminate their services and engage someone else.

To end, I would like to reiterate that delegation or outsourcing does not mean dereliction of duties and responsibilities or abdication. It is a well-thought-out distribution of some of your tasks and responsibilities to appropriate persons/agencies in terms of competence and commitment, in circumstances right for passing on those tasks.

Is not it mind-blowing how kitchen keeps throwing up such great insights on all the key aspects of delegation and outsourcing?

33. Cooking and Team Building

Sounds too far-fetched and stretchy? Not really. Already we have discussed many lessons and issues in other contexts, which are also pertinent to team building. As stated initially, kitchen teaches many lessons through a single incident/experience, and a single lesson through many incidents/experiences. So, some repetition becomes unavoidable here and there.

Simply think about how you 'create' different dishes. Think again about how you create new dishes by using different kinds of left-overs; how you 'redeem' ingredients and dishes soon-to-become-dustbin-worthy to avoid wastage. Aren't they all shining examples of how to 'bring together' different ingredients/elements with different attributes like different tastes, different textures, different flavours, different nutrients, and different looks?

Unity in diversity is the bedrock on which the world of food is sustained. And that is exactly what lies at the crux of any vibrant Team.

Recently, I was into clearing a bit of left-overs of cooked rice and some soaked sago. I thought of making some delicious roasties out of them. I knew, first of all, I have to bring them together with some binding agent(s), add some vegetables for a healthy touch and increased quantity, and finally add some spices to infuse taste and flavour. I mashed the cooked rice and soaked sago roughly, adding grated boiled potato and a bit of besan (gram flour) for binding. Both potato and besan are good binding agents. I added bits of grated carrots, finely chopped cabbage, capsicum, spring onion, fresh coriander, green chili, ginger-garlic paste, salt, chat masala; mixed and mashed them well. I knew from experience, that this will be okay for a roastie, but it will not make it as crispy as I want. For crispiness, I added a bit of corn flour and made yummy, crispy, healthy roasties, using minimal amount of oil. This (and similar umpteen experiences in kitchen) teaches us the very first lesson in team building:

Find a common rallying point that can act as a binding agent.

What, after all, is the quintessence of team building? Goes without saying, it is 'bringing together' different types of people with different characteristic dispositions, in terms of values-beliefs-behavioral patterns and personal goals, into one ambit with the help of something that binds them together. Like, a shared goal, a common interest. Plus, something extra, to add flavour, taste, crispiness, i.e., motivation/inspiration to keep the flock together with a sense of belongingness. Team-play essentially involves the ability to value *diversity* and knowing how to bring in synergy *in diversity.*

Team is not necessarily a homogeneous group of people. It is the effectiveness of leadership, that acts like a centripetal force needed to keep the members of the team functioning together as one unit despite the centrifugal tendencies due to dissimilar values of individual members and relationship conflicts.

So, the real trick of effective team builders (i.e., leaders) lies first in their *ability to discern what can act as a binding agent* – a rallying point around which all the different people would gather, notwithstanding their differences in many other aspects. It is the *shared goal* and *vision* in the context of the Corporate World.

Then, of course, comes the *second aspect* – having got them around a rallying point, *how to keep the flock together* with that extra bit - the application of all the things you know about motivating and inspiring others. Not everyone can put to practice what they already know. Here, the *leaders' personal qualities* like competence, credibility, character, integrity, and expertise from previous experience and practice, i.e., their own personal example, would decide their ability to persuade and inspire their team mates to work cohesively towards a shared goal. *Official authority helps in managing, but personal power finally decides your success as a Leader.* These leadership qualities of your own, as well as personal qualities/strengths/weaknesses of team members are like the 'ingredients' in cooking, and would work successfully in a cohesive and synergized manner, *when properly combined striking right proportions and balance.* Recall our earlier deliberations on balance and proportion.

There is a third important insight. We have some of the recipes, like crispy cutlets/fritters, non-veg kebabs/tandoori etc., which require more than one marination and coating for great taste and crispiness. You marinate and leave for the flavours to seep in, then again marinate with another set of ingredients, then dip in some batter, then roll in and coat with stuff like breadcrumbs, again dip in batter and roll in coat material for extra crispiness. Then deep fry in hot oil, not on high flame for a short while, but on moderate heat for a longer period so that the exterior becomes rightly crispy without getting burnt. *This has a lesson for leaders:*

Motivating your team members is not a one-shot affair; it is a continuous process with right doses at right times at right intervals.

Fourth, and one of the fundamental insights for doing or getting done anything is, of course, on how to build competence. Ultimately, performance is a result of competencies (knowledge, skills, talents, and attitude). As a leader of a team, it is not enough to be competent yourself; you must build competencies of your team members also. By now, we have talked enough on this aspect-how to motivate, train, mentor and supervise your people. In coming segments too, we would be shining light on this. Here I would like to give just one example for drawing a parallel between a commonplace chore in the kitchen with how we approach building capabilities in our people.

When we boil milk, we first ascertain if it is raw, or pasteurized. If pasteurized, it is already boiled, cleared of impurities, and packaged well. We can simply give it one boil on high flame, or use it straight away. But if it is raw, we follow a process called '*aauta*' (let me call it *ladling*) in my mother tongue Odia, which means: Put the milk pot on high flame; stand right there and go on stirring milk with a ladle at tiny intervals till a boil comes; keep taking out ladle-full of milk (as it boils on high flame) up above the milk level by say, 4-5 inches and pour it back into the boiling milk; repeat this process along with stirring for about 10-15 times (more or less depending upon quantity); and finally stop this when milk is boiled well and ready to be left on lowest heat(sim) without having to be supervised, for another 5-10 minutes. By stirring and ladling, even as the milk is boiling on high heat, we manage to build up as well as diffuse pressure at the same time ensuring proper boiling of raw milk without spillage.

Strikes a chord? Yes, in corporate world, we usually are 'given' our team members and as team leaders, we are required to bring each of them up to certain levels of competency. Not each one is of same mettle. So, we have to first ascertain if someone is 'raw milk' or already 'pasteurized'. If raw, i.e., new to the work/system, we have to work on them vigorously right from the beginning (put on high flame immediately) through training, mentoring, appreciating, pressurizing as a combo. But for a beginner, all of this might feel like too much pressure (high heat). So, *keep stirring and ladling (build pressure to get trained, but* keep on releasing pressure simultaneously with building pressure) *under constant watch by being 'present' there.* Like watching how training is being received, how it is translating into performance, small but continuous 'pats' for learning/ doing well, hand-holding for correction/improvement etc. These small things can go a big way in averting build-up of harmful pressure, while retaining creative pressure to learn and deliver. Once these team members are ready with a threshold level of competency, leave them on 'sim'. That is, they are not yet fully ready, so heat/pressure should be low to moderate, though not yet turned off, so that they do not feel the heat too much to break down. Similarly, for the already talented and known to be competent team members (pasteurized milk), you may just go for one boil on high flame (to check out their level and give their creative tension a push) and switch off, i.e., give them the specific necessary training and guidance, and leave them to perform on their own under moderate supervision.

Thus, a team, to be full of aliveness, enthusiasm and needed commitment, must have something more than a basic binding agent (i.e., a shared goal). Just as in the roastie. Something to make it healthy, something to make it appealing with taste and flavour, and yet something more to make it crispy and interesting! Once you imbibe these lessons from your humble kitchen and cooking processes, it would also help you to carry these *perspectives* to other areas including the tough workplaces with challenging team building exercises.

No wonder, great teams not only boringly pursue their professional common goals, *they also engage in and enjoy the less formal or informal inter-personal relations amongst the team members*, involving small personal get-togethers, family celebrations, mutual care/help/learnings, and feedback/ appreciations etc. *Idea is to know about each member in terms of more than what they do in the professional set-up.* In an effective team, every member must do more than what is expected of them as per job sheet. No leader can ensure this unless they know each member as an individual - their overall family background, other qualities, talents, strengths, and weaknesses! This *extra knowledge* about the team members enables the leader to synergize the potentials of all members for a greater team performance.

We have heard it often: TEAM=Together Each Achieves More! Unless that happens, team building in its true spirit is yet to happen.

The great sense of proportion and balance that one can develop from regular kitchen management/cooking comes truly handy in this context. '*Know thy ingredients*' in kitchen, when carried forward to workplaces, becomes the fundamental principle of '*Know Thy people*' for team building.

Effective leaders invest themselves in knowing every team member in terms of their job competence, temperament/attitude in work atmosphere and prospects for professional development, just as a great cook would try to know the distinct qualities of every ingredient before combining. But when human beings are involved, each is to be known both as a professional as also as a 'person.' As already mentioned earlier, a leader must know/spot the other skills and qualities of each member beyond the prescribed skills-set laid down/expected for their jobs/role, as also have some critical information on everyone's personal/domestic situation. Only then, you know your team members enough to develop them and draw on their strengths. Only then you can decipher if your members are individually great employees - reliable, proactive, diligent, creative, great followers, leaders in their own right or not; and if they would stop expressing their individuality to fit seamlessly into the team when the situation warrants.

Only when you know your team members individually in the above manner going beyond their role-sheets, you can fathom how to combine, synergize, and build on their talents, skills and strengths ensuring they complement one another in a balanced and proportionate manner.

A great team is not about all great followers under one leader at the top only; it is about great followership harmonised with local leadership at every rung, just as in kitchen, every dish is a play of balance, proportion, and synergy amongst individually distinct and great ingredients, and when placed on a platter as part of a meal, each dish complements all other dishes placed together for a wholesome meal experience. Underline the parallel – each individual must have competence and effectiveness for various roles individually, but when placed in a Team, each must bring to the table one's competence and uniqueness in a *synergised* manner, *not* to work at cross purposes with other members' talents and uniqueness, but to enhance overall Team performance.

The significance of 'Know Thy People' does not end there. In fact, I would say its greatest advantage is that it helps the leader develop *the ability to assess ability*. Yes, ironically, in the real corporate scenario, there are more instances of persons in leadership roles *lacking* this critical ability to assess ability. May be so, because you don't value a full spectrum view on any individual's situation before writing a confidential report on your team member's performance and potential; or you have not invested enough in knowing your people in a true sense, that includes knowing at least the important dynamics in their background that can constrain them despite their great talents and commitment. The direct outcome of knowing your people going beyond their job sheet to have some ideas about not only their strengths, weaknesses, unique talents, but also their personal background, especially constraints therein, if any, would facilitate a well-rounded assessment of performance vis-à-vis potential and circumstances.

Let us now think about the Doctors in the Kitchen, as also how kitchen is also a great SPA.

Yes, our humble kitchen can be a source of perhaps the best of ingredients for healing, and for our homely SPA! Turmeric, salt, papaya, banana, cucumber, potato, onion, gram flour (besan), milk, fresh cream, ghee, olive oil, oats, avocado and what not! When you invest in knowing your very familiar ingredients for cooking a bit more beyond their food-worthiness, their inherent properties can startle you with what greater potentials they hold in terms of their *medicinal and cosmetic uses*, apart from merely being a food-ingredient. We will separately talk about some examples in a later segment on 'Kitchen: The Doctor and SPA'. Here, I just made a mention to bring home this perspective in connection with knowing your people.

Mothers/any regular cook playing with variety of food ingredients – their real 'Team Members,' usually get curious about their other utilities as mentioned earlier, and when carried to workplaces, this inquisitiveness takes them far in 'knowing' their team mates. As already emphasised enough, 'Know Thy People is a foundational, inviolable dictum for effective leadership.

Cooking helps us in cultivating the art of building 'teams' *outside* the original team (of employees) by making us alive to the need for knowing the *special* qualities of our team members over and above their job-relevant ones. Observe, how corporates mentor and sponsor players, musicians, performing artists – i.e., other talents, amongst their own employees, that adds to their company's brand image, as well as strengthens internal team spirit for organisational goals through a greater sense of belonging, ultimately leading to a greater degree of employee *engagement*. Goes without saying, when an employee feels treated and respected as an individual, and is recognised as someone gifted with more to offer than what the job sheet asks for, bonding with the team/organisation is taken to a next level.

Dealing with emotive/incendiary situations:

This is one more highly useful lesson that kitchen teaches us in connection with team play.

After all, kitchen is where you handle FIRE, as the primary element. Yes, cooking is about ingredients and recipes, and all other things. But who, err. what, *causes* the ingredients to get cooked? It is HEAT. What is the source of heat? It is FIRE! No wonder, any mindful person managing kitchen day in and day out would pick up great insights and dexterity in matters of handling fire to our benefit, guarding against/averting dangerous accidents.

Team dynamics are not always cool and cordial. Occasional conflicts and clashes can be expected as normal even in the best of teams. After all, it is a fact that vast and significant differences can exist amongst different individuals in a team, which may clash from time to time, unless moderated and handled suitably at every level, especially by the team leader. Kitchen has real good tips on how to handle such situations. Let us take a few examples.

At the cost of repetition, I would take the example of boiling milk again, that we have already talked about in the context of motivation under pressure earlier.

In kitchen, watch what happens when you leave milk on gas for boiling on high flame, and forget to keep a watch over it. It spills over – no great application of mind needed to guess that. But mothers know about this *property* of milk, viz. its volume rises *uncontrollably* after boiling point, if left on high flame. So, they do not let that happen in the first place, by *using a sufficiently large vessel* for boiling milk on one hand AND *controlling heat appropriately*. Very important! Either they put milk on sim from the start itself, or first on high flame *under watch* till the boiling point and then reducing flame to sim immediately after that. In both cases, if there is sufficient space left above the level of milk in the pot, milk will rise and fall on its own without spilling over, and you need not be around all the time to watch over it. But if for some reason through oversight you leave it on high flame and suddenly notice that the boiling milk is about to spill over, you still can save the situation by rushing and immediately switching off the burner, instead of changing it to even sim. Because you know the property of both milk on the boil, as well as fire – your two team members in this example. You know, once the boiling milk starts swelling, even a bit more of heat would cause it to *uncontrollably* expand and spill – *so stop the source of heat first*. You may again switch on and put it on low flame if you want milk to boil a bit more. Or, you may first pick up the milk vessel with the help of a grip away from fire, let it lose the swell, then put on low flame again for more boiling, if you want.

At times, if you use a relatively small vessel without enough space over the milk level, you have to keep monitoring once the boiling point is reached, even if it is on sim. You might have to take the vessel up with a tong a few times to keep the rise in check; or you have to blow onto the flame even on sim to disperse heat beyond a point. But essentially what you have to continuously address is: HEAT!

Point is: Just as while cooking, we must deal effectively with heat and its source, similarly, while handling a Team, the leaders must always be on the vigil to sense quickly when conflicts arise amongst team members and their source-the reasons. They must realise that their first job is to *control heat in the group*, instead of immediately jumping to judgements or imposing discipline. These steps can effectively be brought in only after the fire is dowsed, and situation cools down.

Every human being is subconsciously driven by emotions and feelings, and these can be seen as the parallel of 'Heat', while the causes of such emotions and feelings are the source of heat, i.e., the Fire. So, handle the incendiary situations in workplaces as you would handle fire in the kitchen.

Controlled fire rightly cooks food; controlled emotions of both the leader as well as individual team members lead to right group dynamics and desired productivity.

Another example.

By mistake, you have left your stove burners on when the gas cylinder is also on. What happens if you do not know the property of gas? Disaster waiting to happen with one single spark of gas-lighter! But if you are a regular cook, you know the critical properties of what you work with – your team members. In such a situation, you get to know about the gas-leak from its smell; would rush to switch off the cylinder first (the source), then the burners AND immediately you would also open all windows, doors, and fans to *disperse* leaked gas without allowing it to stay concentrated inside the kitchen. And of course, till it clears out completely, you will not light a matchstick. You would find many parallels to this in workplaces with team plays. Leaders to be effective stay ever alert to avert such incendiary situations converting into fire. They find out ways to dissipate the negative energies first, even before working on a positive solution.

Kitchen thus teaches us in many ways *that issues are not to be handled at the level of external symptoms of manifestation alone, those must be dealt with at the root level.* Just as heat is at the root of cooking, fire is the source of heat, fuel and a spark of fire are at the root of fire, and oxygen is at the root of fire continuing to burn, every situation in life, including Team dynamics, runs on these four fundamental angles. If something has to be cooked (i.e., if some result is to be achieved), we must have right fuel (build a good team along with ensuring other needed logistics), set it on fire (bring team members together with clearly shared communication about target outcomes, processes, shared goals and purpose, and start work), allow oxygen to keep the fire burning(ensure/provide conducive conditions to awaken people's inherent achievement motivation, encourage appropriate performance with training, mentoring, rewards/disincentives, inspire through personal example), and last but not the least, keep on managing and controlling heat at right levels (closely follow up, supervise and intervene) as needed at different points.

Coming to communication, which is the life blood of any teamwork, it is amazing how kitchen teaches even this lesson with clarity. First, communication with Self! We tell ourselves clearly on what is there on the menu, what are the ingredients, how much of each is needed, what exactly are the steps of the recipe etc. And we ensure mental clarity on these; i.e., we communicate with self, and make sure we have received the messages clearly. Ambiguity is just not an option in cooking, as once you start, it is about fire. We communicate with others when we *delegate* cooking-related functions in our small family kitchen, or manage a joint-family kitchen or a professional kitchen. Any large kitchen, having to dish-out large quantities of quality food on time (but usually having less spacious work stations than required) can be functional only when clear communications are made and unequivocally received by each. This is done in professional kitchens through written recipes, clear distribution of work etc. In homely kitchen, you are the one doing everything, or at the most you have one or two more aids. But whichever kitchen it may be, *food management can go messy without clear communication with self and others. We have talked on communication in detail* in delegation segment.

Actual/strategic presence, active listening and co-creating solutions/responses through collaborative and consultative processes – which are the hallmarks of any vibrant team- can all be observed in large kitchens, which can be picked up as great lessons.

The lesson that keeps coming up from kitchen is: Go to the *Source (*the root cause) to handle a problem; dowse the 'fire' first, disperse negative energies, then work on a solution, with adequate knowledge on every person/situational dimension involved.

And of course, 'Know Thy Ingredients' in kitchen gives us the cardinal lesson on team-building: Know Thy People.

What great lessons!

34. Appearing Versus Being: Self-awareness and Integrity

A little diversion here, before we deliberate on many other practical lessons we can pick up from our humble kitchen. Ideally, I wished to talk about this, i.e., appearing versus being, at the end, as *this, to my realisation, leads to perhaps the most supreme value getting ingrained in any one taking care of food and kitchen for themselves and their loved ones, and which, to my understanding, is one of the learnings from kitchen that results in the greatest spiritual transformation!* But, thought of shining light on this insight mid-way, so that you could introspect and check if you have seen this underlying every useful lesson that we have discussed so far, or are going to discuss.

When our purpose is clear to us, and when our purpose transcends our own mean selfish interests, we also come to realise that for the 'purpose' to be achieved, *we must 'be' what we are needed to be*, not just *'appear to be'*. *We must live and become what we learn, and not just gain the knowledge*, and rest over it. We *have to 'be' what we think is right, and not just profess!*

<u>It is about integrity.</u>

Kitchen shows us on multiple occasions the lines of difference between 'appearing to be' and actually 'being'. It dissuades us from settling for mere appearing, as ultimately the interests of our dear ones are at stake. As we know, repeat a behaviour recurringly, and it becomes a habit; repeat a habit on auto mode recurringly, it becomes a *samskara*, a part of our character. *Once our character transforms, this trait, viz., integrity, gets invoked in every situation.*

Let us take a few examples.

Self-discipline: We have already seen how it gets imbibed into your character if you are regularly taking care of your homely kitchen. Does it mean you demonstrate self-discipline only for cooking and managing kitchen? No. The lessons that kitchen bombarded on you in this regard since day one also make you, in all probability, a disciplined person in all other walks of your life as well. You do *not only know* that self-discipline is required to succeed everywhere and that mere show-off is not going to work, you *become a disciplined person.*

Hygiene: It is one of the critical pre-requisites of a healthy kitchen. *And this is one area in which mere 'looking hygienic' without actually 'being' can spell disaster.* And what is interesting to note is that *appearing* is very easy on this parameter, as you are mostly working without being watched over. You can always do a cover-up operation at the end not attracting attention of others who rely on you. But as a caring mother, do you do that? NO! *You learn not to fake it from day one. Not only because you care for them, but this also has serious implications in respect of trust reposed by others in you and your credibility! A genuine person never compromises on this aspect.*

At the cost of repetition, I would go back to the example of soiled utensils. Many a times, the homemakers have issues with their maids over cleaning the utensils. I am not saying all, but most of the maids in our Indian small cities are not so professional about the quality of their work. They work for too many houses for a little extra money, and in the process, end up doing a shabby job everywhere. Especially doing the utensils. Most of the times, even if the utensils 'look' clean, they are actually not. *Utensils can look 'clean' even if simply rinsed in water* under a tap running on full force, with just a touch of detergent, or even without. *But to be clean, the utensils must get free from bacteria-dirt-residues of food or cleanser,* and that requires right amount of detergent as well as proper washing with water. No wonder, almost all homemakers end up re-doing some of the utensils, already washed by the maid, before use. Because they cannot afford to put the health of their family to jeopardy.

Kitchen teaches you every day how whatever appears clean, or fresh, may not be so, and how important it is not only to find this out, but also to take remedial action. In workplaces too, very often what appears to be is not that! For an effective manager or leader, not only it is important for oneself to actually 'be', but also one must develop a *keen sense of observing beneath the surface* to stay constantly aware of the chinks in the armour, manipulations, mis-projections and duplicities.

Here the converse is also true sometimes. What looks 'dirty' sometimes may not really be dirty and may be clean from the perspective of 'being'. For example, cotton towels and clothes used to clean kitchen platforms, to wipe hands etc. very often continue to look dirty with stains even after real good washing. But these are free from dirt and bacteria and are good for reuse. You will find it difficult and expensive to manage if you start throwing these towels after every 1 or 2 uses. *Thus, kitchen teaches us to go beneath the surface and apply our mind* to examine if something appearing as something is for real or not, instead of taking anything on face value -good or bad. Is not this a great lesson for life?

On a larger canvas, this awareness (of the importance of being, and not just appearing) can be the greatest gift from the humble kitchen. Because, having infused this awareness, the kitchen also drives you towards 'being' by throwing up repetitive situations of similar nature that makes you bring the earlier lessons learnt into action again and again, till it becomes a habit and default mode behaviour.

There is a dangerous difference between 'appearing to be' and 'being.' A genuine person, a person with integrity, would always go for 'being' rather than just appearing/looking *in every walk of life.* Take for instance any great value, like honesty, compassion, care etc. They would not just care about looking compassionate, but would actually be that in action. They would bring all the values they truly value into their dealings with everyone in all situations, as called for.

A small example in empathy, compassion, and paradigm shift from our humble kitchen, as it happened to me personally!

Once there was a Bandh here in the entire state on some sensitive issue. My maid did not turn up. Honestly, I was pretty annoyed first, as she had already absented on 7 days earlier during *that month*. She was employed only the month before and the previous month too, she had absented on 4-5 days in one fortnight.

So, as she entered the following day, I asked her, "What's the matter? You did not come yesterday!" She said, 'bundh'. "Bundh? How does that affect *you*?" I was really irritated inside.

I was *under the impression* that she stayed nearby at walking distance – because she comes to my house quite early in the morning. It never even occurred to me while engaging her to find out where she stayed, as she had *readily* agreed to my early morning timings. Moreover, she was already working in many flats in my complex. Further, till then my experience had been that maids in our area usually preferred to work nearby so that they could attend to their own household chores also. Obviously, for *working women* – it is always a balancing act. Well, my bad that I was presuming things.

She replied, "Buses were not plying, how could have we come? I stay near Khandagiri area (pretty far off from my residence). I and my sis-in-law leave home every day around 5.30 am, come here, do all our houses, and by the time we get back, it gets almost 7.30 pm." It is true that during daytimes, while taking my car out of our parking space, twice or thrice, I had seen these two ladies having their *dabba* (lunch). Her sis-in-law worked at some apartments here and it was she, who had arranged this lady for my house, as my timings were not convenient to her.

When I heard this, suddenly something *changed inside me*. My anger sort of evaporated! I felt truly bad that without knowing the whole facts, I was attributing insincerity to her. To be precise, *I could see things differently from her position to feel empathetic and compassionate. Why?* Because, in her absence, I had to do all the dirty and tedious cleaning jobs, that she did every day. Without practice, those appeared very challenging and energy-draining for me. When I pitted that discomfort against hers, what she was going through multiple times a day doing the same things in several houses every day, I did understand how difficult it might be for her as it was and how more difficult it must be when she was not well etc. And I felt compassionate, instead of angered!

Certainly, there was a *paradigm shift in* me towards compassion and empathy for her– does not matter even if it was in a very limited context only. The *nature* of experience of a small paradigm shift and a big paradigm shift is more or less similar; what could be different is the context, the *canvas*, that gets impacted by the paradigm shift and the *quantum* of change – small or radical. In my case, due to the paradigm shift in this particular case, I may change the timing to suit her more, I may change my opinion about her and be more understanding of her problems etc... etc... In a bigger context like the role of Employees in an Organisation, a paradigm shift may cause the employees to be looked upon as the most critical *asset to be possessed* rather than just one of the *resources to be used*, which, in turn, would bring in *fundamental changes* in HR areas for organisational development.

In every paradigm shift, there is a spontaneity of change, that makes one see things differently. Seeing things differently is the first step in the thousand miles journey in a new direction. That is actually what we mean when we say "paradigm shift" - probably one of the most talked about concepts in organisational development and personal development (telling this from my own experience in HR; it was one of the most over-used terms that I had come across in articles, speeches and deliberations.) When there is a paradigm shift, you see things differently, from newer angles, so you understand the *composite* and *bigger* picture better and it enables you to know better paths, more effective ways and means to address the issues involved, ultimately impacting the whole *state of being.*

This is what I got from Wikipedia on Paradigm Shift – just checking out whether what I am calling a *paradigm shift* is, in *essence*, in line with what Thomas Kuhn, who originally coined this term, meant it to be.

"Paradigm shift, sometimes known as extraordinary science or revolutionary science, is the term first used by Thomas Kuhn in his influential 1962 book "The Structure of Scientific Revolutions" to describe a change in basic assumptions within the ruling theory of science. It is in contrast to his idea of normal science.

It has since become widely applied to many other realms of human experience as well even though Kuhn himself restricted the use of the term to the hard sciences. The term "paradigm shift" has found uses in other contexts, representing the notion of a major change in a certain thought-pattern — a radical change in personal beliefs, complex systems, or organizations, replacing the former way of thinking or organizing with a radically different way of thinking or organizing."

So, that's it. Kitchen has its ways to push you to break away from the old thinking patterns, old paradigms. Think of how much improvisation, innovation and creativity happens in our humble kitchens – some of them do involve an absolutely different way of treating ingredients. Every major breakthrough in this world has been possible first through a paradigm shift, small or big.

It is also significant to note how Kitchen helps us in *'being'*, in various other ways. *To be, you must do, i.e., translate what you know and learn into action.* Let us take a very simple example. You know/learn that alkaline foods are generally very good for heart health. So, mothers build in such foods, like beetroot, sweet potato, carrots, turnip, radish etc. into their recipes, instead of resting happy with that knowledge only. I find beet root an odd vegetable for our common Odia curry recipes. So, I use it in recipes like pav bhaji, sambhar where its colour enhances the look, plus slight sweetness adds to the taste. I boil slices of beet root and store in the fridge for ready use while making veg sandwiches, or veg cutlets, in which it really goes great. I know, curry leaves are great for health. So, apart from the regular uses in tempering, chutneys, I also add the leaves to different dosa/pancake batters, while grinding, or use chopped leaves. To build in tulsi and mint into regular diet, I frequently add those to my morning tea, for both a great flavour and lots of health benefits.

So, the point I wish to make is: *kitchen is a place, where learning, doing, being-all keep on happening seamlessly!* Sometimes, you *be* and *do* (your feelings drive your actions); sometimes you *do* and *be* (your actions drive your feelings). You are happy, you cook a delicious platter for your family, they are happy too; or you cook a delicious platter for your family, they are happy and that makes you happy. Either way, you are happy and so are others! One, who is mindful and consciously observes this seamless process, learns that such seamless integration of doing and being is possible, and must be so, in all walks of life for true evolution of a person to a higher self.

The true story of self-transformation begins with realising what is and what ought to be; and finishes with becoming what you ought to be – not just 'looking' like that through fake behaviour. Yes, learning lessons is important and indeed the first step towards self-transformation. But actual transformation happens only when we start "being" what we learn and understand. Managing kitchen on a *regular basis for people you love and value* including your own self, does not let you *cheat* – that is the catch! When you care for people from heart, your sense of responsibility automatically expands, and you do whatever is beneficial for the others. So, once you notice the lessons, you actually apply them the next time, and over a period of time, those learnings get into your system deeply as your auto-mode of behavioural patterns, your characteristic traits, your *samskaras*!

Do not *samskaras* (personality traits and value dispositions) get developed and deep-rooted like a groove through *habitual repetition* of behaviour patterns leading to reacting on auto-mode? You start becoming what you do repeatedly in unaware and default mode.

Kitchen offers the needed situations and multiple opportunities to learn a lot many valuable life and leadership lessons. No wonder, mothers are mothers! Typically, great human beings – genuine, loving, caring, sacrificing, empathetic and usually very compassionate.

35. Maintenance for Sustenance

Kitchen has taught me clearly the critical importance of maintenance. Cleanliness is the most important aspect of a working kitchen: every surface, every cutlery, every tool, every gadget, sink, filter, chimney – everything must be kept clean, i.e., 'maintained' hygienically. No one wants food coming from a dirty, unhygienic place. Neither would a caring mother take that chance.

What is necessary is *"being"* clean, not just *"looking"* clean! That, too, on a sustained basis.

Imagine what would happen if your maid only rinses the used utensils with water without detergent and keeps those for you to re-use! We do use many utensils made of fine China clay, glass, non-stick materials, microwaveable stuff, unbreakable cookware which "look" clean if you merely rinse in water; but that does not rid them of the bacteria which feed on the left-over food crumbs and dirt. We ensure that our cookware and cutlery are *cleaned* properly, i.e., *sanitised* rightly to be bacteria-free, before a reuse.

Not only what we use regularly need be cleaned before reuse in kitchen, there are also large number of items - utensils, exquisite crockeries, cutleries etc.- stored in kitchen without regular use. What stays exposed gathers dust. So, cleaning them up periodically, whether used often or not, becomes necessary in a kitchen.

It is a truism that for sustaining anything, it must first be 'maintained' on a regular basis. In the corporate world, they always talk about 'growth' – growth in business, growth in client-base, growth in market share, growth in profit! But unfortunately, many *tenure-based* leaders forget that if care is not taken to first 'maintain' what is already there, a blind chasing of growth may not really yield a 'growth' eventually due to sliding base of existing clientele/business.

Working mothers learn from kitchens how it is important to watch and remedy the maintenance lapses in professional areas. In corporate sector where the property and business belong to no one in particular, see how many times areas needing a real overhaul end up getting a periodic wash-up only, or a bit of sanitisation, or just a face-lift/beautification/ window dressing, and hiding the dirt under the carpet, instead of doing neat works.

How many in leadership roles truly *value* the *maintenance functions*? Even though everyone knows that *growth without maintenance* can never lead to *sustainable growth over a long range,* why do bosses often fail to notice or appreciate regular and great work done in maintenance roles, like say, accounts?

While lack of cleanliness and maintenance in the Kitchen can show up its bad effects over a *short* period through your health (stomach upset and other common illnesses), that in corporate sector takes a longer time which usually happens after *the current incumbent's tenure* – hence the lure to *show off* 'results', play the number games, and carry away the trophy! Who bothers what happens after they leave those positions?

True managers and true leaders do not fall prey to this kind of temptation. No wonder, they (and many women leaders trained from kitchen) tend to "clean up" first in case they see something untoward and dirty in what they have inherited in an assignment before launching their growth initiatives. Not only that, they *stay constantly watchful not to allow maintenance functions run into fresh arrears, and not to allow fresh dirt getting added to their achievement figures.*

Another life lesson from maintenance works in kitchen. Just as we clean everything in kitchen regularly to maintain cleanliness and sanitation, so we must take care of the 'maintenance' of our body and mind. We bathe every day to clean our body, as it is exposed to many types of 'dirt' literally. *What about mind?* Mind also stays exposed to many negativities in the external environment that seep deep into our mind unless cleared on a regular and sustained basis, and hence mind also needs regular cleansing of 'dirt', i.e., negative thoughts and limiting beliefs, to 'maintain' sanity and absorb wisdom.

36. Marketing also happens from kitchen

No lesson in leadership is complete without having inputs on how to market. Although marketing is commonly seen as that of some products/ services created by the organisation, it, in fact, boils down to marketing *ideas on solutions to people's needs* –existing, felt, and perceived (as created through marketing or supply side). As they say, *every sale is eventually a purchase of some solution idea. And every marketing strategy is a thought, not a tool.*

Watch the functioning of mothers intently, and you would be startled to observe how intuitively and how consistently they also 'market'! Mostly unaware, they employ some of the very fundamental strategies/ principles of marketing.

1. *Creating value* (i.e., products/services) to market. No prize for guessing, mothers in kitchen cook and create their products, which is food.
2. *Advertising to spread awareness as well as to entice potential customers.* Again, simple to find the parallels from kitchen. You must have gone to your mom and asked inquisitively, licking your lips, *'Aaj khane mein kya hei?' / 'What's there for dinner?' /*

'Huummm... What's cooking today?' Etc. But when you don't ask, you must have noticed how your mother would come to you and announce the delicacies/family favourites she would be preparing, or simply announcing, "Hey guys, some delicious surprise is waiting for you... Don't be late on the table!" to grab your attention and create excitement for checking out her food, and eating.

3. *Creating a basket/array of products and/or services.* Very often, corporates can't rely on merely one product/service. They create more options, more varieties of the same core product, or products complementing the core product. Idea is to recognise that tastes and preferences differ; so, with a *basket* of products/services, more people would find something or other of their choice under one brand. *Think of all the meals mothers place on the table.* It is always a basket – some staples (core) with diverse accompaniments. Mothers always take care to bring in diversity to cater to different needs and preferences of family members, ensuring complementarity and compatibility.
4. *Collecting customer feedback* and making amends/innovations in products/services, or creating new ones as per perceived need of potential customers. I think, the example of mothers asking soon after some dish is done, 'Chakh *ke bata, kaisi bani hei'* (meaning, please taste and tell me how it is), even before serving, is very common in every family. Not that, she herself has not tasted it to know how it has turned out, or to correct lacks, if any. But she puts premium, and rightly so, on how it appeals to those she is going to serve. *Early feedback* very often makes it easy to amend features or address flaws. In corporate world, many new things are first launched on a pilot basis for a very small group of target customers to collect early feedback on how these are working, before letting it out to the whole market. "Kaisi bani hei?" "Namak Mirch sahi hei?" etc. are the parallels to the pilot runs of the corporate world. 😉 *The second layer of feedback,* of course, is sought after the product gets introduced to the whole market; just the way, mothers never tire of asking all on the table about how the food is. *User*

Feedback not only helps you refine your creations, it also boosts your morale.

5. *Packaging.* No need to repeat. Pl go back to 'packaging also matters' discussed earlier. How mothers make their fussy children eat the nutritional, but bitter or not-so-tasty, food items!
6. *Customer surveys.* Many a times, corporates conduct surveys on people's needs for some new products and then go on to introduce that product line, if viable, for sure shot marketing. Similarly, mothers very often discuss the menu with their loved ones before finalising. At times, they even employ the technique of *reverse psychology* to include in the menu the dish *they* would like to prepare, but making it appear as if it is the will of the others☺I recall here my grandmother's weird habit. If you suggest, let us fry the fish today, she would say, Oh... this fish tastes so tasty if curried with mustard paste! If you say, let us make a fish curry today, she would say, Oh... fish fry, crispy and fresh from the tawa would be so delicious...! Just the reverse of what you suggest. So, my mother used to tell her that she would do this (opposite of what she actually wanted to do) today, and pat comes, No, let us do that (the opposite). So, my mom gets to do what she originally intended to do – she 'marketed' it using reverse psychology! ☺
7. *Customer delight and goodwill through unexpected thoughtful add-ons/gifts/incentives.* Observe how mothers coax hyper children to eat the normal, or healthy but not-relished, food with an enticement to give them an ice-cream or any favourite sweet, or allow them to play outside/watch a comic show etc., if they finish their food without throwing tantrums. At the core, these are some of the marketing strategies that mothers deploy, just like corporates give add-ons, like one free with two bought, extra of the same above a threshold etc. etc. The strategy here is to pair up your product on sale with something else as extra, that the buyer gets only when the core product is sold.
8. *Creating Memories.* Apart from food, the core product from cooking, kitchen also creates something else which is highly powerful in driving customer choice, hence marketing.

Memories! Cherished nostalgic memories of *'Ghar ka khaana' (Homely Food)*, *'Ma ki hath ka khaana'* (Mom-made food), that we subconsciously keep on searching even in hotel and restaurant food, when away from home and mother. *The warmth, comfort, and trustworthiness of home-cooked food with mother's love lend extra emotional dimensions to our dining experience.* Corporate marketing advertisements also try to create a parallel emotional dimension, at least through a tag line, to make their target group find a connect to their own cherished memories about that product, or similar products. Even in the food market, you must have noticed how some food-joints, advertisers of food items try to rekindle that memory (with taglines like, "Ma ki hath ki swad yaad aajayegi" (meaning... Brings back the memories of Mom's food). After all, memories are not just memories of what happened (i.e., facts without feelings), they are triggers for evoking similar *emotions*! And any great market strategist knows how *very often* eventually a sale is all about purchase of some thought/idea that *connects* to a client's emotions and feelings *based on a past delivery* of a similar product/service. Consumer behaviour does not necessarily get driven by logic/rationale always. Here it is interesting to observe how mothers go about creating these memories in us about some specific food, not just as a one-time short-term memory, but as a long-term memory that gets triggered even after ages with proper cues. Memories need grooves to become long-term, capable of evoking similar feelings and emotions as the first time. Mothers are brilliant at spotting the specific taste preferences of each of their children. Once they catch you relishing specific dishes/recipes, they re-create these at intervals as a gesture of love, and/or as a reward for you for doing something positive/necessary. "Finish your homework before going to play outside, and I will make ... (your favourite dish) for dinner." "Be a nice kid when the guests are here, and I will bake you your favourite brownie this weekend once they leave." This way, by repeating the relished food and combining it with positive behaviour, mothers create grooves of happy memories in the deeper level of a child's mind, that get carried forward into adulthood, even old age. A small trigger of smell, hunger, storytelling, reminiscing creates a craving for that food again and again, ending with that feel of happiness.

Mothers may be doing this to elicit some behaviour change, and not exactly to 'market' that specific food. But observant mothers do notice how this also amounts to marketing. After all, one of the strategies of marketing is to *influence customer choice* for purchase by creating and triggering happy memories about same/similar products. If I had loved using Dove soap the first time itself, very likely I would stick to my choice for long even after launching of other brands in the market promising same properties. Memories lead to repeat customer choices, as well as prompt you to act as goodwill ambassadors. When you love the food in a particular hotel, not only you come back to it, you bring your family and friends. You refer and recommend that hotel to others!

Thus, creating a happy memory is tremendously important in marketing! No wonder, every marketing strategist draws upon this. Example of the marketing initiatives of Nestle India to revive their Maggi market is brilliant in this context. As known to everyone, Instant Noodle has become a comfort food for a whole new generation that has virtually grown up with it. Comfort food is usually the ones with which lots of warm and happy memories go. Nestle cashed on this idea of marketing memories. and ran a wide competition of *Maggi stories, stories with pictures of your memorable incidents with Maggi, the myriad ways you have re-invented this ready-to-cook dish at different places in different situations.* And it clicked! Maggi is back!

So interesting to note, how all these basic principles of effective marketing keep on getting practiced from kitchen, mostly without being noticed. For a mother who handles both a kitchen and a leadership position, the lessons get carried forward from one space to another seamlessly.

Mothers not only market whatever tangible they create in kitchen, i.e., food, but amazingly they also market and transmit important 'values' like say, sense of punctuality, sense of responsibility, sense of dependability, sense of trust and being trustworthy, sense of belongingness etc. Because what they create is not a mere food item, *it is a statement of their personal values*, too, like love, care, integrity, creativity – and their attitude, which impacts the people at the other end significantly.

Is it not said, mother is the first teacher of a child? Not only in formal education, but in transmission of values and life skills. How many times one sees a mother literally running after the child to make them finish their food so that they do not get delayed for the school bus? Umpteen times, I am sure. This is an every-family-drama in a certain phase of life. Here, observe, unless the mother brings the food to the table on time, every time, day-in & day out, will she be able to really convince the child, or rest of the family even, to imbibe punctuality as a critical quality? Managing the kitchen not only drives her to be punctual always, it also helps her market 'punctuality' to her family members. It is usually observed, a professional/job-holder/a working couple is ordinarily punctual, if the spouse–in-charge-of-kitchen (ordinarily wife), or the maid, is punctual too, especially in cooking and serving meals.

37. Learning how to make choices in Trade-Off situations

Regular provision of food for your family is a game of various kinds of trade-offs. Observe at a deeper level. Start from the menu itself. You select dishes, major ones on health and nutrition parameters combined with one/a few side ones that excite the taste buds. Clearly the primary trade-off is between healthy versus tasty food, i.e., between what is good versus what looks/tastes good. Next you deal with the trade-off between *appeals to all* Vs *favourite of one/a few*. Then between recipes requiring *readily available ingredients* Vs *have to get from the market*; between *fast cooking* (less time taken) Vs *slow cooking* (better retention of nutrients and taste); between *organic* (expensive but pure) Vs *regular* products (reasonable quality at normal price); between *what budget permits* Vs *what is beyond*; between *diversity in each menu* Vs *quick repetition of dishes*; between *wastage* Vs *innovative reuse*, etc. The list goes on.

Just as in all life situations, any decision involves weighing pros & cons, and so, in spirit, becomes a choice out of a trade-off, kitchen also throws up similar situations regularly. Mothers soon learn to make these choices thoughtfully and judiciously. This trait also gets carried forward from kitchen to their other workspaces. It undoubtedly helps in cultivating a habit of *discerning the visible as well as invisible trade-offs in every situation*, while making a decision. *More significantly, the invisible ones, because what is essential is very often not visible to casual eyes.* Mothers *care*, so they put in extra efforts to weigh the situation, see the trade-offs, and make a considered choice. It becomes such a deep-rooted characteristic trait in them that after a while, it comes to them as a second nature without they even being conscious of it.

Undoubtedly, when you are in a habit of looking at both pros and cons, able to 'see' what is visible and what is hidden, your decisions are more likely to be well-rounded and beneficial.

38. Creating Buffers

Almost habitually, we mothers use large, over-sized vessels on stove when we are going for open cooking of say, lentils, or dalma (a typical dish of Odisha in which dal and vegetables are combined), or biriyani etc. Or for that matter, when we boil milk. Cooking regularly gives the mothers and cooks a fair idea on what is likely to swell in volume or rise a lot with a risk of spilling over. So, to be on the safer side, they start with *a larger pot than what they think they need.* This works as *a cushion* against fluctuations in volume, and the risk of spilling over.

You don't fill the vessel/pot/container up to the brim while cooking, as you learn from your own experience that some extra space must be left for the liquid to rise on boiling, the lentils to create some scum and foam on boiling, the lentils/beans/grains to swell up in size on cooking etc. You learn that it is better to have less final content in a bigger pot than needed, than content spilling over the brim from a small pot. This is one brilliant example of *creating buffer*, in the context of space.

There can be umpteen examples from kitchen on buffers. Mothers always cook a little more than they think would be consumed by their family. This especially happens for sure when guests are to be entertained. This principle of *better to be left with some extra than falling short* is a greatly helpful tactic in many situations in life – both in personal and professional spaces. *For example, in the context of punctuality, it may get reflected in a habit of leaving home for office/any destination a little earlier than required keeping in view the normal travel time plus a sufficient margin for sudden eventualities on the way like unexpected traffic, or diversions or a vehicle problem.*

In professional work spaces, *when you are in charge of leading teams, this insight from kitchen puts you in a safe spot, by keeping you ready for unexpected eventualities.*

- You will always create buffers in timelines for important goals by setting deadlines for your team members which are not the real deadlines for you as the person eventually responsible for an outcome, leaving a time cushion for yourself to intervene. As a head, I always used to intervene at the *11th hour* if things were not going right.
- It will then be your habit to always be prepared with something extra for *strategic retreats in negotiations,* i.e., putting into your deal some extra clauses/conditions, or margin over your true intended price etc. which can be given up easily in a negotiation without harming your interests. Great negotiators always shout out for more than they really want/need, so that they can roll back their demand a bit without compromising with their real interests, and the deal can end on a win-win note for both sides.
- You will also tend to stay ready for exigencies in terms of talent buffers. To face exigencies, effective managers very often train more employees than required, i.e., some employees other than the ones assigned to the specific jobs, thereby creating *stand-by teams* as buffers. These are very important managerial strategies for effective operational management.

Basically, creating a buffer reflects an attitude of preparedness with something extra in terms of time and resources to meet exigencies, if any. Kitchen definitely helps one imbibe this attitude.

39. Secure Your Connects

Kitchen keeps reminding us: *Mind your Connects!*

Connects must be under thoughtful watch always, if you value that connection.

In kitchen, various types of cookware are used. Many of these, especially pans, saucepans, kadais, woks, griddles usually have *handles*, or some kind of grips to help us hold these when the main body is hot, for convenient use. These handles/grips are connected to the main body by fastening small screws, nuts etc. That is for our convenience of use. But that does not mean this connect is permanent. *Over time, through use/misuse, these screws get loosened and unless tightened in time as soon as slightly loose, they fall off unnoticed and we face much inconveniences in using their main bodies without the handles.*

Screws are small connects - but must be under watch for tightening before they fall off, for the bigger part of the cookware (the main body of the pan) to remain as useful as it was intended to be.

Similarly, in our relationships also, both personal and professional, we must always be careful about small gestures that keep the connect intact. A small "Hi", "How are you", "What's the matter, you look stressed", "May I help you", a pat here, a call there, a show-up just to comfort etc. There are many little gestures that must always be *visibly made for the relationship to thrive, get renewed and refreshed, without being taken for granted.*

Have you watched the movie "A Dog's Way Home"? Wonderful! Ends with, the Invisible Leash... that is of LOVE! In our lives as social beings, we are *connected* to people of all kinds and relationships. *What truly binds us is this invisible leash of care and love. Stronger it is, stronger is the bond.* The moment this leash converts to that of non-concern/hate, the bond truly weighs us down as bondage. *Not only people, we are also chained to past events (dead weights) through an invisible leash.* In those cases, however, we have to snap that leash to move ahead. So, it is always beneficial to be mindful of all connects – most connects need be secured, and some limiting ones need be snapped.

Kitchen in many ways as discussed in various contexts in this book teaches us to identify how to secure our connects by strengthening the invisible leash of love, care, and concern.

As one carries forward this apparently small lesson from kitchen to other spheres of life, one realises how small gestures are absolutely necessary for deeper bonds.

40. Dealing with Problem of Plenty

Everything matters in some way or other. But you must learn how to let go of those that matter the least, or have outgrown their utility. At least periodically. This is also the most significant part in the art of organizing.

Kitchen teaches very well how to notice this problem in the first place, i.e., *what is in plenty,* and then how to deal with it.

Before proceeding further, let us first awaken to the *Problem of Plenty*, as ordinarily we go with *'The more the merrier'* in most cases.

There is a real problem in plenty, and it is very discernible if we analyse one case only – that of *information* we go on gathering. With mushroom growth of social media and Internet alone, we are all the time bombarded with information, and the more we consume information, the more our attention gets squandered away in unnecessary information of little value. We are left with attention-deficit for focussing on matters which truly matter to us. Not only in case of information, but practically in *excess holding* of anything, we also hold an avoidable problem. Reason is simple. It *consumes your attention*; *over-fills your space*; it makes it *messy and problematic to retrieve* when a specific piece, soft or hard resource, is actually needed.

A typical experience most of us have in life is: over a period, we tend to gather huge information on something, constantly postponing its sifting for segregating chaff from the grains (insights, knowledge, wisdom, and application). Somehow, we love to hold on to all in our mind space, majority of times, without any mental prioritization for relevance and importance from time to time. Result? If you are asked on anything specific, you might draw a blank first, unable to choose where to begin from. Worse still, with computers around, you save information even without reading with the pious hope of reading *someday*, and the junk in your digital memory merely keeps growing, filling up scarce space for new materials.

A simple example from singing. I sing, people know that and request me to sing on every possible opportunity. But believe me, I start wondering which one to sing from the large number of songs that I know, although I recall many songs and keep singing extempore while in kitchen or bathroom! I just fail to recall on tab! It is a problem of plenty for me. What I should do to tackle this issue is to make short lists of songs for public performance. But even that involves scanning through a l..o..t.., and that never happens.

Similarly, over 2-3 decades of cooking, I have already explored, learnt, and made literally scores of dishes with the same major ingredients. But ask me one which is my favourite, I cannot answer. Ask me to share 2-3 of my most liked recipes, I will pause and start thinking. *Issue is: so many are there that my recall button takes time to scan through memory and cull out.* Like stored files in computer on any one topic. Longer the file in memory, more it gets pressed down, longer the time to retrieve if your hard disk is also otherwise full.

Of course, I have *acknowledged* this problem, and learnt to deal with it in case of at least issues involving *physical space* management, like kitchen storage, house organization etc.

Once we acknowledge and comprehend the problem, we also start learning to get to its solutions.

Yes, the solutions to the problem of plenty lie in periodically pressing the *delete* button, or *discarding.* Our humble kitchen throws up these lessons frequently. *You just need to observe how you are behaving in kitchen and carry that forward to other spheres of your lives.*

Utensils/cookware in kitchen: A real area of concern from 'problem in plenty' perspective. We do have a tendency to hoard, especially in today's world of Amazon/Flipkart/Marts/Malls. How much do we really need or use? In the process of accumulation, we only end up over-stacking our limited racks and drawers, overhead storage spaces in kitchen, in fact whatever little space is available anywhere in the house. What a mess! But ordinarily, we also run through our "treasured possessions" periodically and heartily discard/donate away the old/already-much-used stuff. *Subconsciously at least, in kitchen we are alive to the limitedness of space as well as limited genuine need for these cookware and utensils. We do periodic scan of the store-worthiness of our kitchen belongings.*

If you consciously observe this pattern, you can pick up the fundamental rule of dealing with the problem of plenty: *Discard the useless tangibles and delete the unworthy intangibles.*

The above solution pre-supposes its earlier steps: i. certain things are rendered unusable through wear and tear while still in use (coating coming off from non-stick pans, handle breaking from an already much-used pan, for example); discard or donate them asap; ii. run through your stock periodically to sort out and shorten the list of store-worthy items/ documents.

A great headache in kitchen for me personally is having plenty of recipes. Ordinarily it is helpful, but a problem beyond a point. For example, let me take two examples – fish curry and mutton curry.

We are fish eaters and fish curry is a common dish on most of the days. So, it helps to have multiple recipes to beat the boredom of cooking and eating. Usually, I document recipes for passing on to my daughters (knowledge management process, you know 😊). When I go through my documentation of various recipes on fish curry, many with slight twists, I myself get confused and often forget all those recipes unless uniquely different from one another. So, I created a list of only 8-10 recipes that bring in variety, *and deleted all others*. It helped. In any case, while actually cooking on a day-to-day basis, I do give twists often, so there is no *need* to document them, for they are rarely referred to; plus, for on-the-spot improvisations, mind works creatively without a reference document.

Coming to mutton curry, it is not a regular dish. On special occasions, or at long intervals of a few weeks, we eat it. Due to obvious health reasons to avoid red meat. So naturally, although there are a large variety of *Indian* mutton recipes that I know, that I have learnt from YouTube and Cookery Shows alone, *my tendency is to prepare it the way we love it the most*! So, retaining too many recipes is just a wastage of time, energy, and space. I, therefore, retain just 3-4 recipes, which are way different from one another and are made if mutton is prepared in slightly shorter gaps, to infuse an element of diversity. I have simply deleted the rest to avoid getting trapped into the problem of plenty. Guess what, when I try out some recipe different from the most liked 3-4 ones, my family members comment "Oh! our usual recipe is way tastier; why did you make this?" So not worth maintaining a long list of recipes that are not going to be made.

Thus, an important lesson from kitchen is to realise that it is very important to *take stock of* all you have in your mind, or on hard disk or in your house; *sort them out* on priority/importance/relevance parameters; and *let go of* them as per need, as far as possible.

These are all very common lessons life teaches us in all domains. Kitchen certainly is one of them, and you merely need be mindful to listen to what it is constantly trying to tell you.

41. Kitchen and Neuroplasticity

Sounds apparently like a tall claim. But No.

What, after all, is Neuro Plasticity? Broadly speaking, it is the ability of the brain to modify, change and adapt! *It is about ability to create new neural paths in the brain by doing habitual things in different ways, and/or doing new and different things.* It is about *re-wiring of brain*, reorganizing its structure, functions, or connections. It is the ability of neural networks in brain to change through growth and reorganization. This happens when the brain gets rewired to a function in some way that differs from how it previously functioned, and gets facilitated through *creative pursuits* - art, music, writing, learning a new way to go to the frequented destinations, learning to do daily tasks differently etc.

Neuroplasticity is a must for agility and change!

Simply reflect on what happens when we go creative with most tasks related to kitchen, from recipe explorations, to multitasking tiny tasks, to continuing to manage when injured in say right hand or certain key fingers! We have already seen how our creativity gets stimulated, and how we keep finding many other ways to manage the same things.

In multi-tasking of a bundle of tiny tasks that we were talking about, it is never done in the same order/sequence/way. That stimulates neuroplasticity.

Similarly, the usual staple recipes that we generally have on our daily menus. Say, dal (lentils and legumes). Mothers don't cook the same dal every day, though some dal preparation is almost a *must* on an Indian lunch platter with rice and roti. They change the dal, or dal combo or the spices and tempering, that really makes the dal taste different, look different, acquire different texture each time. That way, the brain does not get stuck with one default mode recipe of this often-cooked ingredients. Brain keeps getting rewired and becomes adaptive to frequent changes.

One more small example from personal experience. Preparing Saaga (green leaves or entire tiny plants of some kind like amaranth, spinach, Indian spinach, morning glory, fenugreek etc.). In my region, the most basic/standard process to do Saaga is: have a tempering of phutan (seeds of mustard, cumin, black cumin, fennel, and fenugreek) in mustard oil, along with chili, chopped onion, and lots of crushed garlic, and then add the chopped Saaga, salt to taste. Saute till done and serve hot and fresh from wok. It is super simple and ultra tasty, besides having a high health quotient.

But, I don't necessarily do it this way every time. Sometimes, I skip onion. Sometimes, I skip the phutan, and just use green chili and lots of crushed garlic. Sometimes, I add fried and crushed badi (dried lentil dumplings) on top. Sometimes, I add badi and grated coconut on top, with a tempering of just cumin and dry red chili. Sometimes, I add some finely chopped vegetables like potato, pumpkin, ridge gourd, brinjal etc. Sometimes, I add a bit of mustard-chilli-garlic paste towards finishing, and a sprinkle of raw mustard oil on top, especially when I use small prawns in Saaga like poi (Indian Spinach) or pumpkin/bottle-gourd leaves.

So, the point is: since I keep doing even a basic recipe in very many different ways, my brain gains in neuroplasticity. In other words, get creative and keep your brain agile to adapt.

In fact, the entire discussion on improvisation, innovation, and creativity in kitchen shines light on how kitchen promotes neuroplasticity.

Add to that, what mothers do when they get injured while chopping, frying, draining hot liquid etc. Or otherwise. They no longer can use the same fingers/hand usually utilized for these purposes for quite some time till they heal at least partially. But that does not make them stop doing those chores. They find out alternative ways, alternative fingers/hand to do those immediately. I understand, it might be slightly difficult to visualize and understand this for readers who have never had such experience. But it keeps happening in kitchen and is a good example of neuroplasticity being promoted.

Let us remember something here. Auto-mode/habitual reactions in familiar situations are not always bad for us. Familiar experiences travel along well-established neural networks that already contain the information of a particular way of relating, a habitual pattern of response based on past experience, and its predictable outcome, *that works for you.* Reactions become automatic so mind doesn't have to waste valuable time in processing information and making a new decision in each situation. *That helps in many ways in our day-to-day normal functioning. But in critical situations, auto-mode behaviour patterns mostly prove harmful as you react, instead of responding.* So, changing your behaviour patterns becomes necessary for a fuller life experience. And to effect change, you need neuroplasticity.

We are not hard-wired for life. With new experiences, new neural pathways are created. This rewiring of our brain from time to time makes us better adaptive to new experiences. Now scientific researches have already shown that we can rearrange brain cell connections (neuroplasticity) as well as produce new brain cells (neurogenesis) *throughout our lives* by creating new experiences consistently.

As we age, we are always advised to keep our brain agile, enhance/at least maintain neuroplasticity by doing daily routines in different ways, reading, and writing and getting into creative activities more to prevent/ arrest mental degeneration. Is it not an eye-opener how mundane kitchen routines and cooking can help us so much in this regard? No wonder, women homemakers are less prone to dementia! My personal observation.

42. Alertness

Alertness that we learn in kitchen over time becomes a second nature to us, coming handy in multiple potentially threatening situations in life. What is significant is: kitchen makes us realise that there is a huge *difference between 'fear psychosis' and 'alertness', although both start from an anticipation of dangers. While the former immobilizes us, the latter prompts us to act but with abundant caution.* As we have already seen, kitchen works are sort of inescapable and we owe a responsibility to feed; and this does not allow us to stop acting even if scared of potential dangers and accidents from fire and sharp tools. *So, over time what we imbibe is alertness and mental presence to avert accidents.* Alertness, not fear psychosis!

I am aware that making a statement like 'kitchen teaches us critical lessons in alertness' sounds like nth order of repetition after all we have already deliberated so far. True. But let me show you *how deeply it gets entrenched* in mothers' character. From personal experience.

Goes without saying, it is a common practice to avoid (as much as feasible) entry of unknown service guys inside the house when the mother or any female member is alone. But let me tell you, that is NOT possible all the time. I have seen, quite often, even if I am alone at home, I must allow outside people, though unknown/partially known like plumbers/electrician/sweepers/occasional cooks etc. or hired aids booked through Apps, simply because they would come during day time only, when your other family members would be out in office/school/college. Every service cannot be slated for holidays. *So, I simply stay alert as they would be working. Kitchen has taught me enough on what happens if I do not stay alert and mentally present in potentially dangerous situations.* So, I have primarily three strategies. First, I make telephone calls to one or two persons, family member as well as some nearby neighbour, telling them loudly enough (so that the outsider can hear it) that someone is doing this servicing. Second, I keep the main door open, bolting just the grill door, which is good enough for carrying sounds, plus for anyone to see from outside what is happening inside. My grill door is specially designed for that. Three, I either hover near the kitchen as I know where my knives etc. are kept (😊), or sit/loiter near the main door, from where I can flee in a second (😊). Don't laugh. And of course, I keep supervising their work, chit chatting with them, with a bold look that shows no sign of fear or nervousness, and always with my cell in hand for immediate use in case of an emergency. Power resides in us only when we believe in our power, transcending fear of 'what if's.

My dear kitchen, please take a bow!

43. Attention, Focus and Concentration

Kitchen is an effective learning platform to make us grasp the correct meaning of important concepts like attention, focus and concentration.

Especially, what these terms mean in a *functionally-wise* sense. Focus and concentration that we are talking about here would be in the context of how to work better in our daily lives, not how to meditate. Meditation starts with attention, gradually building up to focus and ultimately to concentration. Let me keep that deep ideation aside.

In our humble homely kitchen, we learn how it is not *concentration* (the centralisation of attention on one thing), but attention as such (i.e., awareness, peripheral awareness, or total awareness of the immediate surroundings), that takes us far in *engaging* most productively with all the jobs on hand, whether routine, mundane or intellectually stimulating. We need not follow the much-harped-on advice, *'when doing something, just concentrate on that'*. Sorry, it may sound against the conservative wisdom, but what we need is *focus*, not *concentration* in its strict sense which is neither easy to achieve, nor required every time.

At times, we just need to do our own interpretation and have clarity of understanding for ourselves, even if it goes contrary to common sayings. Just like multi-tasking! Albeit, it must stick and work for us in most situations, not just in one specific instance, lest it becomes an excuse for some undesirable comfort of ours. Let me explain.

Attention is what we all understand it to be in general: *mindfulness.* So, it is simply about *awareness* about self and the immediate surroundings, *i.e., inclusive* of awareness about the periphery. If I am cooking, say, stir-frying vegetables, I know *consciously* that I am stir-frying; but I am *also aware enough* to notice and drive out a fly that is moving towards me. *I am aware* when the pressure cooker on the other burner on high flame gives out the first whistle and I have to change the switch to sim mode. *I am aware of what is happening around me. So, attention is inclusive.*

Attention becomes *focus,* or focussed attention, when we pay *maximum* attention to the *point in centre* (the primary task on hand), but with a peripheral awareness, i.e., all the time alive to what is happening around. So, *focus is also inclusive awareness,* but with a higher degree of attention to what you are doing currently.

Concentration, on the other hand, is centralization of attention on one thing, completely oblivious to what goes around. So, its nature is exclusive. While concentrating, we put all our attention on one single point exclusive of everything else. We might have heard of stories of sages in ancient times going into deep *meditation* in seclusive places for spiritual enlightenment for long periods completely unaware of the surroundings, so much so that even termites/snakes used to build their mound nests covering their body and they were not even aware of it. That is concentration. Deep meditation certainly needs concentration.

"Attention is not the same thing as concentration. Concentration is exclusion; attention, which is total awareness, excludes nothing." J. Krishnamurthy ('Freedom from the Known')

I found this statement very enlightening in gaining clarity on these terms myself.

'Focus' and 'concentration' ordinarily get used in colloquial language interchangeably, which is flawed. What we mean most of the time is *focus* that makes more sense in the context of day-to-day lives.

Take the example of a *table lamp*. It casts maximum light on a tiny area for reading, but simultaneously spreads out its beams on the surrounding creating a ring of illumination that gets lesser and lesser bright as beams go farther. This still makes the surrounding objects visible enough. Similarly, when we talk of focus, it is about the *central* task of highest priority that we must do at/during a certain time period, while our attention is like the 'light' of the lamp, most of which is getting beamed onto that central task, but at the same time, all other tasks and happenings in the surrounding are also receiving this light (attention) as well, though faintly. We are *aware* of all that, though not attending to them at that time so long as we keep working with focus on our central task.

There is another side to focus as well. There are times when you are not attending to the prime responsibility at the moment, and yet you keep it at the centre of the ring of your attention. *Think about a mother with a baby.* Even if she is a stay-at-home mom, check out how occupied she is all the time with the house hold chores! But in the midst of all these household chores, how she focuses on her baby; how her attention is all the time on her baby as the centre of her world! No, she cannot afford to hold her baby in her arms all the time to protect her *to the exclusion* of all her other duties and responsibilities. Even when she is, say cooking in the kitchen, she makes sure that the baby is made to stay nearby from where the latter could be heard, or watched over. She goes on doing her chores as neatly as needed or possible at the moment, but she stays attentive, alert to the safety and need of her child. Attention does not stray away from the centre of responsibility.

To reiterate, focus does not mean exclusion; it means attention. Complete awareness of what is going on around, what all are our duties and responsibilities; and you go on attending to them one after another as per the hierarchy of priority, while at the same time keeping the top most priority at the centre with full attention even if you are not attending to it right at that moment.

Observe a driver. As he focuses on his driving, he is not only paying attention to what is in front of him, but also to what is behind, the traffic movements, the traffic signals, road conditions etc., i.e., the general environment around him. Recollect your own experience on a road trip along ghat roads to a hill station. The driver is busy driving along serpentine roads, soft music is playing, captivating views of the mountain, the lush greenery, the rustling river flowing by the side over rocky beds... Nature presenting its pristine beauty in a majestic way! You are enjoying this deeply with a mind that is *sans* tension or too many thoughts. *Yet* when the driver negotiates a sharp bend, or a narrow stretch, or crosses other vehicles, you do get mindful. *You are engrossed, yet not lost but aware! Cooking is almost like this – you stay engrossed, yet not lost. Focussed, yet aware of other things in the surroundings. You simply cannot manage cooking and kitchen if you must concentrate your attention exclusively on doing only one thing at a time.*

In our day-to-day lives, what we need is focus in say 99% of times, not concentration, although we say loosely, concentrate on what you are doing. Yes, we need concentration of attention in a few cases, like meditation, or say while writing an exam paper, or say working upon some complex tasks that need your exclusive attention at some particular stage. For example, those specific few seconds when you are going to put stuff for deep frying into hot oil, classical music rendition, a scientific experiment in some critical stage that does not simply allow any distraction etc. In fact, not many examples are there when concentration is truly required. Success is all about focus in most cases, *as it is not in our control generally to shut off all the stimuli that keep coming at us from our surroundings.* As I am typing this,

I am aware of all the honking from the street, birds chirping, wind making rustling sound in the leaves of the nearby trees, faint sound of random people talking etc. *We seldom live in a vacuum.* So, for success, we must learn to develop the ability of being simply aware of our periphery, yet continuing to do what we are doing with *utmost* attention (not *exclusive* attention), by managing the distractions.

We can say, focus is continuing work without getting distracted *uncontrollably.* And this is what we need the most in life. And this is what mothers learn in the kitchen very soon and very effectively, as they keep their antennae up for say, the baby crying, the other dish on the other burner that is cooking simultaneously, the other mini tasks that she is multitasking as she cooks etc., but all the time paying enough attention to what she is on at a particular moment.

Kitchen thus gives another insight, that paying attention to your environment, i.e., peripheral awareness, doesn't necessarily reduce the attention you pay to your work. It could be quite the opposite. Similarly, in corporate life when you head, you work on your personal focus areas, while paying attention to overseeing delegated areas. You cannot obviously 'concentrate' on your work with exclusive attention shutting off to a score of issues that come to you as the leader in the middle of working on your personally responsible tasks.

Cooking teaches us how to *focus* on the dish we are cooking, and when to absolutely *concentrate* on it to avoid a disaster. For example, suppose we are sauteing the spice paste for a curry. We have to focus on it for a few minutes until it can be left on low fire; otherwise, we would simply burn the spices. Say, we are roasting semolina in clarified butter(ghee) for halwa/shira/kada prasad. Even if it is on low to medium heat, we have to constantly stir it till golden brown and fragrant. We cannot simply leave it, and do something else even for a few seconds. Here it is very close to concentration. Whereas, suppose our recipe for curry is done till water can be added. We can add water, cover, and leave on high heat. Till a boil comes, we just have to stay attentive though we can shift to something around that place. Means, we still have to focus on our curry. But once the boil comes in a few minutes, we can reduce heat to sim and leave it unattended to for a good 10-15 mins as per the cooking time needed, and do other things, keeping the time factor to finish it in our *peripheral attention*.

While working in kitchen, situations would abound which teach us not only what focus is and what attention is; but also let us understand how through peripheral attention, we can better manage all our tasks.

If we observe ourselves keenly, we can realise that while working seriously, our mind *seeks to* minimize sources outside its focus. However, it *cannot* completely shut off all its attention to the surrounding environment. Rather, you would observe that your mind keeps *perceiving sensory signals from it* though a bit unconsciously. This becomes very evident when you are deep into reading or writing, but still aware of and in fact enjoy, the chirpings of birds, at the same time! At other times, when you are working, there may be TV sounds, smartphone notification sounds, machines making huge noises in the nearby construction site, continuous traffic, and horn sounds from nearby main road etc. etc. If these sensory signals perceived through peripheral attention disturb you, then only these become harmful distractions. But if you can ignore, manage, or enjoy these signals, these might actually act as productivity boosters. We will talk more about the value of even distractions, in the context of focus, in the next segment.

Personally, I can tell you, as a child, I used to do Maths very well as I would be listening to music/songs on radio. I have seen many youngsters working seriously on computers with music playing very softly. This is peripheral attention, which is a part of attention and focus. You don't really concentrate, in its strict sense, on one thing ever.

Many final year school children often ask: how to concentrate on studies? I say, do not try to *concentrate, try to focus*. Concentration means you forget everything else and direct your entire being onto one thing. If you concentrate on studies only, you would end up studying or worrying about studying all the time. Then what about your food, sleep, play, other engagements, and interactions? *A relaxed state of being is required to 'absorb', 'retrieve' and 'present' what you have studied, when writing the examination paper.* And that needs FOCUS on studies, not concentration! Always remember the examples of mothers multi-tasking and how a table lamp lights up the focus area. Similarly, as an individual you have a number of things to take care of, and that include your own self, for the simple reason that if you do not take care of your own well-being (achieved only when you stand integrated on a healthy body-mind-spirit level), you cannot take care of things relating to your other roles. But the good thing is, you have multiple goals through which to reach your ultimate purpose, and they are spread over various stages of life and timeframes. During any specific phase of life, or at any particular point of time, all goals do not come as important and urgent. This understanding helps in focussing on one goal while keeping others in peripheral attention.

So, the key to finishing well lies in prioritisation and focusing on tasks which are important and urgent during that specific period, while at the same time being mindful to the need for other things which are important, so that you can focus on them at the appropriate time before they become urgent due to non-attention.

For students, "studies" is the 'baby' that is at the centre of all their priorities. So, they must focus on it, while still paying attention to and attending to other priorities like food, play, sleep, and normal social life.

Paying attention is awareness/mindfulness.

Paying *precise/utmost* attention is focus.

Paying highest and exclusive attention is concentration.

So beautifully our homely kitchen brings out these important perspectives!

44. Value of distractions

As mentioned earlier, we do not live in a vacuum, nor can we shut off to the multitude of sensory signals perceived through peripheral attention in order to focus attention on what we are doing. If these peripheral stimuli disturb you, then only these become harmful distractions.

Well, we commonly believe that distractions are harmful. Mostly this is the case; but *not always*.

Kitchen helps us learn why and how to avoid distractions so that we can focus. But the beauty is: it simultaneously gives us a valuable perspective on why we should also allow some kind of *distractions in certain cases to help us re-focus*. On when and what kind of distractions would benefit us rather than harming! No need to elaborate on how kitchen teaches us to avoid distractions, failing which disasters can strike in the world of cooking and kitchen, while literally playing with fire and dangerous tools. We have already discussed it enough. Now, let us understand, how kitchen teaches us to discern *helpful* distractions in certain situations.

Focus on one thing at a time! We all have grown up with this stricture from our elders and well-wishers. No issue with that so long as we are clear on what it really means. Please recall our deliberations in previous segment, as also in multi-tasking.

I usually keep my mobile in an open rack adjacent to my kitchen, which is almost at the centre of my flat. While at home, I can hear the rings and beeps wherever I might be. The other day, I was cooking. Was finished with sauteing the spice paste, had poured water for gravy which had come to one full boil. I lowered the heat to sim, covered it, just when a phone call came. I came out of the kitchen and took the call. It was from a well-known ex-colleague. As we chit-chatted, he asked, if I was free. I said, for the time being, yes! I told him, I was mid-way through cooking, but 'relatively' free as my curry does not need my presence or hands or even full focus for a good 10-12 mins. So, I took the call. If I were mid-way through, say, draining steaming hot cooked rice, I would not have taken this call; as my hands would not have been free then, draining could not have been left mid-way, plus I would have focussed on draining to avert accident. This is the difference – you need not focus on just one thing (standing near the curry waiting for it to get over), if simple multi-tasking is possible due to *an empty time window* popping up, or different faculties and body parts are required for other tasks, even as you generally keep the primary task within the range of your focus. *The other tasks in such cases are distractions, but beneficial ones that act as time-savers, or mood boosters.* So, we must have clarity that the 'one thing' in 'Focus on one thing at a time' must be such that it cannot be combined with something else at the same time and calls for your full attention, i.e., distractions would adversely affect its performance. Usually, this means focussing on one 'project' at a time, not always on one 'task'. Even in some circumstances, you can focus simultaneously on separate projects, but that requires availability of robust support systems for effective delegation. One person singlehandedly can never do that.

In fact, every activity that we attend to other than the primary task in any multi-tasking in kitchen is a 'distraction', as it *pulls us away from* the primary task. But these are welcome as time-savers, or mood-boosters. Interestingly, some examples of multi-tasking even fly on the face of the claim that mind cannot do things simultaneously! We do, at times. But yes, only *habitually* wherein mind does not have to 'process' or 'decide' much. I sing while cooking, and that is possible, because singing comes as a *habit* to me without zero stress in kitchen (as I am not singing for others) in respect of correct lyrics, or correct tune, or a good voice. A large part of cooking also comes to me as a *habit* involving not much thinking. On top of it, motor activities (not too much mind application) predominate in cooking many oft-cooked dishes. So, a distraction like singing while cooking acts rather as a *traction* by keeping me closer to the cooking task, taking the boredom element out of it.

And yes, while drafting an analytical article on some complex theme, or writing a book, rightly chosen distractions are not only beneficial in the sense of recharging you to re-focus, but also can become necessary for getting *splashes of fresh ideas*. When you concentrate or think hard, your mind might get jammed, or stop responding for a while. If you notice this, don't try harder dwelling on that point; take a break, or just leave it for the day, if you can. You would observe how miraculously ideas start coming at the most unexpected moments, or after you wake up the next morning. When your consciously thinking mind is allowed some rest, the sub-conscious mind takes over. So, chill! Distractions may just be misnomers at times. Check out yourself how it is working for you, and decide.

What is distraction, after all? Something that *interrupts my attention and draws me away from what I want to do primarily* with focussed attention. If distraction becomes a habit, or some distracted activities are such as to *suck* me into them uncontrollably, or lead to a mind *dispersed over* many other things at the same time, then I am unable to sustain focus required for success in my professional as also personal life. So, it is of critical importance to know if the specific distractions in any situation are harmful or not.

My thumb rule: Ask the following questions.

Why do I need some distractions at some point of focussing on something important?

How long do I engage in the distracted activities?

Am I getting *sucked* into these distractions?

Am I getting into a dispersed-mind mode, thinking about/trying to do too many other things, moving away from the primary task on hand?

Etc.

The answers to these questions lend clarity to me on whether those distractions are good or bad for me at that time.

I am sure, all of us can relate to all/some of the following examples.

- You are in a family get together after a long time. Notifications keep popping up on your cell phone screen and you go on checking them out, faking an embarrassing smile as if these are about very urgent and important matters. You are supposed to have conversations with people who matter to you, as that is highly important to keep these relations nourished. Instead, what are you doing? (harmful)
- You are drafting an article or a book. But every now and then, you scroll your WhatsApp messages to check out, or you get up to munch on something. (harmful)
- You are drafting a manuscript for a book and are working on a particular chapter. But a new idea comes in a splash, that is relevant to some other chapter of the same book. You stop; *land* that idea on a piece of paper, or on a scribble pad, or in a place in the document itself, which can be retrieved later to build on the idea, because sudden ideas, if not landed, get lost. You immediately come back to the chapter you were working on. (beneficial)
- You are cooking, and must finish it by a certain time. A phone call comes from a friend. You put the gas on sim and go on talking and talking, forgetting that your dish is on the verge of getting burnt. You got sucked. (harmful)
- You are sipping a cup of tea, but thinking about the clothes in the washing machine to be dried, the soiled utensils to be done, the menu for the day, the left-over batter that you must use up

today, the breakfast to be made, the application that you must draft today and submit in the bank, the kid's friend's birthday party that you all must attend in the evening, the next chapter in your manuscript, blah, blah...! *Are you in fact drinking your tea?* A typically dispersed mind! Yes, it happens very often when you have too many things to do within a short span. But unless reined in, a dispersed mind would produce no result. (harmful)

- You are deeply into solving a mathematical problem, and get stuck at the last moment despite repeated attempts. You get up, take a round, come back, put some soft music, and get back into the sum. Something magical happens and you solve it! You took a break to get re-charged. (beneficial)
- You have been working on the computer for long hours. Your eyes, your neck, shoulder and back have started hurting and feeling strained. You get up, stretch a bit, and move around. May be, pick up a cup of coffee, too. But you get back after a short break and re-focus on your work. You allowed some distractions to take a break. (beneficial)
- You are humming, singing, listening to music as you are cooking, or while taking your morning walk. (beneficial)

Etc. etc.

So, what is happening? Since our behaviour always gets prompted by external or internal triggers, those same triggers are also responsible for our attention or distraction. Some triggers in the external environment like notification sounds, ringing of a phone, someone calling, loud noises in the environment, or internal triggers like boredom, fatigue, stress, uncertainty, burden of performance, feelings of inadequacy, loneliness etc. make us take our attention *away* from what we really intend to do/ are doing. If it is for reasons of easing our work-related fatigue (physical and/or mental), taking a small break is a distraction, but is beneficial in most cases and can help us in focusing back on the job with a refreshed body and mind. But if it is because subconsciously, we wish to *avoid* performance stress or, feelings of inadequacy/inability to perform, and so we allow ourselves to get triggered to shift to something else, mostly frivolous, then usually these are harmful, and unhealthy distractions merely to escape from bad feelings. Not only we allow our attention to be interrupted, we also get drawn into these distracted activities uncontrollably. Suppose you get distracted and start playing video game, or watching TV, then most likely you stay stuck there, and find it difficult to get back to your original important work. As we are driven by an urge not to face some *lack of our own,* we lose control over ourselves, and allow 'distraction' to get stronger than '*traction*' (any *action that moves us towards what we really want).* Interestingly, even in such cases of avoidance of bad feelings, distractions might sometimes act as powerful tools to ease mental pain, or reduce the impact of painful or negative experiences. You can bounce back after this kind of a break, involving distractions that shift your attention much away from the pain of the negative experiences.

The same activity could be a destructive distraction for one person and helpful for another. It all depends on why you are engaging in the distraction and for how long. Eventually, problems can arise if you *habitually* embrace distractions as a permanent escape from some uncomfortable reality.

Thus, what we should be clear about avoiding is: i. a *dispersed mind*, a fickle mind which starts hopping from one thought/task to another so quickly and serially that nothing gets even the minimum attention span or time required; and ii. a *habitually distracted mind* trying to escape the pain of uncomfortable realities. Other distractions can be managed with a bit of mindfulness.

So, it is of paramount importance to identify and face your own feelings or thoughts behind your attention getting diverted away from the intended primary work. Once you get a hang of it, although you cannot avoid distractions altogether, you can definitely *manage* them to your advantage; or ignore, or at least stop just before it gets harmful. And managing is your own responsibility. You can't go on blaming your lack of success to external distractions all the time, because whether you like it or not, this world will always be full of distractions.

Our humble kitchen awakens us to these important aspects in the context of focus and distraction, too.

45. Diversity is the spice of Life

The need for diversity not only fuels creativity, it also is an absolute *must* to prevent boredom in life, and thus keep up our zest for life. What is life if it is not interesting? So having an appetite for diversity is a great value that each must imbibe and demonstrate always.

Kitchen not only teaches us how need for diversity in food drives creativity, it also demonstrates why it is important to embrace diversity in all spheres of life- not only in kitchen.

Literally, we cannot do without diversity in our food menu across meals. How would it be if you see the same food, even if that one dish that you love the most, in every meal of yours for days together? Does not take rocket science to guess. The law of diminishing marginal utility will start operating immediately, and then you start deriving negative satisfaction. Even if multiple dishes are there on the platter to your choice, but the same menu gets repeated even a second time, forget about for days together, how would you react? Needless to mention, we get bored with repetitions in food very soon. Everyone, without exception, likes to have diversity in meals.

Similarly, look at the ingredients that go into any one dish. These are also diverse. You don't create a dish with one single ingredient only.

It is similar with our day-to-day lives. We would drop dead with utter boredom and lack of zeal to go forward in life if we have to do the same things every day, follow the same routine, interact with only the same set of people, stay inside the same geographical limits. We do create our comfort zones in respect of highly important and sensitive aspects of our life to stay safe. For example, daily morning ablutions! This is an area in which a habitual routine rather serves us well. But say, you only focus on your official duties, ignoring your hobbies, family time, social meets or doing other stuff that really make you come alive. Will you grow as a human being? How long can you survive in a meaningful way? *No wonder, it is said, keep checking the comfort zones you are getting yourselves trapped into. And purposefully, keep coming out.* Travel, read, have fun time with family and friends, make friends with strangers, take new routes to your daily destinations. Even hop and quit jobs to spread your wings to newer skies. Yes, need for neuroplasticity here too!

It is interesting to note how kitchen teaches the significance of diversity in many ways. We have already discussed above taking our dishes and meals as example. We have also deliberated earlier in innovation and creativity how kitchen drives diversity. Just to add a bit more. Take the example of 'Ghanta Tuna' – a typical Odia delicacy (mixed vegetable curries) [other Indian communities also have their typical mixed veg curries, like Undiu of Gujuratis). Literally a large variety of vegetables, almost 20+, go into this traditional curry of ours. Also get added to vegetables are mixed sprouts (whole green gram, whole Bengal gram, whole yellow peas/whole chickpeas), grated coconut, fried Nadi etc. The ghanta truly turns out yummy. There is everything in this dish-taste, texture, fibre, protein and other nutrients, minerals, and water. Exemplifies, *how unity in diversity brings about an elevation in each element's individual character and usefulness.*

The point not to miss is: some of the vegetables used in the ghanta, like over-ripened cucumber, ash gourd, have virtually no taste or flavour *of their own*; *but when mingled with other ingredients* in the mixed curry, *they acquire flavour and taste*, and nicely come together with all other ingredients.

Brings forth a great lesson as to why we need to happily accept and merge in family lives, professional teams as also social groups *despite differences* in temperaments and characteristics of group members! And allow others to do so. *Just as in kitchen, diverse ingredients come together to create amazing dishes, similarly diversity in the workplace can bring about refreshing ideas and perspectives, skills and unique talents that will help drive organizational growth.*

TEAM = Together Each Achieves More. (Recall our discussions on Team Building)

Others in our life can really complement us, if properly appreciated and accepted.

Whatever you are in, wherever you are, *do allow diversity to thrive*, if you truly want an exciting, vibrant journey of work and life. Kitchen shouts out for diversity loud and clear!

46. Importance of having a Not-to-do list alongside a To-do list

There is no need to elaborate on the *To-Do* lists that most of us routinely maintain to attend to tasks on hand as per priority, as also to keep under constant watch all the important milestones we wish to achieve in life, so that we can plan and move forward accordingly.

But we rarely talk about Not-To-Do lists. Well, in kitchen, there is always a *mental* Not-To-do list at least, if not a written one. Items on this list might be things like:

'Don't leave the Gas Cylinder on at night.'

(It can be on To-Do list as well, reading 'Switch off gas cylinder every night'. But it receives much more attention when in Not-To-Do list because now it is about a *danger* to be averted and becomes *non-negotiable* for security reasons. In the maze of too many To-Do items, this might have gone out of sight.)

'Do not light the gas-lighter/matchstick at the slightest smell of gas.'

'Do not leave anything on high flame and go away from there'.

'Do not use ingredients beyond expiry dates especially if not stored in refrigerator.

'Do not use bitter vegetables with other generally favourite vegetables of your family members.'

(It completely ruins the taste otherwise. Bitter vegetables must be included in menu for health reasons, but as separately cooked items. Of course, I know, for a Bengali delicacy named *Shukto, bitter gourd is a must along with other vegetables.* We can treat that as a rare case.)

'Do not multi-task when dry roasting something like semolina/split green gram that need constant (not merely frequent) stirring with attention and heat control.'

(Otherwise, you are sure to burn the bottom layer partially/fully.)

'Don't add salt at initial stage to dishes, if Chinese sauces or cheese are going to be added later in the cooking process.'

(Because these ingredients already contain good amount of salt. So, seasoning must be perfected only after tasting towards the end.)

Etc.

If we observe carefully, the Not-to-do lists in kitchen are often short and contain items which are more in the nature of warnings, to avert dangers, and do not move out of the list at any time. Like permanent items! Moreover, even if we can convert these Not-to-Dos into To-Dos in an affirmative way, I still prefer these to be on a short Not-to-do list. Or, I might call it Not-To-Miss list, instead of Not-To-Do list, for added seriousness.

Idea is: it must receive exclusive attention. To-Do lists usually run quite long and get longer by day, items changing spots with priorities changing often, and items getting scored off on completion. Very often To-Do items keep *getting carried over from one list to the next,* with a risk of some items getting lost in the process. Non-negotiable items running high risk of disasters if not acted upon *without fail* simply cannot form part of a *long and perennially changing list* like the To-Do list.

Kitchen teaches us that the Not-to-do list is as much/more important than the To-do list.

In life, especially in professional life, many leave the items on Not-to-do list unticked in an ambitious pursuit of accomplishing from To-do list by hook or crook. Pause. Always keep checking if you are doing this. That would cost you your soul power and inner peace at the end! Your Not-to-do list may have an item "Never compromise own integrity." An unethically ambitious person, or even a person of weak character may leave this item unticked *when inconvenient,* out of greed and/or fear of backlash.

Realise that it is as important, and in matters of *core ethical and moral values, it is* more important, to tick the Not-to-do list even if that leaves a few items on to-do list unticked. For example, if you are ethical, your Not-To-Do list will have one item "Never cut corners for personal promotion". Your corresponding item on your To-do list will be "Sincerely work and try for elevation to next level by such and such time". In contrast, an ambitious person not caring for values and ethics will simply have a target for promotion on to-do list without a corresponding value-based not-to-do item.

I must add something here. Often it is said, our mind cannot process "NOT" as it processes inputs mostly in visuals. So, it better absorbs ideas framed positively and as concretely as possible. For example, if I say,

'Do not leave the gas cylinder open at night', mind might get confused in visualisation. Whereas, if I say that in affirmative format, 'Switch off the cylinder every night', mind is quick to create a visual of me switching off cylinder, and stores this dictate easily. Perhaps, this is why, not many talk about "Not-To-Do" lists. Personally, I am not sure if this is true or not, as for me 'Nots' also work fine, especially in respect of *value-based non-negotiables*. May be, because I *believe* too strongly in them; and hence they get grooved in my sub-conscious. If I have a principle of not doing something, I just don't do that, come what may.

So, *check it out for yourself* regarding what works for you. For me, "Don't ever steal" works stronger than "Use only your own possessions". Call it by whatever name – Not-to-do, or Not-to-Miss; but do maintain a list of *what you must never do*. Otherwise, you may maintain two lists. One To-Do list containing your priority tasks, that move; and another *short* Must-Do list containing affirmative conversions of uncompromisable value-based, or security-related not-to-do/not-to-miss items in spirit, which are permanent refrains. Work the way it works for you, but always be mindful of this lesson.

Kitchen can become your Zen master, I swear! Heed what all it whispers all the time.

47. Learning the difference between *equality* and *equity*

A mother of several children knows intuitively (because she *cares)* which child *likes* what and *needs* what to stay healthy, happy, and motivated. And she provides accordingly! Observe a mother how she serves food to her kids so rightly according to their age, body type, hunger pattern, health requirements, and taste preferences etc. Some get more, some less. *Is she being unfair and inequal?* No! What she is doing exemplifies *equity*-i.e., maintain justice and well-being for all by ensuring to each according to need. We all keep hearing of *social justice* through *equitable* distribution of basic resources, in the context of a welfare society and the role of government therein, as also *equal* rights as citizens in the eyes of law.

Put in right perspective, when we talk of 'equality' in the context of social justice, it only means equality of 'opportunities' after ensuring some basic critical level of necessities (like food, shelter, clothes, education etc.). Leaders are always looked up to for ensuring this aspect of justice and equity. Observe our mothers and learn how she ensures this in her world of food and nourishment. The key to her insight lies in the fact that *she cares for all her children equally.* 'Equity' follows as a natural consequence, when we ensure 'equality' in *caring,* not necessarily in *sharing* always.

When 'equality' is ensured in 'care' and 'opportunity', and not necessarily in provisions and entitlements, 'equity' prevails.

This insight from mothers, when carried forward to team managements and leadership, facilitates the most effective work environment that enthuses each member to contribute their best. An effective leader does not stick to 'equality' in training, appreciating, hand-holding in respect of each employee although in most of the cases the same remuneration is paid to all in the same position (in a public sector at least). *They bestow personal attention to the needs of different employees to bring out the best in them through differentiated treatment, depending upon their capacity. What matters is equity through just differentiation without unjust partiality.* Not equality in a strict sense. It is said, an equal treatment of unequals is a form of inequality, in fact. We have to get this perspective right for effectively discharging duties and responsibilities as a leader.

48. Moving from Dependence to Self-Dependence to Interdependence

Kitchen is a great learning portal for many life lessons. One of them surely is the perspective we can develop on the triad '*dependence-self dependence-interdependence*' which is essential for clarity on how to reach our potential in any field drawing on self as well as others. That too, quite early on.

In life, it is neither possible to live being completely 'dependent' on others, nor being completely 'self-dependent'. Nor it is warranted. In our normal process of growth, everyone moves from being fully dependent on others as a human baby to a 'partially self-dependent and partially inter-dependent' social being in course of time for living a normal and fulfilling life. But there are some amongst us who would not like to grow up in the sense of taking responsibility and making efforts for their own wherewithal, and as far as possible would like to stay in the comfort zone of drawing on others, especially on parents and close relatives who, they know, would never ditch them. Such people gradually lose their ability to fend for themselves, and ultimately do not make much headway in life. These are dependent people who have failed to learn the value of Self-Dependence.

There are some other people, for whom, dependence on others is an anathema, and they would like to do everything by themselves, which according to them, is self-dependence. But even these people seem to have got it wrong. *Self-dependence does not mean always depending only on your own self, and doing everything on your own.*

We are not born in an ecosystem that can run on 100% individualism. Look at the design of our body itself! Every part dependent on every other part in a coherent, synergistic way for the full body machine to function effectively. Look at Nature all around! So complicated, varied, dynamic, yet inter-connected in a seamless manner, drawing on one another for survival and growth. We, as human beings in a civilized world, similarly need to *live the inter-connections optimally, i.e., learn to be inter-dependent,* to be able to manifest our best potential. We are not here just to manage our *survival* on our own. Even for that, we have to depend on sources of food, air and water from elsewhere, as we cannot create these natural resources. We are here to become our best versions. And that requires each of us to *learn healthy ways of inter-dependence.* When I say, 'healthy', it implies not parasitic dependence on others from one side only; it has to have a healthy give-and-take to it to become right kind of inter-dependence.

Self-dependence only means the willingness and ability to manage on your own, should the situation so warrant. It is not about actually doing everything on your own every time, forgetting about the better choices you can have with others' help, as well as the opportunity cost involved in doing everything on your own. Plus, it is about being secure enough in yourself, being confident enough in yourself, to turn to others and consider different points of view, while at the same time being clear that you and only you are finally responsible for your decision and working it out with/without others' help.

Yes, self-dependence is a virtue; but it lies more in the ability and attitude, rather than in action only, as discussed earlier. *Cooking is amongst many life skills that you are likely to require till your end.* You need food till you breathe your last. *So self-dependence in this area, i.e., having the ability to cook when required, is a great quality* that each of us, irrespective of gender, age, or status, must imbibe and demonstrate. But that does not mean you MUST cook all the time for yourself neglecting other necessary jobs, without drawing on available, dependable sources of help, like a hired good cook, little helps from other family members/aids, outsourcing at times etc.

From kitchen and cooking, we can pick up a perspective on how an optimized life requires both self-dependence and inter-dependence in a balanced way. Here, we may do well to understand the difference between inter-dependence between two predominantly dependent persons, and inter-dependence between two self-dependent persons.

The first category, i.e., inter-dependence of dependent people, may lead to unproductive/ineffective/disastrous outcomes. Whereas interdependence of self-dependent people can lead to a better than individual-best outcome. Because in the first category, it is about incompetencies joining together; whereas in the 2nd, it is about synergy of competencies. Thus, entrusting cooking to a hired hand, who is equally devoid of cooking skills as you are, or who is simply not punctual or dependable, is an interdependence of 1st kind that can spell disaster. Whereas even though you are a great cook, effective delegation of some of your cooking tasks to right persons (like say, kneading of flour for roti/making of roti, preparation of masalas and pastes, or just chopping of vegetables etc. to a hired cook or even a new-cook, employing a dependable good cook, outsourcing food at times, getting rations and vegetables through others or online instead of going by yourself etc.,) are interdependencies which are beneficial. When two self-dependent people unite, there is cross-fertilisation of ideas/skills and enhanced confidence level; hence improved results.

The Corona Pandemic of 2020-21 must have made many people face the harsh fact as to how important it is to be self-dependent in cooking. At the same time, it must have also brought to surface the opportunity costs (time spent on cooking that could have been otherwise utilized to work for your career or passion), thus making it clear how crucial and useful it is to *strike a balance between being self-dependent and being inter-dependent,* making clear choices depending upon your personal necessities, priorities, and own skill levels.

It is good to be confident and to have the ability to manage things on your own. But it is arrogance and counter-productive *to insist* that you must manage everything on your own only. As already explained, that is a skewed understanding of self-reliance.

Basically, when we understand the importance of graduating from self-dependence to inter-dependence, we stop resisting and allow gracefully others' help and expertise to improve our life; and *in mutuality,* we become available to them for their needs too. This is fellow-feeling that automatically enriches your other social skills, too.

In kitchen, everyone is like a baby when they start. The beauty of running a kitchen for a long time regularly is that it gradually makes you grow self-reliant, but at the same time it also eventually makes you inter-dependent over time. You learn to take others' help. You learn from others' recipes and kitchen tips. You share yours with others. You volunteer to help others in necessity of help. *A sense of mutuality sets in course of time.* You honour and encourage others. You gratefully accept others' encouragement. All this not because you cannot depend on self if required, but because you appreciate that together with others, everyone does more! *This is inter-dependence of self-dependent people, that empowers each for more.*

Carry these lessons to your work situations, to your team-building initiatives where premium is placed on team work. Look for how to leverage the positives/strengths of others to build a synergy in and outside the group - be them your team members, superiors, juniors, or anyone you come in contact with, along your supply and demand chains. Carry these lessons to your personal lives, and you start living beautiful relationships based on mutuality, as against self-centeredness.

If you have picked up these lessons correctly, you would also be able to know exactly where you must draw the line between *managing on your own alone* and *pooling together with others.*

Kitchen never ceases to surprise me with profound insights.

49. Kitchen: The Doctor and SPA

All of us know the Great *Vaidya* (Doctor) we have in kitchen – Turmeric! There are, in fact, many ingredients in our homely kitchen with great healing and cosmetic properties. Let us talk about just a few:

Turmeric (Haldi), with its great anti-bacterial, anti-inflammatory, and anti-biotic properties, is very effective for healing, both internal upsets as well as external wounds. But you must know this to use for a quick heal. Mothers get to know this and just recall, how many times, *haldiwala dudh* (turmeric infused warm milk) or *haldi ke lep (turmeric paste)* becomes the first medicine to cure you from many illnesses, like fever, body ache, scars and injuries etc. *As it cures* facial scars, traditionally, it is used even to brighten up and lighten dark face skin colour; and make the face and body glow. In fact, Indian marriage ceremonies have a 'must' slot for the *Haldi* function. 😊 And as I understand, these properties are the reason, turmeric earns its pride of place amongst spices.

Salt, our almost indispensable ingredient for food, is also an amazing healer. Remember what you do the first thing if you have sore throat? Gargle salted warm water! What is the homely first treatment for canker sores/dental/jaw pain? Rinse mouth vigorously with water with a slightly high amount of salt, swish and spit out a few times! What do the toothpaste companies advertise? Theirs have salt in their dental cream. Soaking feet in warm salted water eases pain when we suffer from ingrown toenails, or have tired feet. And of course, salt is a major ingredient in ORS to beat dehydration. Etc.

Observe, how the cheapest and the commonest of food ingredients like salt and turmeric heal us in many dis-eases.

Cucumber, low in calories but high in water content and rich in many important vitamins and minerals, is very good for balanced hydration, digestive regularity, weight loss, controlling constipation, and lower blood sugar levels. Because of its great cooling property and hydrating power, it is also great SPA element for facials and very beneficial for eyes, as well as skin.

Papaya has special enzyme called papain and chymopapain. Both enzymes digest proteins, thus, help with digestion and reduce inflammation. Papaya contains special lubricants and enzymes which help in cleaning the colon and keep it healthy. High in vitamin C and antioxidants, it is also very good for immune system and heart. Papaya leaves are used for curing Dengu fever and other illnesses. Papain removes skin impurities. Hence, it works as a great exfoliator in SPA for clearing dead skins from your face.

Bottle gourd, rich in dietary fibre, vitamins, and antioxidants, alkaline in nature, is great for heart health, digestion, controlling diabetes and acidity, cleansing toxins from skin, healthy immunity system etc.

Tomatoes are the major dietary source of the antioxidant lycopene, which has been linked to many health benefits, including reduced risk of heart disease and cancer. It is used widely as a SPA element too as lycopene in tomato acts as an age-defying ingredient that helps clear black heads, helps fight pimples and acnes.

Oats contain saponins that helps expel dirt from pores, and its oil softens face skin.

Avocado, full of Vitamin A and other essential nutrients as also glutamine, can lighten pores and make the skin glow.

Bitter gourd, Herbs, Pure Ghee, vinegar, lemon skin, banana peel...... And the list goes on.

Most of the ingredients used in kitchen for preparation of food possess many medicinal and cosmetic values. Mothers in course of their long experience in the kitchen learn these, going beyond their regular food-related uses, and apply as first-aid whenever required. These doctors in Kitchen give us a clear perspective on why we must make conscious efforts to know about as many properties as possible of whatever we use, whatever has been given to us by Nature, or whoever we interact with in our daily lives. Carried forward, this leads to development of a healthy tendency to stay curious about the people in our lives; their special qualities, strengths, weaknesses, passions etc. Needless to mention, the more we know another individual personally, the greater is the chance of a stronger and healthier relationship.

50. The Teachers in the kitchen

By now, we have seen quite elaborately how regular involvement in processes of managing food and cooking imparts many valuable lessons/ perspectives, which we should carry forward to other relevant life situations, including the formal and professional situations involving management and leadership issues. These lessons help us immensely in handling people and situations with more competence and effectiveness.

So, virtually we have been talking about *'teachers' in the kitchen* so far- in terms of a situation, an experience, a tool, an ingredient, a process and so on. Nevertheless, I would like to talk about some of them again, for the sake of highlighting and greater comprehension. *Some ingredients, dishes, tools in themselves are huge lessons that we can decipher if only we have a keen sense of observation.* What is more, the same lesson many a times gets hammered from different elements and experiences in kitchen in such an impactful way that you simply cannot miss it. Let us now reflect on some of them.

Fire - We have already talked about this basic element enough in the context of Team Building, learning from mistakes, motivation etc. Let us just recall how wonderfully fire teaches us about constant alertness while dealing with potentially hazardous tools and resources, how to ably handle the 'fire' of motivation in pressing situations, how to deal with sensitive and incendiary situations to keep your flock together etc. Invaluable insights, indeed.

A hot stove – Touch something hot with your bare hand; you will get burnt.

It happens to everyone perhaps while cooking, more frequently during the initial stage till we learn to be careful. Accidentally, you touch a hot pot, or a hot stove, or the door of a hot oven, or inadvertently get your hands too close to fire/gas flames or steam/heat, and you know what happens! *This teaches us at least three key lessons:*

1. *Know your job hazards*, i.e., the potential risks of what you are handling, *and observe caution proactively.* The tools and "others" will behave as per *their* own nature, not necessarily personally against you. So better take care of your own safety.

2. *Don't repeat an avoidable mistake.* That is, if you have once got burnt, it is foolish not to be careful the next time and commit the same mistake again. You could have avoided it with just a little mindfulness.
3. *Don't stop doing something if it is essential, merely because it is dangerous. Just exercise caution and use safety-aids.* We may use a clutch/tong/grip to hold hot pans, or wear kitchen gloves/oven mitt etc. Just because you have got burnt once does not mean you would stop cooking.

In life, there would be umpteen examples of such things as in dealing with which, we have to make *caution* as the watch word. Riding a bi-cycle, riding a two-wheeler, driving a car etc. all have become necessities now; but must be done with required caution. Similarly, in work situations, there would be many emotionally charged and explosive situations involving other human beings as well as sensitive issues, from which we cannot simply run away, and which we must face, but with caution and safety-aids (in terms of calming tactics, creative problem-solving skills etc.)

A piping hot dish – you don't dig into it without stirring it first.

When we are having something like, say, a bowl of hot soup, or hot porridge, or hot lentil rice, we don't just dig into it. Instead, we take a spoonful and put it into our mouth carefully. We first stir, or blow air into it, so that some heat escapes and it cools down a bit and does not suddenly burn our mouth or stick to our tongue/mouth. This experience gives out a loud message: *do not just jump into conflict situations to solve the issue at stake without first taking some initiatives to take some 'heat' out of all involved.* An agitated situation does not lead to a real solution. Situation must be made to cool down a bit to see things as they are and sort them out.

Knife

Let me repeat the example of knives at the cost of some repetition.

Keep Sharpening your knives

Observe yourself in the kitchen doing the chopping jobs. You will notice that every now and then you sharpen your knife, otherwise it gets blunt and useless. If you notice this consciously, you will draw a huge life lesson for yourself. That unless you keep working on your own talents, skills, and competencies in any area whatsoever, soon they would be unusable for you. If you are a singer, you must make time for practicing your vocal music; if you are a writer, you must make time for writing and reading widely; if you are a chef, you must make time for experimenting with new combinations, new recipes, and new techniques of cooking, and the like. You must 'sharpen' your skills, learn new things, and evolve continuously. Then only you, as a member in any group and in any capacity would become an asset to that community. Just like a knife in a kitchen sharpened from time to time!

A sharp Knife – Handle with care, or you hurt yourself.

Similar to lessons from fire for cooking. Knives are meant to cut and chop – to help you cook your ingredients. We have to hold it properly first- the sharp edge away from our fingers. Plus, we have to hold the thing to be chopped keeping a safe distance from the likely place on which the knife edge is likely to fall. *So, the lesson is again Caution*. Don't cut others short, ensure your own safety.

Fire, hot equipment, sharp knife, or any other potentially hazardous stuff in kitchen - all carry a loud spiritual message in the context of life philosophy: Always take care of your own Karma! Fire does not know whether you are a good-hearted person or an evil one. It will conduct itself as per its own dharma to burn anything that touches it. If you do some prohibited or sinful or careless action, even unknowingly, you shall reap the results that go with it. So, be mindful and careful about all your feelings and actions.

A blunt Knife – there is a right use for everything, as also a scope for redemption

In every kitchen, I am sanguine, there would be both rightly sharp knives along with a few which have gone blunt with use. You don't throw away the blunt ones right away. *Blunt ones are sharpened and put to use again.* That is redemption. Mother knows that the bluntness of a knife is a result of its long use, *and not a core defect*, which cannot be corrected. It has been useful, and it will be, if properly serviced again. Carry this lesson forward to your relationships and you would be sensitive to the causes behind 'bluntness' in any of them which can be corrected.

Many a times, even a blunt knife has its own use. You don't always need a sharp knife for everything. Personally, I find a blunt knife very useful for shaving off potola (pointed gourd), as I just need to scrape out a very thin layer of the peel of this vegetable. Regular peelers and sharp knifes cannot do this well. Further, I have observed, if a regular sharp knife is used for such light peeling a few times, that also turns blunt. So, the understanding that comes is: *everything has some right use and we must choose our tool accordingly.* Immediate discarding of anything once it runs out of one use (its original use) is not optimisation.

A burnt curry

It teaches us something very useful in personal as also professional life. *Keep control over fire (raging emotions), or your best of curry can get burnt and will have to be discarded!* When emotions run high, acts with even the best of intentions become counter-productive. So, learn to maintain calm and poise in all situations. It also teaches one of the important lessons – when and what to discard. We have already discussed this in waste consciousness.

Spilt Milk – Don't cry over the spilt milk.

What do you do when boiling milk spills over in kitchen? Well, there certainly is an instantaneous moment of overwhelming regret. But just a moment, literally. Next moment you spring into action, almost reflexively – switching off the fire first to stop the spillage asap (deal with the root cause), then get onto cleaning off the mess created with the spilt milk (gather back your life), and get going with your kitchen chores (move on). *Let bygone be bygone.* Close the past stories.

Salt -It is said, homemakers are like salt in the curry, whose presence is never noticed or appreciated; but whose absence simply kills the dish and everyone immediately notices its absence! Such a regular, cheap ingredient in kitchen like salt gives us *a life-transforming lesson: Conduct yourself like salt wherever you are.* Do not be frustrated if your presence is not visibly acknowledged. Rather, *make your presence so useful and beneficial for all that your absence would automatically become conspicuous!* In corporate world, perhaps everyone carrying out maintenance related jobs must follow this dictum like a gospel. And then, see their morale soar up magically.

Another great lesson from salt is: *it is better to err on the lesser side in many cases*. Less of salt can be adjusted afterwards by adding some more to taste, but it may become difficult to salvage a dish gone over-salty. Yes, some dishes with gravy can be mildly corrected by adding more liquid, or at times by incorporating some more of some ingredients like boiled potato, flour dough etc. But these cases are not many. Spoilt cases due to overdose of salt are rather many. *Hence, in cooking, the ground rule with salt is to use it on the lesser side, taste before finishing and adjust*. It is said, always taste before you serve. This can have a deep connotation for real life, too. We should always consciously 'taste' our words and actions before we express lest it becomes too late. *The wisest of philosophies: Pause!* Especially when you are angry or in a foul mood, Pause and taste, i.e., think about what you are going to say or do. Control your negative emotions and their outward expression before you end up with a situation of irreversible harm.

And yes, what happens when salt is rubbed on an open wound? No need for me to describe. If you have a wound in your hand, be careful while working with salt – better still, keep your wound away from salt. *Have this sensitivity for others too. Don't hurl hurtful words to someone already in pain.*

Salt always reminds us the dictum that excess of even an indispensable item (like motivation tools in management of people) turns counter-productive. In everything in life, we ought to set a healthy limit for use. Even in creativity! Using the infinite power of mind is the call for us in everything, but to achieve what? *'For what purpose?'* should be the guiding principle for setting the boundary. Look at the scamsters and fraudsters and criminals. Don't you think, they use their creativity way too much, beyond the limits of ethics and morality, losing sight of the outcomes? Point is: creativity must get a free run, but always with eyes on the *nature* of outcomes you are trying to achieve.

Moreover, it is salt in the kitchen that keeps reminding us all the time about the difference between 'value' and 'price' of a thing. Many of us attach higher 'value' to a higher priced object, which is clearly a misconception. The sooner one realises this the better. *Value is intrinsic, while price is more a game of supply and demand*. A leader sensitive to this aspect would never fail to recognise the contributions of a janitor in their excitement to applaud some high-level executive's achievements.

Amazing how a common ingredient like salt can be a great teacher in so many different ways!

Lemon: Squeeze it too much for its juice, it turns bitter!

In my mother tongue, Odia, there goes a saying: Ati lembu chipudile pita. Meaning, if you squeeze a lemon too much for its juice, eventually there will be bitter juice.

A great lesson there, especially in the context of management, managing people and using their services for an outcome. Managers, who are more bosses and less true leaders, often put unreasonably high pressure on their employees to perform that eventually turns counter-productive. Employees get frustrated in being pressurised further and further even when they are giving their performance with sincerity. The process of squeezing out optimum quantity of juice from a lemon teaches the mothers how carefully and optimally pressure need be put from all sides – lightly first, then slowly increasing the churn, till the right point, and not beyond.

To motivate and move people effectively and powerfully requires genuinely accepting them as collaborators, as members of your Team who are out to achieve the common goal, who need clear communication, proper training & guidance, and facilitative operative environment, that involves both incentives and disincentives aimed at creative tension for peak performance, yes, but not debilitating pressure to demoralise/destroy.

Air-tight Containers

In kitchen, in order to keep certain ingredients/preparations fresh and long-lasting, they are stored in air-tight containers. For example, Bournvita, Coffee, Horlicks etc. get hardened very soon if not kept in air tight containers. Many spice powders like coriander powder, cumin powder, red chilli powder get damp and spoilt if stored outside unless prevented from getting in contact with air. Even Pickles, unless stored in air-tight jars, get spoilt sooner than they should, by coming in contact with air. In fact, there are many food items which get rancidity if left exposed to air due to reaction with oxygen. Rancidity not only changes their taste and smell, it also makes them harmful to consume. Further, air tight containers prevent growth of some harmful bacteria in food, and also restrict entry of foreign substances that might cause contamination of food.

There is also an opposite situation in which food gets spoilt in air-tight, vacuum-sealed containers. There is a form of bacteria called anaerobic which thrives in the absence of oxygen. So, it flourishes in an air-tight container.

Similarly, inherent moisture in green leaves, even after being made apparently dehydrated, tends to spoil the lot, even if stored in air tight bottles, *without* something like a tissue paper below the bottle cap to absorb moisture after the bottle is closed.

Even without lessons in scientific reasons behind these storing practices, mothers know these things by following elderly guidance, coupled with own intuitive understandings. A keenly observant mother goes a step further and captures the deeper lessons:

1. *Insulate your Inner self from external negativities to preserve your own inherent positivity!*
2. *Yet, do not be so closed-minded that even beneficial external ideas do not get a chance to enter and kill your own negativities that might be flourishing in the absence of new and fresh ideas from the outer world.*
3. *The key lies in a balance – be open but do not get swayed away without applying your own mind!*

Profound lessons from an ordinary kitchen ware like an air-tight bottle, indeed.

Pressure Cooker

Hard ingredients like dal become tender easily in no time when cooked in pressure cooker. But *the key is to know how much of pressure cooking would cook it right* as per your need. Overcooked, its texture might become slimy and repulsive. Undercooked, there is no point of using Pressure cooker just to save time. *Not to forget, pressure cooking kills nutrients* instead of releasing them as it happens when we cook normally. Similarly, in every work sphere in life, some degree of creative pressure makes it easier to deliver. But extra pressure usually turns counter-productive. This is another huge learning from pressure cooking: *Over-pressure kills ingenuity. Keep a watch while applying pressure.*

Another lesson also comes up in the context of Pressure cooking. You develop a knack of choosing right in a trade-off situation. On one hand, pressure cooking takes much less time than normal cooking. On the other hand, it kills nutrients to a considerable extent. You will make situation-specific choices to minimise adverse effect, though cannot rule out nutrient loss completely. Similar awareness of trade-offs while making decisions in life situations always helps.

Serving Bowls and Plates – perception management

Some mothers are truly ingenious in managing perception of their children about quantity of food. When the child is fussy, and the mother wants her to eat a specific quantity, she would simply serve it in a bigger than required bowl/plate, so that the quantity *looks* small. Managing the proportion of covered and empty spaces on serving utensils! Similarly, if she wants her child to have a limited quantity, but knows the child would fuss for more, she would serve up to brim in a small bowl/plate. 😊 I had learnt this too well while serving my old mother. She could be made to eat the right quantity served in over-sized containers.

Perception Management is not akin to cheating. It is a very necessary tool for *persuasion* in managing people and situations. Its objective is benign, to make those on the other side feel comfortable, reduce resistance, or accept certain things for their own benefit. To persuade others to do something necessary and positive in the face of apparent doubts and misconceptions. To mould attitudes on the other side by showing the truth, but with a larger or deeper context, to enable them to appreciate what is desirable. It also helps in convincing others involved to perceive themselves as participants and collaborators in the solution being worked out.

Hilsa Fish

Life is like eating a Hilsa fish.

I am a bigtime fan of this fish and my children simply love watching me relish a fried Hilsa piece! It is full of fine bones, but so tasty that it feels divine.

Ask any Hilsa fan – would they stop eating it just because of the bones? No way, I bet! In fact, many would even assert: Come on, it is so very sweet and tasty only because it is so bony. And observe closely how skilfully they manage to eat the fish, all the way averting any of the fine bones hurting their mouth or worse still, slipping down their throat!

I know how that becomes possible – i.e., to eat it despite the hundreds of fine bones. In fact, if you sit down to de-bone the flesh that you are going to eat, it is next to impossible. So, the trick is: take out some big bones as you can, don't bother about the finer ones, take a small bite straight into mouth, start chewing carefully (almost like a cat) constantly *feeling* the bones as you chew and keep taking out the bones with your tongue/fingers, as you enjoy the fish.

Well, quite some skill! Not many people can do it with ease; but I can. *I can because I love it way too much.* I relish it so much that you would not find wastage of any flesh portion in my left overs.

So, the lesson is: Life is like eating Hilsa fish. Just as this fish is extremely tasty yet full of bones, life, too, is very beautiful and enjoyable-but full of hardships (bones), which cannot be segregated from life fully. One needs to take a mouthful, *taste* hardships, and keep on *throwing them out* skilfully without allowing these hardships to hurt you deep down. And yes, the most significant thing is: you must love life for that.

If you can relish Hilsa fish, why not relish life with its million stings?

Garlic cloves

What's the use of a garlic clove, safe in its skin within a bulb joined with some more of the same? Ever noticed how a garlic clove gives out its best aroma only when finally crushed and fried in hot oil? I feel at times, each of us should be like these cloves- you skin us, crush us, and chop us rough; do not stop at that, saute us in hot oil and we give out our best flavour!

Garlic carries a very clear lesson for us that life's trials and tribulations are meant to make us our best version, not to break us.

The process of boiling

Carrots-Eggs-Coffee beans!

These three ingredients, when boiled, turn out to be great teachers on how to handle adversities.

Most of us know this story about how a mother taught her married daughter, complaining about hardships in her marital home, about an important life lesson. In three separate pans, she filled water. Then in the first pan, she put the carrot, in the second, she placed the eggs and in the third pan, she put some ground coffee beans. She left them to boil for some good 20-25 mins. Then she asked her daughter, "What do you see?" Daughter replied, "Boiled carrots, eggs and coffee, of course!"

Mother then took out the carrot and egg, and ladled coffee into a cup. Asked her daughter to touch, feel and tell her what changes she found now. She did as her mother told. Then she said, the carrot felt soft now on boiling. After peeling off the egg shell, she touched the boiled egg and it felt hard. She sipped the coffee. It has now coloured the entire liquid (water) in its own beautiful colour and is giving out its nice, rich aroma, tasting very refreshing.

The mother then explained: All the three elements had faced the same adversity, the boiling water, just like we all go through traumatic phases. But each responded/changed differently. The carrot went in strong and hard. However, after being subjected to the boiling water, it softened and became weak. The egg had been fragile. Its thin outer shell had protected its liquid interior. But, after being through the boiling water, its inside became hardened. The ground coffee beans were unique, however. After they were in the boiling water, they had changed the water.

Similarly, each of us must ask ourselves: Which am I? A carrot, egg, or coffee? When adversity stares me in the eye, do I like the carrot wilt and lose my strength with pain and problems, though initially I seemed to be strong? Or, am I like the egg – starting with a softness within, but harden and become stiff as I go through heat?

Or am I like the coffee bean, that changes the hot water itself, i.e., changes the very circumstance that brings the pain? When the water gets hot, it releases its rich aroma, taste, and colour. *If you are like the coffee bean, when things are at their worst, you get better, not bitter, and change the situation around you for better.*

Coffee beans teach us to elevate ourselves to higher levels in the face of adversity and transcend it. To change the situation for better instead of changing yourself for worse!

Goes without saying there are many such things in our kitchen which are all great teachers of some lesson or other.

At the end, kitchen is no less than a mini-battle field in the context of usage of tools and resources. Your perennial enemies on the other side are the potential serious bodily hazards, which must be continuously fought with your own 'carefulness' and 'skills' as weapons on your side-both to defend and attack. These teachers continuously teach you how to fight and win, as also how to heal and bounce back if harmed at times.

51. Value of 'Completion'

Taking things to its logical end. Closing a communication loop/circle.

No one can deny how crucial these are in the context of effective leadership, as also bliss in personal life.

In kitchen, you don't leave dishes half cooked, or half-baked or half-done. You take it to its needed state of being cooked. *You complete cooking*, irrespective of whether it is an ordinary or a gourmet dish.

Similarly, in life, we must develop a quality to take things to their logical conclusion; deal with issues *conclusively* instead of handling half-heartedly and/or leaving mid-way. Abandon if you must, but in that case, it must be for a cogent and larger reason, not because you suddenly lost interest for some reasons, or because of your lackadaisical attitude.

Closing a communication loop after dealing with an issue conclusively is also utterly important for any relationship. For example, in organisational set up, many a times, the dealing functionaries do not pay attention to intimating the customers even after resolving their small issues. Suppose a customer comes with some issue, you seek further details or documents, which he complies with. You promise him you would look into the matter on urgent basis, and he leaves. You do look into the matter and fix the issue, but don't intimate him. What happens? To your client relationship? To your goodwill? You did the job, but just for that last part of the communication loop that you did not close, a lot of the intangible gains are lost, which otherwise would have accrued to you and your organisation through a satisfied customer–one of the best brand ambassadors! Simple 'thank you,' or even simple acknowledgements from the last party involved must not be ignored for completion of a communication loop. Personally, I have seen many who would see your messages on WhatsApp, yet not acknowledge or reply. It is not a good situation for a relationship when the sender knows from the green ticks that the message has been seen at the other end, yet neither acknowledged nor replied to. *In kitchen, not only you, as the cook, know how important it is to complete cooking, you also know how important it is to receive feedback constructively and act on possible action points, seek further feedback, till 'you are happy, I am happy' status is reached.*

It is said, you are judged not for what you start, but for what you finish.

Success is not achieved if, along with *character* and *competence*, you don't have the *willingness and ability to complete*. We must have seen thousands of examples where someone flags off something fabulous with great fanfare, only for it to lose steam on the way before reaching the destination. In sports parlance, sportspersons are always goaded to *reach the finish line*, even if you get to know mid-way that you cannot make it to the top slot even if you try your hardest. *Sportsmanship lies in best participation till the very end.* If you have started running a race, you must *complete* it; otherwise, you are already a loser!

Yes, there might come occasions, in respect of on-going projects, when on comprehensive review of the same you are thoroughly convinced about the net benefits of abandoning it for cogent reasons to work on a better alternative. *For example, in kitchen*, when your curry gets really burnt and irredeemable, it is a well-considered decision not to go ahead with it. *But on normal occasions, you don't start cooking a recipe, and leave it mid-way without completing.*

Kitchen very silently and consistently drills this value of completion into anyone in its charge. Carry this forward to all life situations. True leaders always give their best to something they started in the first place thinking it to be worth their while and keep going till they complete it. Abandoning mid-way without completion is rather a warranted exception in very special circumstances. We have seen how kitchen teaches us valuable lessons on purpose-orientation, planning, goal-setting, strategizing and execution. These skills, coupled with many core values and right attitude imbibed in kitchen, keep our resolve and *ability to complete* till the finish line is reached.

Have you ever realised what role your kitchen experience can play in building your leadership qualities through such numerous insights and lessons we have been talking about?

52. Humility

Humility is the ability to give up your pride, yet retain your dignity. *Humility is about respecting others' worth, without degrading your own.* Humility is perhaps the one fits-all-purpose trait of a truly strong person, who bows down to everything worth learning, but bows down to none in weakness!

How kitchen teaches it? Very simple. Primarily, cooking is an acquired/ learnt skill. No one is born with culinary skills. Hence, it makes you realise very soon that *you must learn it from others.* You might develop an aptitude and passion for it as you go along and become proficient at it. But not at the start. So, to approach and learn from others, you automatically must shed your pride/ego first. It is normal that we respect and stay humble towards our *Gurus* at least out of an inner feeling of gratitude. In fact, if you don't drop your pride, you do not learn in the first place.

Admitting your own ignorance to yourself is the first step in any kind of learning. And that is also the starting point of feeling humble, without demeaning yourself.

A hunger for learning is a mark of humility as a strength, not as a weakness. Who has ever become great in any field without it?

Secondly, the learning process in the kitchen also humbles you in many other ways:

-when you find how so many others are coming out with so many better and newer recipes continuously even if you have already reached a very impressive level of excellence as a cook/chef. *There is always something better than yours,* and you can see that if you remain open to newness.

-When *you, despite your great culinary skills, occasionally spoil some dishes.* And this happens with even the best of cooks and chefs. *Your own failures, despite your great talents, can be huge teachers in humility.* It does not make you feel ashamed; it makes you feel human and humble, as to err is human. At least it busts the myth that you are infallible and takes away your pride. At the same time, it makes you introspect on what went wrong that you should not repeat the next time. True humility lies in learning, not in a feeling of unearned guilt or degraded self-worth.

- when *you are hit with some discouraging feedback* from a loved one on a dish you have cooked with great love and care, and as per your taste, you are satisfied with it. Differences in tastes and preferences are bound to exist even in a close-knit family. Even your best of dishes may not appeal to the taste-buds of some, and their negative feedback may not necessarily be due to any lack on your part.

So, kitchen magically leaves you wiser on how to shed ego, and how to take negative experiences with grace, humility, and a great sense of humour.

Yes, you cannot imagine a great leader without a genuine sense of humour, that essentially flows from humility only. Not only you show the humility and courage to laugh at your own mistakes, *and learn*, you also never stoop down to laughing at others in disdain for their mistakes or shortcomings. You look for anything hilarious in the situation, even while going through stress, and heartily laugh it out with others, which lessens the stress for everyone and leaves all re-charged. Anyone fortified with this characteristic trait, *humility*, has way higher chances of success in every other field in life.

53. Trust and Credibility

To be an effective leader, you must inspire trust of others in you and earn credibility. But for that you must possess honesty and integrity yourself; demonstrate your commitment through repeated action and posturing, stay dependable always, take responsibility and walk your talk. No shortcut.

We have already seen in various ways how kitchen helps you imbibe the precious values of *honesty and integrity*, and shows you how to be trust-worthy, dependable, committed, and responsible as a person on whom one can count!

Let us recall our discussions in "Mindscape and Skills" against Example 3: Integrity.

No point repeating. Integrity gets deeply ingrained in kitchen.

I just want to highlight the single most significant perspective on what we could, and should, mean by integrity. Yes, it is about doing the right thing even if no one is watching. So, by inference, it is *not* really about whether other people think they can trust you. It is about whether *you are integrated or not! Whether all of your being, within and without, is working together as a whole regardless of who may or may not be watching, or what others may be thinking about you.* So, integrity is something that is first known to you yourself. Others get to know, of course, but in course of time as they notice whether there are frequent divergences between your talk and walk, or not. Without integrity, your credibility would be lost in time shattering your personal as well as professional relations. So be careful the moment you find yourself floundering. You have to maintain your own integrity not only to live in authenticity, but also to live up to the trust others repose in you as a leader, or simply as a good human being.

Kitchen makes you alive to the paramount importance of living up to others' trust in you.

By default, everyone trusts that whatever is being served on their plate has been prepared in at least a non-harmful manner. At home, there are more things presumed:

- that it is prepared the healthy way.
- that it is as per my specific taste and preferences and health requirements.
- that I can expect the meals on my table *on time* and *every day.* It is not like my mother serves me food as per her whims and fancies, whenever she feels like. She *ensures* it, so you can depend on her, trust her that she will not let you go hungry.

Etc.

So on and so forth. When a mother stays alive to these role-expectations, she inculcates a deep sense of responsibility, a strong commitment to her job-role-responsibilities, a sense of punctuality, a habit of regularity and shapes herself as a *trust-worthy, dependable, honest, and credible person,* whose integrity is beyond doubt. Highly required personality traits to succeed in any relationship – personal and professional.

As you live these values daily, they automatically get ingrained/ strengthened in your character; and get carried forward to all other spheres.

Interestingly, kitchen teaches you on 'trust' factor in a well-rounded manner. It not only teaches you why you must be 'trust-worthy' yourself, but also how to trust others, yet how not to trust blindly. Moreover, it keeps us alive to the fact that blind mis-trust is equally harmful as blind trust. Please recall our discussions on delegation earlier. We cannot delegate if we start mis-trusting everyone else's efficiency or intentions. However, we are not supposed to blindly trust everyone either. Here comes the need for supervision. We must trust and delegate, but follow it up with right supervision to find out training, motivation, and other kinds of needs, if any, for a desirable outcome on time. *Trust begets trust* essentially means *trust with responsibility*.

Must have heard, "Trust in God, and tie your camel."

54. Value of Patience

Kitchen is not a place for you if you do not have patience! Good news is: even if you are impatient as a beginner, it pushes you to imbibe this quality soon enough.

In the world of cooking, everything needs to be rightly cooked – some are best fully-cooked, some crunchy-cooked and some just raw! A broccoli, fully cooked, not only loses its nutrients, but tastes bad too; while a potato half-cooked is sheerly uneatable. Tea/coffee, not rightly brewed can just taste garbage. Gravy of a curry not cooked for long enough do not absorb all the tastes and aromas of ingredients used. Chicken kebabs, tanduri/grilled chicken not marinated for the right length of time do not absorb all flavours to be tasty enough. Perfect dry roasted semolina needs patient and constant stirring over low to low-medium heat for a fairly long time. Etc.

So, basically, you mess up a dish, if you do not allow it to get cooked just for the right length of time, controlling heat to right levels all through. *Cooking needs patience. Kitchen shows you the great difference between being quick and hurrying merely to be done with a task on hand.*

Similarly in life, certain efforts need an optimal time for fructifying – want it sooner or later, it will come with its undesirable side-effects. So, we must cultivate patience as a core value.

These days, most of us use pressure cookers and microwaves due to time constraints. But we know, these are not generally good for health and taste buds. Microwaves are generated in the oven to stimulate the water molecules in the food which then warms up the food. So, while heating and cooking in microwave may be fast, it can lead to dry, chewy food if not timed rightly. Similarly, in pressure cooker, ingredients do not get 'cooked' but burst under pressure and heat, that kills nutrients of the food to a large extent. Here again, unless timed right, your food would either get over-boiled/under-boiled. Loss of nutrient is still the concern to be kept in view. On the other hand, slow cooking, and simmering lead to release of such nutrients. Thus, the very purpose behind food, i.e., to get nutrients from what we eat for the body, gets lost in our hurry and preference for fast cooking most of the time out of impatience. *Only a cook with patience can strike a balance in use of normal, slow, and fast cooking tools to manage time without much loss on nutrition.*

I am sure, while working in kitchen everyone must have spilled some stuff on the floor accidentally. Recall how a mother handles a situation when a glassware slips from grip and breaks into pieces over the entire floor with its contents spread all over! Clearing this mess requires real patience, not your panicky reactions of O..M..G... blah... blah! The other day, a hot deep pan of cooked rice which was just drained and held with two cotton towels with two hands suddenly slipped from my hand. Lo and behold! Entire cooked rice fell all over the kitchen floor. On top, it was steaming hot and sticky. Unless cleaned asap, it was impossible to function there, forget about lamenting over wastage and re-doing a fresh batch of rice. In Hindi, they say, *khud raita failaya... khud sameto turant (you have created the mess, you only have to clear it now).*

In such situations, the only thing needed at that moment is a determination to act asap with patience. Patient action of cleaning from one end slowly, followed by repeat cleanings as necessary. No howling, no crying over the spoilt milk, no blame game would steer you through such situations. At times I feel, it indeed amounts to 'bravery' when one gears up for patient action in crisis situations, irrespective of the work space or work load.

I repeat, kitchen is not a place for you if you don't have patience. Patience is what connects efforts to outcome. In kitchen, healthy food takes time to cook and one must have required patience to let the dish cook properly Similarly, everywhere else too, *efforts made with sincerity takes time to fructify, during which one must maintain patience.* Further, kitchen is a place of hazardous stuff – fire, sharp knives, and tools, boiling and steaming hot stuff. You lose patience, either you serve something un/under/over-cooked; or you trigger a dangerous accident.

There is another critical perspective that you get to develop easily in kitchen. And that is on the importance of Sequencing, which also helps us imbibe patience. Not only right choice of ingredients, but also the right process of cooking that involves right sequencing of adding ingredients at different points of the cooking process, apart from right levels of heat through various stages, is essential for right cooking. You wait with patience to introduce one/more ingredients at the right stage of cooking, instead of skipping the needed sequencing. Similarly in life, various experiences and milestone achievements come in some order/sequence, for achieving true 'success'. Try to fast forward, or jump stages, the result might not be beneficial. As they say, for an infant just learning how to get up and walk a few steps is "success", while for a 2 year old, it might be getting rid of the habit of bed-wetting! And we do wait patiently for the baby to achieve the milestones in right sequence. In professional spaces, too, moving upward from lower responsibilities to higher ones with right kind of patience ultimately yields great dividend.

I have personally got many insights and ideas while *patiently* dry-roasting semolina. It needs *constant* (not frequent) stirring; otherwise, the fine granules on the bottom layer are sure to get partially/fully burnt, rendering the whole lot unfit for use due to a burnt, bitter taste. Your hand is constantly occupied, so cannot even multi-task. But that turns on my thinking mind. 😊 Mind, in any case, keeps on thinking irrespective of what your motor/muscle network is up to. When with habit, my dry-roasting happens on auto-mode, yet attentively, I slip into observation mode and many relevant thoughts start popping up. A patient mind is calm, and a calm mind thinks clearly.

Amazing how patience as a basic value gets imbibed in kitchen over a period, almost on auto-mode!

In all life situations, patience is a required virtue. "Do not rush" is a watch-phrase which cannot be discounted in life. Is it not great that working in our humble kitchen helps us so much in imbibing this value?

Patience and fortitude conquer everything!

While talking about patience as a value, I cannot but get drawn to its spiritual aspect. In Vedic philosophy, 'Titiksha,' which means forbearance/patience, is said to be a profound quality, pre-requisite for the spiritual seekers. *Because patience is ultimately not about waiting only, but about maintaining a positive attitude while waiting.* Very often, you have no option but to wait, but inside you would be bubbling with irritation and all negative energies. That is not patience.

Sahanam sarva dukkhanamapratikara purvakam I

Chintavilaparahitam sa titiksha nigadyate II

(Sankaracharya's Vivekachudamani 24)

Meaning, Titiksha or forbearance is the capacity to endure all sorrows and sufferings without struggling for redressal or for revenge, while always being free from anxiety or lament over them.

Sai Baba used to say, *'Saheb mile saburi mein...', meaning we can realise God through patience*. How inspiring!

Just observe mothers in kitchen (as also elsewhere)! The trait of patience that they continuously demonstrate is nothing lesser than titiksha, if you understand their plight with gratitude and compassion.

55. The joy of sacrifice

Observe your mother, or yourself if you are a mother, as we go on bringing food to the table day in and day out. Look at the simple sacrifices that we, as mothers and cooks, make many a times to delight our family and friends, no matter the inconveniences caused to us. Why? *It gives us joy.* Very often, we really work happily despite inconveniences and go that extra mile to cook some special dishes of choice of others, or cook meals at odd hours, or entertain guests arriving sans prior notice!

True joy always lies in doing something for others unselfishly and ungrudgingly. Working in the kitchen regularly provides many such occasions. Every time a mother sets plates for her family, she always serves the best to the rest and keeps the least or the last best for herself. Yes, if she must do this as per an unwritten *command* flowing from an atmosphere of patriarchy, and not out of her own will and pleasure, then it is not a matter of joy. Ordinarily, she does this out of love, but not by starving herself. At times, not having enough left for herself could be because of some other reason. For example, cooking in a homely kitchen runs on estimates, not on exact measurements. Sometimes, the quantity of an already cooked dish may fall short inadvertently, and the mother chooses to forego or lessen her own share both to avoid the inconvenience of making something afresh at the last moment, as also out of a sense of love for others and responsibility. After all, it was her responsibility to cook a quantity enough for all. So, serving others and adjusting her own share gives her a sense of satisfaction, a sense of joy that she did not let others suffer for her own mistake. It is a sacrifice out of own volition, not under anybody else's command. One basic aspect in a mother's sacrifices with joy, though, must be that she is not on a mindless self-harming project.

I am certainly not advocating, nor glorifying, the extremely self-effacing type of sacrifices made by women at large, especially in India, on multifarious fronts mostly as an outcome of a misguided understanding of 'sacrifice.' Very often, you are made to believe by the society that as a care-giver, you must always put the other in front – always, even if your own survival is at stake. And you give in to mindless exploitation by others. No! I am not talking about that kind of sacrifice, which is exploitation, not sacrifice. To give a small example, in patriarch families especially in poor families in India, the women would work the whole day, earn, cook, do all the household chores, but would serve everything to their family first and starve themselves on most of the days. In a poor family, there is usually a situation of insufficient food for all in the family. As a common practice, the priority for serving food runs like this: Lion's share for the Male Head (enough to fully satisfy his hunger), followed by children to the extent food is available and sharable (girl child being lower on the priority to be fed), and the mother coming last on the list. She is lucky, if there is something left for her: otherwise, she simply goes hungry. This happens rampantly in poor families even when the mother works and earns; and the male head does not earn, but engages in toxic habits like drinking etc. The mother may feel the joy of sacrifice initially; but for how long? Plus, for how long her body can really tolerate this torture? If the family is well knit with love and care for one another, they would most likely know the value of *sharing* in such situations, instead of feeding some at the cost of the women in the family.

Sacrifice must be self-willed, not under duress. But sadly, the fact remains that most mothers are yet to learn how to enjoy healthy and loving relationships without *giving up yourself* in the process.

Kitchen undoubtedly makes us taste the Joy of Sacrifice, but simultaneously it also sharpens our sense of differentiating between sacrifice vs. giving into exploitation. There is a huge difference between *making a sacrifice* and *being made to sacrifice*, the latter amounting to plain exploitation. *When we make a sacrifice* (i.e., choose to sacrifice), out of our love and concern for others, but taking at least minimum needed care of ourselves to be able to continue caring for others, putting their interests before ours, there is joy. A small example. Suppose some delicacy like cake/ice cream is being shared, and one child wants a bigger share for she loves it, a mother will sacrifice her own share and give it to the child with utmost joy! *This is true joy of sacrifice, as it arises out of our ability to take joy in others' joy.* It is said, if you can be happy in others' happiness, then you will never fall short of reasons to be happy. Mothers somehow get to learn this never-failing recipe for happiness in kitchen through the simple, mundane duty and responsibility of providing food to the family.

This sense of duty and responsibility to ensure something for those dependent on us for that service (providing food, in the context of kitchen) even if it calls for some personal sacrifices is the hallmark of a great contributor in any field.

It becomes clear to those engaged in kitchen that there is a difference between true sacrifice and exploitation when *we are made to* sacrifice out of a clear lack of concern of others for us, at times even for our survival. This is no less a precious learning from the world of food. This lesson, in turn, makes them very understanding and compassionate for others while working elsewhere. Such people in management are likely to be more caring of others, and hence more likely to be effective in working with people.

The joy of sacrifice manifolds when everyone shares and sacrifices.

There is *another dimension* in the context of sacrifice that we need to be clear about. When we are talking of the *joy of sacrifice,* we are talking about those *acts of love and sacrifice that are not done with any sort of expectation-quid pro quo, even in emotional terms.* You do it, solely because you find joy in it. Most unwittingly, *when we believe* that we have made a 'sacrifice' for someone or something, we normally start 'expecting.' We expect results or returns, or at least gratitude or praise. If these are not forthcoming, we start feeling like a victim. Strictly speaking, there is nothing like 'sacrifice,' if you have done it out of your own volition. Just like every other decision, it is your own choice. You have a trade-off situation between two sets of interests/actions, and you choose to pick up one. If you had prepared say, exact number of spiced fish fries by head count, and now your husband would love to have one more because it is so delicious, it is up to you to choose- give him your share and be genuinely happy in his happiness/in explicit appreciation for your culinary skill, or give him your share and make one more afresh for yourself but with extra effort, or simply sacrifice your share for him but with unhappiness within. The trade-off was between *to be joyous* even by giving up your share, or having to do some extra work, or *being unhappy* even after giving up your share. Choice is yours.

Small but frequent acts of sacrifice out of love and toil in kitchen make mothers awaken to the aforesaid spiritual dimension of sacrifice, too. This realisation elevates the quality of our overall life as we live all kinds of relationships. We consciously try to minimise our expectations or validations from outside and learn to do good solely *because it feels good to be good.*

56. Courage

Courage as an indispensable value/personality trait cannot be overemphasised in the context of management, leadership, and life. No debate there.

What is interesting and enlightening is noting how our humble Kitchen throws up opportunities practically every day to practice courage, and thus, almost drives us to discover our own inner courage and further strengthen it to take everything head-on in life; be it on personal or professional plane. Let's take a look.

Simply put, courage is feeling fear, yet choosing to act! It is the ability to do something right, necessary, or new, *despite fear, which may be real or even imagined.*

The key point is: *courage must get demonstrated at the level of action.* No action-no way to ascertain if there is courage! *But thought always precedes action.* So, at an ideology level (that precedes action), *courage is of course summoned first in the mind* – at the thought level. You are courageous when you are *not ready to conform* to anything and everything that comes as a diktat, tradition, or common practice. *At the level of mind, courage is the ability to question;* to apply your own mind and then take a decision as to whether something being asked/advocated/followed is to be accepted by you or not.

As rightly and succinctly put by Earl Nightingale,

"The opposite of courage in our society is not cowardice... it's conformity."

I believe, for a rounded comprehension of any term, both *what it is* and *what it is not* must be understood fully.

Keeping the above in view, let us further discuss on courage and its dimensions, along with examples on how kitchen helps us imbibe this great value.

Literature on 'Courage' abound. But Dungate and Armstrong have given very nice insights into understanding courage. According to them, "Courage, very broadly, involves making a decision, or taking action, where a risk is involved – something actual or imagined to fear." Further, for a finer analysis, they broadly categorise courage into six types, and maintain that taken together, these six kinds of courage can enable one to take life head-on.

The six types of courage are:

1. Physical Courage: Bravery at the risk of bodily harm or death. Very often, courage is talked about in this sense of developing physical strength, resilience, and awareness.

   In kitchen, you get minor hurts almost regularly, and at times, injuries can be severe physically. Even experienced mothers and cooks cut their fingers while chopping, burn fingers suddenly trying to hold something hot in a hurry, accidentally expose their fingers and hands to piping hot steam while draining some hot liquid, like say, rice, getting hit by hot oil projectiles (!) over face and body parts while frying some stuff which has moisture inside, or explodes suddenly (like, usually while deep-frying corn for crispy corn; or frying fish – there are many examples). I am very used to all these, especially the last, as that happens even if you stand a bit afar, and is very unpredictable most of the times. I had once cut my fingers and palm just beneath my left-hand thumb when trying out my new silicon knife (super-sharp) over something round, that slipped and *deeply* slit my palm and fingers. If you have experience of cooking and kitchen chores, you know how extremely painful and almost incapacitating it is.

   The fire risks need no elaboration – a gas cylinder bursting, an electric gadget suddenly malfunctioning dangerously, or even at times your attire catching fire especially when using open wood burning chullahs!

   But the show must go on. You must have rarely seen mothers stop cooking because they are injured, or even they fear that they might get injured. As if from the blue, they get the tricks of using their palms, fingers, hands in other uncommon ways and complete the chores. *What is significant to note is: not only that they carry on with their job in the kitchen even after being injured, they also show the guts to come every time to the kitchen, knowing fully well that they are perpetually at risk of getting hurt.* It is courage 'before, during and after'! Driven by *purpose and meaning* in role, as already enunciated in the beginning.

Apart from the risk of physical hurts, there is one more critical dimension associated with cooking and kitchen management, that we have talked about enough earlier – *the physical and mental tiredness* that grip you doing this job every day, day in and day out, for long, without much of a break! Notwithstanding the daily drudgery, mothers come back to kitchen every morning. This unmistakably toughens your physical tolerance/endurance capacity, as also your resilience in mind and body.

These may be small examples of how *physical courage* gets instilled in our humble kitchen; but though small, they do build such courage brick by brick and consistently. The injuries are obviously nothing compared to, say, those of soldiers fighting at the front, in terms of gravity of the injuries. But the *mental quality* that keeps them ever ready to jump into action despite the risk of getting hurt and the physical pain, is similar whether it is in a battle field or a kitchen. *Thus, it is not just physical courage. Even these attitudes reflect moral and spiritual courage. You are acting with physical courage because you realise the larger purpose of your being there in a small kitchen and your grand role in that context.* We have already discussed that in great details, so no need to repeat.

2. Social Courage: Ability to take the risk of social embarrassment, rejection, unpopularity or ostracization. It's about being ourselves in the face of adversity.

   Cultivating social courage is a must for leadership, as leadership very often involves transcending conformity –i.e., going against prevailing social practices and attitudes. Though in a very limited sense, I find a small parallel in the context of food and kitchen, when women working as high-level executives also cook at home regularly against the general expectation of others who believe that such working women must have delegated these responsibilities to hired hands. As already mentioned earlier, many working mothers like me cook for the family for several reasons other than affordability.

3. Intellectual Courage: Ability to discern and tell the truth by demonstrating a willingness to question even *own* thinking, to engage with challenging ideas even at the risk of making mistakes.

It's about letting go of the familiar and expanding our horizons. Obviously, the creativity and innovativeness that mothers and great chefs work with stem from this kind of intellectual courage, that is nothing other than our willingness and ability to explore and experiment, even if we fail a few times. I would just make a special reference to how kitchen infuses *a spirit of inquiry* even into small acts. Innovation and creativity of course require the basic element of an appetite for experimentation. But there is another driver of creativity, too, namely, *questioning the status-quo, or conventional wisdom.* Here I would just add an example which is self-explanatory. Roasted a brinjal (Aubergine) on fire? Ever since I started cooking, I have seen experienced cooks and Chefs applying some oil on the whole brinjal and making a few slits. Slits for the moisture inside the brinjal to escape without bursts as it roasts on fire; and oil on skin to make the peeling of the burnt skin from the roasted brinjal easier and neater. Fine. I did that a few times. But once I just thought of checking out what happens if no oil is applied to skin, as after roasting in any case the skin gets burnt and unless peeling is done under a slowly running tap, it gets messed up a bit even with a lot of care. So, I just roasted with slits and cooled a bit, not fully and started peeling under a slowly running tap – going from top to bottom. It worked so well that, after that I never apply oil, though that is a standard practice, advocated even by great professional Chefs.

4. Moral Courage: Doing the right thing, or standing up for the right thing and justice even at the risk of punishment, shame, opposition, or disapproval of others. *It's about ethics and integrity; about one's ability to walk their talk.* It is not about who we claim to be before our family and society, but who *we are* in terms of our words and actions reflecting our values and ideals. *We have already seen how kitchen helps us in imbibing integrity and honesty as core values.*
5. Emotional Courage: Ability to feel the full spectrum of positive emotions even at the risk of encountering the negative ones. This is, sort of, a beautiful cocktail of all types of courage mixed together. *You cannot be courageous otherwise, if you are not*

emotionally courageous as well. Because everything involves some negative experiences alongside positive ones, and unless you know how to take the former in your stride, you cannot meet anything, any emotion, any situation in full. Fundamentally, it is a positive ability to stay vulnerable. You cannot experience happiness in life, if you don't have emotional courage to allow vulnerability, take upsets and adversities, that may come up as you follow your heart. Kitchen is a responsibility where you are not sure of appreciation of your tireless efforts, nor success every time; yet mothers never stop continuing on their sojourn of taking care of the well-being of their loved ones. Recall our discussions in the segment on motivation.

6. Spiritual Courage: Ability to handle existential questions on purpose, meaning, beliefs and faith constructively. As a result, spiritual courage fortifies us to face pain and adversity with dignity and faith. *Work in kitchen becomes worship for mothers, because they subconsciously convince themselves on purpose behind their mundane role in the very beginning itself* to deal with at least the physical inconveniences of working day-in-and-day-out in kitchen. In course of time, we have seen how positive attitudes and elevated traits like grace, acceptance without expectation, empathy, compassion, gratitude etc. get aroused and ingrained in them. No wonder, mothers demonstrate high degree of spiritual courage.

In every kind of courage, there is an in-grained element of risk-taking ability despite fear of outcome. Nothing worthwhile is achieved if no risk, at least calculated, is taken. NOT taking a risk is also a risk in the sense that it completely blocks the possibility of success, or at least being rewarded in some ways, not anticipated by you. Taking risk, showing up with courage very often opens up unseen/unimagined newer vistas/ opportunities! This is especially true when there is calculated, thought-through risk-taking.

Looking at big picture (feeding your family as a care giver) just makes the mothers toughen their ability to bear. Courage drives them to focus on the bigger goals undeterred by minor irritants, hiccups, and obstacles.

Kitchen is a huge learning platform that hammers in us that courage is a pivotal quality of mind as without it, we can indeed do nothing worthwhile in this world.

57. Empathy, Caring and Sharing

Our homely kitchen deeply instils and nurtures *empathy* as a distinct characteristic trait in *mothers*. And empathy as a value forms the bedrock of *Caring and Sharing*. What is empathy after all? The ability to put yourself in someone else's shoes and look at things from their perspective, so that you can *understand* them and their specific situation. *Goes without saying, no Empathy-> no Understanding of others -> no Caring!*

How important empathy as a trait is can be fathomed when you observe keenly how people behave when there is *lack* of empathy and understanding causing great harm to others, even without having outright malice!

It would be our sheer stupidity if we cannot notice how even a simple household responsibility like providing food to the family regularly can give repeated opportunities to bring in empathy into every related activity and expand our ability to be caring persons. We have already talked about it from many angles. You ensure food on time, *because you care* for your family members' well-being. You ensure *right* kind of diet for special needs of different members, *because you care* for their health and well-being. You ensure including in your meal menus dishes of special liking to your loved ones as per their different tastes and preferences as often as feasible, *because you care* for their happiness and use their favourite food as means to delight them. (Oh, yes, in corporate parlance, this is akin to Customer Delight- getting something you like beyond your expectation!) You make them eat at least some healthy food, which may be unappealing to their taste (like bitter-gourd, bottle-gourd, non-oily/non-spicy food etc.), *because you care* for their health. When sick, you ensure the prescribed diet and see to it that they have it, *because you care* for them and want them cured. *So on and so forth! Yes, you do all this because you love them. But is not love another name of care?*

By the way, have you ever observed how loving husbands take care of their pregnant wives' food cravings during odd hours and fetch that food doing whatever it takes? This is a very sweet kind of love and care that finds expression through food. It is rightly said, food is not just some eatables-it lays out the road to someone's heart!

Food is never *just something to eat* or an island; it comes bundled up with so many emotions! Perhaps that's why it is said, *a family that eats together stays together*. No wonder, when you look after food for others, you yourself turn a new leaf as a human being every now and then.

Care, as a value, does not come to a person without empathy, understanding, love and compassion. A hugely precious bundle of core human values. Big 'Ego's abound, who ask, why should I care for others without minding *only* my own business? But dear ones, is there anything in this world that is exclusively your own business, without an iota of dependence on others? Think deeply, nothing is truly independent in an absolute sense. This Whole Existence is a play of interdependence. So, to become what you are meant to be, you must care for and share with others – no choice! *When done willingly from within, caring about other people becomes an absolute strength in life, as also in profession, as it allows you to connect with others at a deeper level with respect for human dignity in the first place.* Caring enables you to listen actively with genuine emotional presence and empathy, respond with understanding, and compassion, extending needed support with love and kindness. Keenly observe your mothers sometimes and these qualities in them will simply be unmissable. I am not saying, they imbibe all these qualities from kitchen ONLY; all I am maintaining is kitchen also helps them greatly in this respect. Kitchen responsibilities are such that they cannot but help them acquire/reinforce these traits subconsciously. Once imbibed, these values automatically get manifested in other walks of life as well, as *you have become a 'caring' person in essence.*

Mothers also mess up dishes at times, as they are humans after all. But find out who eats that, if not discarded. Mothers themselves! Usually, they fix something else/better for the family quickly. Because they love and care for them. Also, look at how mothers manage to share the quantum of a dish already made amongst the family members. Whatever order they choose to serve, they always keep themselves at the end. At times, having nothing left by their turn comes. But still they remain happy and *share the happiness of others.*

It is said, food always tastes better when you have someone to share it with! Since time immemorial, cooking and sharing the meal has been perhaps man's foremost, even quintessential, social experience. Across the globe, across all cultures, all societies, celebrations surrounding meals and eating together are ubiquitous. Nothing unites humanity the way a simple practice like sitting together and sharing a meal. So, sharing is a value that permeates across food-related behaviour for most of us. *And the sense of bliss is perhaps the most when we share our food with someone hungry and deprived!*

Kitchen is about food; and food is about sharing and caring. Sharing as a precious value automatically gets imbibed in mothers from kitchen.

It is amazing, how since thousands of years in Ancient India, Rig Veda prescribes "Bhojanam Mantra" (i.e., a prayer before meal) to be chanted, that lays emphasis on understanding that food is to be eaten for a well-nourished body, that in turn, is to be dedicated, along with our mind and wealth, to carry out our divine purpose (*Brahma Karm*) through service to the World – service to the Humanity! Thus, food is to be first offered to and blessed by the Supreme, and then taken as "*His Prasad.*" Again, it clearly states in the following portion of the *Mantras* that it is an absolute requirement *to share our food with others, or else that food leads to one's ruin eventually!*

Om... Moghamannam vindate apracetah satyam bravimi vadha itsatasya

Naryamanam pushyati no sakhayam kevalagho bhavati kevaladi

(The foolish man wins food with fruitless labour; that food, I speak the truth, shall be his ruin who feeds no friend, no man to love him. All guilt is he who eats alone.)

(source: Internet)

(So, eat together; give and share.)

What better and deeper spiritual, yet worldly-wise, message can be there about food, which is simply taken for granted when available easily?

In fact, I am sanguine, every religion teaches one to thank God and offer prayers before/after a meal in acknowledgement of Divine Grace to ensure food for the sustenance and nourishment of our body, which is a crucial instrument in achieving all our goals.

Look around with deeper eyes- every action performed with love and care generates positive vibes that get shared with others. Sharing, not only in kind, but also in terms of positive energy, is truly one's invaluable gift to all around. No wonder, we always hear, *"Sharing is Caring."*

Moreover, as one responds to all work, situations, and people in one's life with a strong sense of caring and sharing, it only implies that they are responding fully to the whole of life itself not in a mundane, but in a transformational way.

58. Taste what you serve (Always be Self-Aware)

A fundamental rule that is taught to the students of culinary skills is that you must taste everything, at many stages, and the final creation, before you serve it to others.

Mothers and regular cooks, of course, are always in the habit of doing this - tasting at least once the recipe is done to confirm its taste and balance. [Except when you are preparing ceremonial *Prasad* to be offered to God to maintain its purity out of your own religious sentiments. But you would be stunned to know about a story of the *Sabari* in the epic *Ramayana*, who tasted each berry to ensure it was ripe and sweet before offering it to Lord Shri Ram, out of supreme devotion!]

Some mothers like me even keep tasting at various stages of the recipe to ensure everything turns out as intended. 😊 I have heard Professional Chefs advising the mentees to always taste – taste the ingredients before applying, taste the spice paste, taste the gravy, taste at all important stages to ensure nothing is off-track, and finally, taste the dish on completion before serving.

Reason is obvious. *Tasting before serving ensures correction needed, if any, so that it does not get too late to redeem.* But that is not all. *It also means I now have the choice not to serve it at all, if it is likely to cause irreparable damage.*

The idea is not only to perfect the taste and balance in the dish, but also to *know what you are serving*! *Knowing what you are serving has a profound spiritual connotation*. Our spoken words, demonstrated reactions and behaviour are like arrows already shot, which cannot be brought back. Hence, it is highly important that before speaking, before reacting we must *pause* to consciously witness our own thoughts and feelings, how they are going to impact our words and actions, and their likely effects on those at the receiving end. We must always have a tab on the 'ingredients' used; i.e., our ingrained beliefs and values lying at the root of our thoughts leading to default-mode reactions. I must be careful about what is the 'taste' of what I am going to 'serve' through my speech and action. *Once I live in this awareness mode, interestingly I will be the first one to have the 'taste' of my own words yet to be spoken or action yet to be taken. And this should help me immensely in moderating or changing or discarding the same if I realise that it is going to hurt my valuable relationships or bonding.* In unaware mode, very often we do end up speaking or acting improperly that we regret later. The only solution is to be present in the moment and be self-aware.

It is also interesting to understand from another angle how kitchen facilitates imbibing this uber-important lesson on Self Awareness. Observe yourself in kitchen. When you are cooking, you are cooking; when you are chopping, you are chopping, when you are washing the dishes, you are washing the dishes etc., i.e., being fully conscious of what you are doing, being 'present' mentally as you act physically on even the smallest of the small chores. You don't normally get fickle-minded thinking constantly about, say, the next 10+ tasks you have to do. Because you know, you just have to be done with the current tasks now and here, and then can focus on anything else. Besides, as we know, if you do not focus, accidents/disasters can strike in the kitchen. Food is something we cannot do without; so, while preparing it, we just do that instead of letting our mind run too much off track. My personal experience is: even while multi-tasking many tiny jobs, attention on the particular job on hand at the moment is utmost, as it is just a tiny time window that I get for this task, and in next few secs something else will have to be done. Yes, while doing something in the kitchen that I do regularly almost on auto-mode and listening to an audio on say, spiritual discourse, my attention is divided; but as one task(chore) is *habitual,* and hence, does not need my mind or intellect to be engaged in 'deciding how to do that', not much problem is created if the other task (listening) receives the best part of my mindfulness. *But most of the times, the focus is clearly on what I am doing, anchored in here and right now. That precisely is what mindfulness means for always staying in Self-Aware mode.*

Vedantic scriptures always impress upon us to remain *'Sa-manaska', i.e., staying with the mind here and now*! That is, keeping our consciousness alive to the whole of present reality at every moment – what is going on in my inner space as also what all are happening in my surroundings.

Amazing how just this one practice in kitchen, viz. taste before you serve, is indeed a profound lesson in cultivating Self-Awareness! *Stretched a bit further, this can help us in cultivating total awareness or mindfulness.*

Whether it is our mundane life in this material world, or our spiritual life involving serious inner work on our *Samskaras (deeply inherent traits) and Atmagyan (knowledge of and experiencing* SELF, *the pure consciousness)*, no progress is feasible unless we know what is going on in our mind every moment, in a perpetual *right now and right here* mode. Otherwise, the default modes of our behaviour patterns take over and intellect does not even get a tiny window of opportunity to decide what is right or wrong, before ego-driven mind reacts.

And as mundane and as humble a workplace as our homely kitchen constantly helps us imbibe this profound and pivotal quality of being in a continuous state of self-awareness!

Self-awareness helps us know ourselves much better. In leadership parlance, we always talk of doing a SWOT analysis – Strengths, Weaknesses, Opportunities and Threats – for worldly success. It is a self-analysis through self-awareness so that you can work on yourself.

Needless to mention, for a manager, a leader, or any individual for that matter irrespective of the area of their functioning, to be effective, it is indispensable to know one's own strengths and weaknesses. Interesting to note how, even in this aspect, kitchen can come to help us imbibe the necessary abilities to assess own self.

Kitchen is a work space where you simply cannot avoid feeling the 'heat', literally and metaphorically, too, in terms of many stressful situations that a kitchen keeps throwing up at us. Just like our lives. Even with the best of planning, preparedness, resources, and competencies, no one can be in complete control of one's life. In kitchen, if you are not careful in stressful situations, you can get burnt, or worse, can burn others. *It is highly necessary that you have a fair idea of how much is too much for you.* How much you can stretch yourself without snapping. When you take on more than you can handle, it is very likely that not only you perform at sub-optimal level, you might even break down.

So, kitchen teaches you loud and clear, *if you can't take the heat, get out of the kitchen!*

If you consistently feel 'heat' in any job/responsibility, and you are aware of it all the time, then you should pause and re-evaluate your suitability for the job in terms of your own strengths, weaknesses, and aptitude, and take a decision to continue or to quit.

59. Decision Making

It would amount to redundancy if we go into details on how decision making is involved at every stage of cooking and running a kitchen regularly. All the aspects we have already talked about so far, especially, planning-execution-review-course correction, are nothing but decision-making in varied contexts. Just the simplest example – MENU. What exact dishes would be made for different meals of the day is an important decision-making exercise in the context of daily food, keeping in mind many relevant factors. Is it not? Ask the mothers, what they find the most difficult part of cooking, and invariably they would say, it is the menu! Forget about large families, or Indian Joint families, or when guests are to be entertained, or, festivals are to be celebrated; even in a small family, different members can have widely different tastes, preferences, health requirements, cravings etc. in respect of food. Top it up with the need for diversity (you can't repeat a dish or a recipe too soon, except the staple) and the need for optimum resource management without wasting. Deciding a menu for each meal is not as simple a task as it might appear, especially if you have to do this continuously for a long time. Once the menu is decided, cooking involves much less tension.

It truly gladdens my heart to notice the young working couples of the current generation sitting down together and deciding menus for at least 3-4 days in advance. It helps immensely in execution and delivery. Plus, sharing kitchen responsibilities is a concrete positive step towards true women empowerment and gender equality.

At a deeper level, every moment in our lives, we are making choices, i.e., making decisions, on what to do, how to do, how to be, consciously and mostly unconsciously. So, when we face repetitive encounters with situations calling for conscious and matured decisions, as Mothers encounter day-in and day-out in kitchen, our ability to decide gets fine-tuned and developed.

Mind-blowing to glean from what we have discussed so far, how kitchen weaves many threads of perspectives, lessons, insights, which intertwine to reveal a tapestry of experiences and lessons that guide us toward our highest potential through *right decision-making* at every juncture that counts.

Sense of Responsibility. I think this one trait, one of the greatest drivers of correct decision- making, ingrained in you from kitchen, also makes you learn *how to take charge, when you are in command,* irrespective of where you are placed.

Although taking charge of a situation is essentially a core leadership call in professional roles, I wonder, which 'leader' can indeed lead others, without first being able to lead their own selves in a right way. So, I am convinced, the above edict is as much relevant in respect of self, as it is for others put in your charge. *You ought to put yourself in command of your own well-being in life and take charge, alongside taking charge of your external roles and responsibilities.* You must take charge – of the people, of the situations and of the outcome! If you are responsible for something, then you must own up your responsibility and steer everything with that ownership of responsibility and ultimate accountability.

Believe me, kitchen responsibility may sound very ordinary; but in reality, kitchen is almost like a mini battle field where failure is not an option every now and then. Whether you cook yourself or get it done through others, ultimately it is your singular responsibility to ENSURE food on the table on time, catering to every other associated needs.

Mothers, over time, get into the habit of doing their work with a great sense of responsibility to manage food and kitchen day in and day out, taking complete charge of it. Without wishing to be dubbed as a feminist, I would like to recommend you to look deeper into the functioning styles of most working women, irrespective of their cadre and you would be amazed to notice how effortlessly they bring to table many of the effective leadership qualities and strategies without even being conscious of it. No wonder, because the vast majority of working women also happen to be the ones in charge of kitchen management at home!

60. Role Vs Role-holder

It is not the 'role' but the 'person who holds the role' that makes all the difference!

In an organisational set up, employees are assigned to play various 'roles' at different points of time and it is the specific person who ultimately makes the differences to the role (s)he is holding. If roles *per se* were the determinants, outcomes and deliveries should be the same irrespective of the persons who hold those roles. It is never so. *Role-holders, and not roles per se, bring about changes.* Some persons in whichever role they are put make that role look shiny with great deliveries and great possibilities; while some others, in whichever role they are put, make those roles look lack-lustre due to their own deficiency in vibrancy and competence.

I find a great parallel to this in kitchen.

Kitchen is a great mirror that keeps on showing you the 'person' you truly are. Please re-visit our discussion on how kitchen drives you *to be*, not just *appear to be*. Simply observe the differences when your mother cooks and provides food, as against when a hired hand cooks for a salary. Both the mother and the hired hand are playing the same 'role' – that of a cook. But look at the sincerity and sense of responsibility, love and care with which mother ensures that you not only get, but eat your food on time and as per all your requirements. The hired hand, even if having a commendable level of cooking skill, would most likely not come anywhere near your mother in terms of the caring factors. *Why so much differences in quality of engagement and delivery?*

Clearly, it is because the hired hand lacks the *sense of belonging and ownership of well-being of others* that a mother brings to the role of a 'cook'! When as an employer you transmit this attitude to your employees successfully, you will successfully delegate and bridge the gaps between playing of the 'role' by various role-holders.

On the other side, personal qualities of employees would decide if as '*the* role holder' in specific roles, they can make a visible difference to the functions and glory of that role; *albeit*, impacted by the quality of leadership to some extent.

It is not the 'role', but 'the person who holds the role' that makes all the difference!

So true!

Many a times when I used to be weary of under-performance by some team members, or needed to boost their morale, or even needed to sustain my self-motivation in a less visible role, I used to repeat this one-liner, and believe me, it always worked like a Magic Wand!

Maybe it worked in my case because I never did mere lip-servicing it. I had understood, meant, and *lived* what I was saying.

Quite strange that these miracles are already happening, not because of the bosses, but because of quite a few out there – amongst your employees, who believe and live it out day-in and day-out, whether the boss notices it or not. It is their own commitment to themselves to make the difference as the "role-holder" to whichever role they are assigned – glamorous or lack-lustre.

Let me add one more perspective. Ever thought of your inconspicuous, taken-for-granted role in kitchen from the following special angle?

Food and Art are two unique worlds which do not have borders! Basudevam Kutumbakkam genuinely applies to these two worlds, without friction and fragmentation of any sort. Our highly contentious political relationship with some of the neighbouring countries notwithstanding, travel of food culture and food fusions amongst us keep happening seamlessly all the time. No wonder, Chinese recipes are a rage across India, while Indian recipes are similarly adopted and hugely relished in all Asian countries as well as world-wide. The popularity is mostly a function of awareness created by the traditional owners of recipes. Also, thanks to the Communication and Technology Revolution of the last few decades, such awareness is spreading at a lightning speed and the idea of any specific land/people as original-owners has already lost relevance. *There is a beautiful mingling and churning and fusion of food ideas globally,* and the theme that runs across the globe is good food is good and adopted, no matter where it originated in what form!

Working in a small homely kitchen, if you can see this big picture and your tiny, but significant 'role' in it, is it not hugely rewarding and fulfilling? For me, a huge Yes!

Such kind of *role-consciousness* definitely helps one in every sphere of life in playing different roles with utmost sincerity, authenticity and inner satisfaction.

61. Simplicity is the ultimate sophistication

Yes, the world of food keeps reminding us the above - a huge life lesson!

True sophistication, to my understanding, lies in subtleties, craftiness, artfulness, slickness, and appropriateness; i.e., in *tasteful simplicity* that renders the result just right. Neither overdone, nor underdone. Sophistication does not lie in gaudiness - garish, tasteless ornamentation.

Just for an example (pl do not brand me a patriarch): Look at two beautiful young ladies, one with very minimal/no make-up, simply radiating the glow of her youthfulness and a good heart, and another with/without a good heart, but heavily made-up. In fact, you can visualise your own young daughters/sisters just before and after bridal make-up in one of the common beauty parlours. (I guess, highly rated excellent parlours do not over-do.) Who appeals genuinely? Whose 'beauty' touches you instantly?

That exactly is the difference between *sophistication in simplicity*, and *mistaken sophistication in tasteless flashiness*.

Coming now to our world of food, recall how you felt on being served a glass of lemonade just when you needed it after a long drive - simply garnished with a lemon ring and a tiny sprig of fresh mint; well-made (tasty) and poured into a decent glass. Simple, yet sophisticated. Don't you think so? Would you have expected the lemonade to have more ingredients which are unnecessary or non-complementing? Or would you have liked it more, if, say, the glass was decorated a lot more? Think about it. A lemonade is a lemonade, and *there is a purity in its taste that must be retained without complicating it*. Similarly, in life, there are many things that must retain its simplicity for the sake of its purity. No need to complicate their presentation in an ostentatious manner. That does not lend to it any sophistication.

Have you ever observed your own feelings when you are served a meal consisting of homely, simple, and healthy dishes when you return from a vacation outside in places where you had no choice but to eat mostly spicy, unhealthy, unappealing food in hotels/restaurants? Recall your own experience and you would realise the satisfaction in simplicity. What purpose does sophistication sought in garishness (rich, spicy, well-garnished dishes) serve if it is devoid of the most-needed element of satisfaction for the diner?

Now, let us take the example a poached egg-a perfectly poached one. How simple yet sophisticated it comes across! Well, getting an egg perfectly poached is not really as simple as it looks: the technique is tricky and is perfected through practice. And therein lies its sophistication.

Similarly, take for example a fish fry. Depending upon the kind of fish, you fry it in some simple, but *right* way so that the fish fry turns out crispy on the outside but moist and juicy in the inner flesh portion. I tell you, not everyone gets it right although it is a simple process. *Rightness of cooking technique, when added to the simplicity of the dish, lends it its ultimate sophistication.*

I like Italian cuisine! For its striking simplicity, that in no way diminishes its great taste which is very homely and earthy. Nothing complicated. And I know, many people across the globe love it, too. No wonder, Italian restaurants are flourishing world-wide, including in Indian cities. Even our small-town food joints and hotels spring up the most basic, yet perhaps most relished Italian dishes like pasta and pizza! It is amazing how, every time I enjoy Italian dishes, whether in a restaurant or at home, its simplicity comes across to me as the ultimate sophistication. Even in star hotels and restaurants, I find no garnishing or much less of that just for presentation's sake in case of Italian cuisine, compared to other cuisines.

I gave the example of Italian food for sophistication in simplicity, because I feel, most of the readers in this globalised world can relate to it.

But back home, in my home state Odisha, and other Eastern states in India, typically our cuisine is full of simple, yet truly tasty and healthy traditional/local recipes, that are *soul-filling*! Sophistication in food, in true sense, does not necessarily come from a complicated *presentation* that is only a visual treat without substance. It must come from a fulfilling, comforting, complete meal that makes you relish it, gives you all you need from your food so that you feel soul-satisfied and energetic. Instant appeal to the eye is, at best, a bonus. Look at the pictures of many simple homely dishes, now being uploaded by home-makers and Chefs as well on social media, with no or a very little garnishing (say, a sprig of some fresh herb, or just a sprinkle of grated coconut, or a bit of fresh cream, or a few fried dry nuts, or a few strands of barista etc.).

Emphasis is on quality and taste, as it should be. That ensured, sophistication in your food is achieved!

I, myself, cook very many simple dishes, like Fish fry with only salt and turmeric, fish/prawn curry in turmeric powder, and a few other basic ingredients, No-oil Meat Stew (my father's recipe), *Khechudi, Dalma, Santula* (boiled mixed vegetables tempered with garlic, or other basic ingredients), *Saaga* (green leaves tempered with garlic, onion and chilli), *drumstick-aloo bhaja, pithua bhaja, baigana bharta, aloo bharta* etc. etc. - extremely healthy and tasty, famous and ubiquitous Odia dishes. Too many are there. I will fail myself and all Odias if I don't mention our highly relished, soulful, simple dish of Summer called Pakhala! These, and many more Odia/Indian recipes from other parts of our vast country exemplify how simplicity in fact is the ultimate form of sophistication for comfort, stomach-fill, and nutrition. Every time you prepare these recipes, you know you don't have to, or rather must not, go overboard on presentation part. No garnishing is the best garnishing in most of these cases.

Especially, if you want to experience simplicity as the best form of sophistication, then I would recommend you to have a meal of Sri Jagannath Temple Maha Prasad at Puri (a world-famous town in my home state, Odisha, for pilgrimage). Served on banana leaf. No garnishing, except a bit of tadka. Tadka is a simple tempering of cumin/mustard seeds and dry red chilli in clarified butter, with/without *nadi/badi*-which is sometimes added after it is offered to Lord Jagannath, but before selling, for a touch of enhanced look and taste. Otherwise, Maha Prasad items are one-pot, non-tempered dishes. Sophistication in these dishes runs through their simplicity in both procedure and presentation.

Perhaps the best examples of 'simplicity being the ultimate sophistication' can be seen in our concept of 'Thali.' In India, various regions have their own Thali menus – Gujrati Thali, Maharashtrian Thali, Rajasthani Thali, Bengali Thali, Odia Thali etc. Firstly, these are very representative of the food that is commonly prepared and relished in that region – the typical cuisines, the typical style of cooking, the preferences for taste etc. For example, if you would find a lot of spiciness in a South Indian Thali on one extreme, you would find the love for sweetness in almost all dishes on a Gujrati Thali. Secondly, the dishes on the Thali capture the uniqueness of that region in terms of what is available in that geographical area as per climatic conditions. A Rajasthani Thali would be lacking in vegetables, but buzzing with grams and lentils; while an eastern India Thali would come alive with fish and seafood, along with a variety of greens and vegetables! But one thing is usually found common in all Thalis – *they speak to you and keep you excited with dishes that play with your palate with "Sad-Rasa", the six tastes, about which we have talked earlier.*

The common presentation of most Thalis is a very simple circular arrangement on a large plate. No garnishing, no added visual attractions, barring the neat and simple arrangement of the main staples in the middle on a big plate, surrounded by small katories (bowls) of delicacies as accompaniments. Or, simply served on a banana leaf. But in terms of the variety of ingredients, textures, flavours, tastes, techniques, and recipes that go into the meal served on the Thali, it is just mind-blowing. *If this is not sophistication in simplicity, then what is?*

To reiterate, kitchen is a place where premium is put on quality brought in through simplicity. On one hand, it teaches that simplicity ultimately drives sophistication in taste and quality. On the other hand, it also teaches that sophistication is a journey of many simple steps. In fact, from the angle of how even difficult recipes are *simplified* – step by step, it teaches us that ultimately if you want sophistication, that will eventually come from simplicity, and/or *simplification* of processes. Do not complicate things in the name of sophistication. Simple presentation does no harm to inherently qualitative creations.

What a great lesson for everything in life! Especially, the idea of 'simplification' is extremely relevant in the context of communication for project management in professional workspaces. Once you start valuing 'simplicity', you can get across every message in a way that is *received* correctly by those at the other end; you can capture and get done any complex job as a series of simple jobs; you can place and project your achievements with simple authenticity without out-of-context or manipulated drum-beatings. Etc. etc.

No wonder, we have very often heard: *being simple is rather a very difficult job. Hats off to our humble kitchen for helping us gain this perspective, too.*

62. Attitude matters ultimately

At times, I dare think that cooking is nothing less than a metaphor for life! How? In a kitchen, there are numerous food ingredients, multiple tools, varied cookware, multiple sources of heat for cooking, multiple ways to combine ingredients, multiple ways to cook your dishes and, of course, multiple situations. Ultimately, it is your own choice as to what to pick up and how to go about it, or how to deal with the situations. What you eventually *turn up* is what you yourself have worked towards! *As you sow, so you reap*-the universal *karmic law* is constantly in operation here, in a visible form. You just need to 'see' this happening in the kitchen all the time, just as it keeps happening in our lives. At birth, we all are given, or come with, some 'ingredients' like some behavioural tendencies, and environmental factors like parents, family background, and immediate surroundings. As we grow up, we acquire some more and discard a few, too. How we eventually use and apply those 'ingredients' in crafting our own lives depends majorly on our own *mindset;* our attitude towards people, objects, and situations.

No wonder, it is often said, *'We are the MasterChef of our own lives!' And 'Our attitude decides our altitude in life."* Rightly so.

In kitchen, we are the Master Chef creating the infinite type of dishes through our choices of combinations and processes for our recipes from the finite number of ingredients/inputs/processes. Similarly, we ourselves craft our own lives, like *a delicious and nutritional platter* as we go on making moves or responses every moment, by choosing to behave in particular ways based on infinite types of combinations involving our *inner-compass dimensions and external stimuli.* How to face or handle a situation is our own choice ultimately, just as which recipe to follow is ultimately our choice as the cook/Chef.

I think, everyone should have a shot at cooking. The basket of ingredients is almost the same for many people from a similar background. What matters is: out of those ingredients, what all you pick up and in what ways you are going to combine them to make your recipes interesting and unique!

Same with our lives in this world. The human emotions, the conditionings, the playing fields, that each of us gets to choose from are more or less similar at some level or other. But what one chooses eventually makes all the difference. *Life is always what we make it* – what we choose for ourselves: positivity over negativity, enthusiasm over cynicism, authenticity over duplicity, attitude of quest over fear of failure etc. etc.

Further, a Chef turns a Master Chef only after achieving a high level of excellence, which they gain only by going *beyond the known* – experimenting, exploring, and yes, bungling/ruining a few dishes while experimenting with newer ingredients and newer recipes. Experiment they must – with courage and an increasing knack of flavours. So, why bother if you fail a few times? So-called 'failures" are always "successes" as you learn from them what does not work and what might be done differently. We have talked about it earlier, too.

Eventually, you have to 'eat' what you have cooked – you have to live the life yourself that you have created by your choice of actions. So, why not cook something that appeals to your own palate and helps elevate your skills?

Why not be the Master Chef of your own life and spice it up the right way in right combinations, i.e., always choosing from a rightly balanced matrix of skills-competence-attitude?

When we put together the essence of everything, that we have talked about till now, it is profound to realise what a robust, well-rounded, positive set of attitudes kitchen helps us develop. The only need is to stay alive to the messages, lessons, and insights; reflect on them; imbibe, and carry forward to apply wherever applicable in life.

Kitchen routine almost *pushes* anyone in regular charge of it to develop a *wide and deep* perspective about everything significant in life, and thus a right set of attitudes to look at every situation/person. Especially, that urge to *spread wellness* seeps into our bones and spirit!

Sir Edmund Hillary, the famous mountaineer once said, *"It is not the mountain we conquer, but ourselves."*

All challenges in life – be it in our humble kitchen or in the cut-throat world of professional competition, or even in our journey of spiritual transformation – *challenges are ultimately met in our minds.* And how effectively or shoddily we meet them depends upon what attitudes we bring to our moment-to-moment life situations, along with our knowledge and skills – our *Mindscape*, as I like to call it. We conquer every battle that comes our way, only when we conquer our inner selves – our Mind. In spiritual discourses, subtle distinctions are made amongst mind, intellect, and ego to explain our inner world. But for our general purpose of understanding our inner world, we may refer to it as 'MIND'- a composite entity that perceives, assimilates, thinks, experiences feelings and emotions, and decides on external expressions and actions. *And all beliefs, thoughts and logics that finally get demonstrated in any action in any situation can be taken as the attitude towards a situation.*

With wrong attitudes, kitchen can be a nasty uninspiring workspace which might leave you feeling overworked, under-remunerated, unappreciated, and demoralised. Physically as well as emotionally drained, so to say. As already emphasised many a times, it involves unavoidable, tiresome, often repetitive, mostly unappreciated routine job. But with right attitudes, you develop a pair of 'real' eyes (realise), and see the *greatness* and *worthiness* behind everything that happens in a kitchen and everything that gets delivered from here, and you 'conquer' yourself spreading wellness all around.

Come on, just note what profound lessons can be learnt even from the very commonplace kitchen exercise of washing everything clean – the grains, the legumes, the vegetables, the miscellaneous ingredients, the cookware, the soiled utensils, etc. What purpose does this involve at the core? *To constantly ensure that what you are using and consuming is free from dirt and impurities.* No. 1: you don't throw away these resources just because they look dirty; you know they can be cleaned. No 2: you know *how* to clean – rinse enough number of times till all the dirt is washed away, and the cleaning water becomes transparent. *This is exactly the lesson everyone must learn to keep cleaning their minds of negativities and impurities from time to time.* Because, living in this material world, it is not 100% possible to shut ourselves off to all the negativities. So, it is crucial that we keep on adding a *continuous source of positive feed* for our mind to continuously cleanse our thoughts and emotions, and our inner world. Needless to mention, our external life experiences are in fact projections of our inner world dynamics. A life of peace and fulfilment can only flow from a calm, poised and blissful inner state of mind that does not hold on to impurities and negativities for long.

On the spiritual side on an elevated plane, the ultimate in the matrix of 'right attitudes' is Contentment, as it comes finally from *Gratitude, that always elevates us with a sense of abundance* and satisfaction *here and now*. I get goosebumps when I can see clearly how kitchen helps us imbibe this ultimate value over time. Especially, the contentment mothers derive from feeding their family, as also others, despite all discomfort and sacrifices, is invaluable. Ask them- they would not trade it for anything else. At times, this even feels like a puzzle: if you are so unappreciated and overworked, why do you want to even continue? The answer can lie only in something they *gain* which is much superior and much more valuable to their existence. And that is: contentment. Contentment, to me, can come in two major senses. 1. There is contentment when I am grateful for everything that I have at present. 2. There is contentment in the simple sense of having that blissful feeling of great satisfaction when you do your best in anything, without bothering about the burden, or even the fruits, of your labour.

And let me tell you, contentment as a value and personality trait moves through a loop of universal values like gratitude, acceptance, compassion, and an ability to experience abundance! It is truly enlightening to appreciate how these universal values are fully inter-woven - feeding on and being fed by one another! Start at any point and we are eventually at abundance, from which it creates more and more abundance, joy, happiness, and bliss. When we are grateful, we accept situations and people with understanding; when we accept, we let go of expectations from others/outside. Once we do not really expect, we are contented. Once contented, we feel abundance, devoid of any feeling of envy or longing, or any *sense of lack*. Once we feel abundant, on one hand we *work with greater energy* to achieve more, and on the other hand, we become *generous - sharing with others out of our sense of abundance.* Sharing brings with it abundant joy and happiness. This again creates another virtuous circle of higher positive energy, happiness, gratitude, contentment, acceptance, higher energy, higher achievements, greater sharing, higher joy and elevated energy exchanges.... *And the process becomes not only self-perpetuating, but spiralling upward, continuously expanding!* This is the real and empowering meaning of contentment.

Every value and attitudinal dimension that kitchen helps us imbibe ultimately infuses a sense of contentment in us.

Working in the kitchen regularly, you start realising that nothing - no work, no role, no person - is useless or insignificant to be derided or played down. As someone put it nicely, you must look down at someone's shoes only if you have something to appreciate about it! Every cog has a rightful place in a moving wheel. When you manage your mixed bag of tools in kitchen, you realise everything has a unique purpose, hence use, of its own. A knife is usually expected to be sharp; but we don't need a knife with extra sharpness for every chore. Even a blunt one has its own use at times. A razor is sharp, but it cannot cut a tree; similarly, an axe is strong and sharp, but it cannot cut hair. You must use each tool for what it is *meant to do*, without comparing the incomparable.

What is more, in kitchen one develops a knack of understanding the *value* of everything, not necessarily linked to their market *price* (salt). *This imbibes a great attitude that encourages never to discount or treat as useless anything or any person at face value without an honest attempt to figure out what value they carry.* This is also another factor that enables you to respect others, to be humble and to always strive towards effectiveness/

optimisation with excellence in whatever you are engaged in – dealing with situations or interacting with people.

The attitude that gets imbibed through these kinds of realisation is *respect for self as well as for every other person, and genuine respect for dignity of labour,* irrespective of what the job is. I need not elaborate on the benefits of people with such thinking patterns and how relevant this is for managerial effectiveness.

Secondly, you start learning to learn through a spirit of inquiry without accepting things on face value. You find something or other to learn from every situation, every work, every role, every person! On the side of worldly wisdom, the 'spirit of inquiry', i.e., accepting nothing without questioning and analysing deeply as to whether that works in different contexts, is an *attitude* that carries you far in life. And just recall, how even a mundane functional style like multi-tasking in kitchen opens your eyes to the value and wisdom in questioning even a supposedly scientifically upheld theory that says multi-tasking kills productivity. You learn to assess the context, and that gives right perspective.

Thirdly, as already emphasised earlier numerous times in this book, you start learning *to apply* what you learn – not just 'appear,' but 'be'!

When right perspective develops, right values/beliefs/attitude also get imbibed. Most importantly, your attitude to situations, especially adversities, in life, gets re-shaped. What happens to you (i.e., situations you land into) are mostly beyond your control. But how you respond, take it in your stride, decides the real quality of life that you experience. Recall *the carrot-egg-coffee bean story* from the segment on Teachers in the kitchen. What can be a better example of how insightfully kitchen engagements shape your mind?

Let us recall our discussions on discarding in waste-consciousness section. It mirrors a great mindset developed in kitchen to deal conclusively with unwarranted/unwanted/negative stuff in life that cannot be *undone*.

Closure of past stories of hurt and pain is very essential for moving on. Just discard them or dilute them continuously with more and more of positivity.

In life, we end up with many negative situations that cannot be reversed howsoever we might wish. We cannot, however, go on and go forward with bottled bitterness, and must find out a way to accept that situation post-facto by at least diluting its effects to such an extent that it no longer holds any significant impact on your present and future life. How? *In kitchen, this lesson comes to us succinctly if only we keep ourselves open and introspective!* We have talked about what do we do usually when the dish turns up salty. Since it is not possible to take out excess salt already mingled with it, we try to *dilute saltiness.* Essentially you *introduce some new agents to* normalise the messed-up situation. So, neither you torture yourself with a salty curry, nor you waste the whole dish just because of one mistake. For every messed-up situation, there may be some solutions to salvage depending upon specific situations; or just discard - let go of it, without any heart burn.

Similar with life situations. When the negativities in our life are too much to bear, and are irreversible, all we need to do is: add a whole lot more of positivity to life! One fine day, you would not even feel any negativity left from the past.

That is the ultimate lesson in life: Always focus and add more and more of positivity, irrespective of the negative situations that you might have had to face, and will face in future too.

Motivational speakers always exhort us to be positive. But not many explain how to convert negativities to positivity; how to change our thoughts from negative to positive. Kitchen keeps on throwing all the clues. Just grab them as you go along, treating mess-ups, accidents as lessons and opportunities to grow in life, just as our *Kitchen Garden* teaches us how pruning is necessary for growth and renewal of our herb plants. In fact, observe Mother Nature anywhere, the plants and trees would show you how they grow further after every pruning, every shedding of old leaves and branches!

Let us re-look at the example of maid remaining absent.

In a typical Indian household, maid is an integral part of the kitchen. Almost indispensable. Picture this: Maid overstays leave period, then informs she would be coming on such and such date, then neither shows up, nor cares to inform!

In such a situation when maid does not turn up after long absence even after confirming she would, and does not also bother to inform you in time regarding this, you usually lose patience and get angered. But then slowly you also calm down *as kitchen chores are simply unavoidable. So here you learn slowly there is no point in torturing your own self by holding on to anger and irritation for long.* It will only hurt yourself and nobody else. In this situation, the longer you stay angry without doing anything, it gets too late in the day to arrange for an alternative maid also. So, wisdom dawns and you sober down, and get going without wasting more time. Try for some other temporary maid, or do it yourself.

So, what happened exactly?

1. ***Acceptance of the situation.***

We learn the lesson that things in life that we have no control over must be accepted first. The best and most powerful example is past hurts and adversities. They are past – passed and simply cannot be undone or reversed. So, accept, learn lessons from it, let go and move on! In current situations, similarly, we must accept parts of circumstances not under our control as quickly as possible and start taking action for alternative solutions instead of wasting time in annoyance and blame game.

2. ***Introspection.***

You understand that although you might have quite convincing reasons to get angry, wisdom lies in not justifying an intense emotion that is harmful to you yourself.

3. ***Living in Awareness.***

You learn that even though you could not help getting angry in the first place (as that might be a very deep rooted *samskara* in you, creating default mode reactions), you must *consciously decide how long you can afford to hold on to that turbulent energy within*, i.e., anger in this case, in your own interest. That is living in awareness. You get a sense of what thoughts and feelings are about to grip you, or have just gripped you, but immediately pause and let that pass if negative.

4. ***Not reacting and being empathetic.***

You learn to give yourself just a bit of *time to respond to the situation instead of reacting. Taking a pause, you* can now see things in a different perspective, more so from the side of the other person. Not from the same angle that made you angry in the first place. For example, in the instant case, the first reaction of anger could have been a thought, like

"How irresponsible and uncaring the maid is!" But as you consciously start looking from the maid's side giving her the benefit of doubt, thoughts like, "May be, she is genuinely in some problem, so could not return even after intimating.", "May be, her cell has some issue of balance or battery or anything else, so she could not call later" etc. will dominate your thoughts bringing out *empathy* in you.

5. ***Compassion.***

As you start looking at her probable situation, you realise, your anger has in the process given way to *compassion*. You end up reflecting, how difficult their life is in any case! While we get so worked up doing the cleaning and other jobs pertaining to merely one house (our own only) during her absence, how tedious it must be for her to be doing these every day for several hours in several houses non-stop. No wonder, when they get a break, they prolong it on some pretext or other, or for genuine reasons. Aren't they also human? Don't they also get fatigued? Sick from overwork? When we start putting ourselves in their shoes, naturally our anger vanishes and gradually compassion takes over that space.

6. ***Gratitude.***

Last but not the least, now you remind yourself that actually you must thank God that you have a support for the number of days she comes, instead of cribbing about the few days she does not. *Gratitude....* That's what you end up feeling. Living in gratitude leads to an inner shift that allows you always to find your power back and become more self-aware and grounded.

What more lessons do you need in life? One episode in kitchen, and it teaches you acceptance, introspection, living in awareness, self-control, empathy, compassion, and gratitude!

In every sense, kitchen prepares us to be the MasterChef of our Lives!

The lessons are manifold as we have seen till now. There can be many more subtle and explicit lessons that one might pick up from our kitchens, depending upon one's specific circumstances. It is not possible to list all. But the good news is: when assimilated, they can be grouped under 5 pivotal lessons that we must learn, imbibe, and apply on the ground, no matter where we are, in which role we are or in which situation we are. These are:

- Be mindful
- Observe keenly
- Reflect and spot lessons
- Learn to learn
- Apply, Review and Apply

We would be then crafting our lives beautifully very close to our *purpose of being.*

What is more, everyone carries an energy field wherever they go. Routine rigours at home, be it in kitchen or in other areas in our home like regular cleaning, re-arranging space, discarding stuff beyond utility for us etc. to de-clutter without undermining still-useful basic tenets of our daily living, though appear to be mundane drills, indeed work towards *cleansing our energy field from time to time* with right attitude towards life. So, not only we behave in a positive way in kitchen and at home, we also end up carrying forward these ways of response and engagement wherever we go – our professional space, our social life, and our overall life in general.

Amazing how the learnings from our humble kitchen go spectacularly far beyond the ingredients and recipes, the diner and the dining, the brunch and dinner, and the pots and pans and platters. 😊

PART III

(Concluding Part)

Spiritualty and Our World of Food

Vedantic Scriptures explain about human *existence* in this mundane body. Our *existence* is primary, everything else like I am so and so, or such and such, is secondary. For most of us, there is no concept of 'Self' apart from our identities and personalities, which get manifested through our body, mind, and intellect, and our *karma*. Out of ignorance, we identify our 'Self' with our body. We think, "I exist so long as my body exists". We do not realise that I, the SELF/SOUL, is *apart from* my body, mind, and intellect. All these are mine, but I am not them, as I am the Subject, the *experiencer* of them. I cannot be the same as what I am aware of, or what I am experiencing. I simply use these as instruments to manifest my existence in this material world. We lack the understanding of the Self, the Pure Consciousness, that shines on everything to make us, i.e., the Self, *experience*.

Vedanta explains how the human personality manifests through *Panchakosha* model. We come into this world (are born) wearing 5 sheaths (coverings) - *viz. Annamaya Kosha (the body), Pranamaya Kosha (the vital energies), Manomaya kosha (the mind), Bigyanamaya Kosha (the intellect) and Anandamaya Kosha (the causal body). You (Self) are NOT any, or all, of these 5 sheaths. You, i.e., your Self/Soul, is your pure being, pure consciousness, apart from these coverings. The expression of the Self through these panchakosha is what we call 'life'. You require all these instruments to manifest in this world. Snapping only of the annamaya kosha from the other 4 sheaths and the Self or Soul, is called death. The gross body only dies, not You (Self),* which moves on to other planes after death. The pranamaya kosha does the separation.

I made a brief narration as aforesaid just to highlight why food is so important in the larger context of what we call life and death! *Anna* means rice, symbolic of all types of food and our gross body is equated with this - the annamaya kosha, snapping of which leads to death. Imagine, thousands of years backs, our great wise men had put emphasis on *food* at such a pivot level of our existence. It is also said commonly, *we are what we eat*. This warrants that we appreciate and value the importance of taking *right* food, prepared with *right* energy, and eaten with *right* state of mind too. Though gross, body is important as it is the *only means* to *exhaust our basanas (desires)and karmaphal (results of previous karma), as also to do appropriate karma now.*

Thus, body, and hence food, acquire high significance in our spiritual journey, too.

Work is worship.

We must have read it many times; must have heard it often from wiser people. This is one of the resounding universal messages that literally keeps coming from all sides. Even from spiritual angle. In Vedic philosophy, it is clearly asserted that each of us is a mere instrument of the Supreme Creator to carry out HIS jobs, and so whatever we do must be done consciously as an agent of The Supreme, in complete surrender of the deed itself, as also its results, to The Supreme; so that our 'karma' does not bind us to the cycle of births and deaths. This is *Niskama Karma* – action without expectations of fruits. Thus, there cannot be any room for whining as we do any work, including even the tedious tasks in kitchen. All we have to remember is that, the service we are providing to others through our work is in fact service to God alone. *Work is merely another name for worship!* And as we have already seen in our deliberation on motivation, mothers in kitchen learn soon enough not to expect any reward, recognition, or reciprocation as they go about tirelessly attending to their responsibilities and serving others as nothing less than *worship. No desire to be desired is undoubtedly a spiritually much-elevated state of mind!*

Even if we do not indulge in explaining anything regarding food, or work in terms of any scriptural interpretations, and look at WORK simply *pragmatically*, we would realise how absolutely it is necessary for every person to have 'work' – something to do. For, an idle mind is a devil's workshop, and *work* banishes boredom, poverty and evil from an engaged mind. Moreover, work that is indispensable to your daily routine is a great *detox* for your mood swings and stress. Simply because, it diverts your attention from *what is troubling you* to *what needs to be done* at *the moment*.

May be initially, we do work assigned to us, and/or accepted by us, only as duties as per our role and responsibilities. *But in course of time as we do the same work with interest, enthusiasm, and passion, alive to the purpose behind, it inspires a great sense of being relevant and inner bliss. Almost a feel of divinity!* Because we have been created for some purpose and that purpose gets actualized through our 'work' only. *The abilities, unique talents, and gifts we are born with are meant to be put to use in our work.* Without work, nothing fructifies – neither can we survive nor grow without taking some action or other, in some field or other. Is there any living human being who does not do anything? So work is essential for our very existence, and we better enjoy it, do it with utmost commitment and dedication, like worship. And I am sanguine, most readers are likely to agree with me now (having gone through all the detailed deliberations made till now in this book) that *kitchen is, indeed, a great platform to experience this truth.* This only takes us forward in a positive, more constructive manner in life, no matter what the situation is. We know situations are not entirely in our control, but how we respond and deal with them, is certainly within our control.

I think, kitchen has taught me *compassion* like no other field of work. I cut my finger or palm while chopping, the little pain I feel instantaneously reminds me of the risks of unimaginable physical pain that the soldiers out there are constantly taking to protect us. I accidentally burn my fingers or hand, and the immediate burning sensation reminds me of the millions of brides being burnt to death for dowry! I see the working ladies returning from work and travelling in local trains in Mumbai peeling green peas, or doing some preparatory work for the family dinner to be made immediately on reaching home, and I feel deeply for them for the drudgery they are going through daily to make both ends meet. I also feel grateful that at least I have the capacity to engage a hired hand for helping me in the kitchen. I look at the maids doing a lot of rigorous chores every day in multiple houses, and then go back and do all the household chores in their own homes, and I feel compassion for them. Also, gratefulness inside. Thank God, I am so much better-off!

Fasting is a very common religious or social custom across cultures. Apart from health benefits like cleansing of internal organs, abstaining from food makes you *experience hunger*. When you yourself experience the hunger pangs, you also become alive to the pain that the poor and the underprivileged undergo frequently for want of food! Observe yourself. What fasting brings out in you is: compassion.

Etc. etc. Examples are many and frequent. I am sanguine, many others share my experience.

Compassion, gratefulness, unconditional love... all these are basic tenets of a genuinely spiritual life. Kitchen and our world of food arouse/strengthen these divine personal qualities in us from time to time.

In our modest homely kitchen, we *feel* this divinity in work deep down in our innards. After all, over a time, either consciously or subconsciously we realise that we are serving and tending to *relationships, not just individuals who happen to be our family members.* We pass through umpteen occasions when one family member might have upset us tremendously through their behaviour, yet we continue to make and serve food to them without a trace of negativity infused into our work. Our mood does not decide if there will be food for the family or not. Just like irrespective of what we are going through in real life, if we are spiritual and are in the habit of 'connecting' to The Supreme through prayers, good karma, and surrender, we shall continue to do that, no matter what. Similarly, when we are upset about someone in the family, we appreciate that the fault lies in the *conduct* of that person, not in the *relationship, which must be taken care of and nurtured at all times.* This is the reason I preferred to talk about homely kitchens rather than professional kitchens, as the existential importance of relationships served through a homely kitchen is not there in professional kitchens. Yes, professional relationships with customers, suppliers, employees etc. are also very important to stay in business. Yes, many of the lessons we learn in homely kitchens are also there to learn from professional kitchens. But there, the underlying interest being *quid pro quo* and profit, relationships are to be maintained with professionalism, not unconditional love that lies at the core of strong familial/personal relationships. *The crux of spirituality in relationships across the board lies in unconditional love; and there is a greater scope to experience this in homely kitchens* as compared to professional kitchens.

Yes, deeper awareness on many things about food and kitchen takes us nearer and nearer to comprehending our deeper, existential queries in the realm of spirituality.

Post Script

Irrespective of where we are from, where we are now, discharging which role; and who/where we want to be in life, let us note that at the core of any understanding of how to find meaning in life and live in fulfilment lie the undernoted two perspectives:

1. **Learn to learn**

There is so much to learn in this world! Always be a keen student and position yourself on an ever-expanding learning curve. If we cultivate a habit of being *mindful in the present*, and *observe keenly*, we can *learn something or other,* from every situation, every individual and even most of the inanimate objects. Even a failure contains a direct message on what does not work. So, stay hungry for learning; develop an insatiable *hunger to learn* by looking through what is apparent, delving deeper than what is visible, and viewing wider beyond the proximate. And the rest will fall in place. *Learn to respect. Ability to learn* shall never be robust unless you genuinely *respect* the value of every other job, every other situation, and every other person you come across. Your learning can be well-rounded only when you develop an ability to appreciate *differences* with respect, so that you find something to learn all the time. Not having respect for something or someone will always deter you from even believing that there could be anything to learn from them. Your ego sets the impenetrable wall! *So, stay humble, respect others, and convert every situation into a learning experience!* As already elucidated in this book earlier, humility is not about degrading your own worth: it is about respecting others' worth.

2. **Learn to 'be'**

Learning is of no use if not applied in real life. Faking ultimately damages our own personal development and spiritual transformation. We are now living in a world wherein veneers are the norm, unfortunately. Look behind the facades, and the true quality would shock us for its unimagined lowliness in many cases! May be, acceptability of this can be thought of in the context of objects in some situations to make something look more appealing. But allow this in our own character as human beings, it will be extremely dangerous at some point or other, not only for our own selves, but for the entire humanity.

So, learn and live the positive lessons you have learnt. Do not just *appear to be* honest; *be* honest! Do not just *appear to be* humble; *be* humble! Do not just *appear to be* kind and compassionate; *be* kind and compassionate! Do not just *appear to be* appreciative; *be* appreciative! Do not just *appear to be* grateful; *be* grateful!

Miracles unfold only when we persistently learn and work towards 'becoming' what we ought to be!

www.ingramcontent.com/pod-product-compliance
Lightning Source LLC
LaVergne TN
LVHW041015150826
845672LV00001B/100

9798891337527